Fun, Sun and Sadness

a life of ups and downs across the world

Angela Barry

Fun, Sun and Sadness
a life of ups and downs across the world

Matador
9 De Montfort Mews
Leicester LE1 7FW, UK
Tel: (+44) 116 255 9311 / 9312
Email: books@troubador.co.uk
Web: www.troubador.co.uk/matador

ISBN 978 1848760 660

British Library Cataloguing in Publication Data.
A catalogue record for this book is available from the British Library.

Typeset in 11.5pt Bembo by Troubador Publishing Ltd, Leicester, UK

Matador is an imprint of Troubador Publishing Ltd

Printed by the MPG Books Group in the UK

My thanks to all the friends who have inspired and encouraged me to write this book; to Haulwen and Graham Fagg, my computer mentors, without whom the manuscript might still be floating about in the ether; and to Jackie and Peter Armstrong for providing the photograph from the Berlin production of Richard III.

Contents

Introduction

It was Peter Mackintosh, a friend of a friend, whom I met briefly a couple of years ago in Spain, who in the course of three conversations galvanized me into writing about my life. In the first of these conversations his opening words were: "Now tell me about your life". To my surprise he seemed genuinely interested, amused, appalled and curious at the bits I recounted and told me to put it all on paper. You, reader, be you family, friend or stranger, will be able to judge for yourselves how sound his judgement was in this respect. (Sadly Peter died before these memoirs were finished, but I would like to record a posthumous thank you to him).

I left the UK for Spain in August 2003 aged 72 years. I left many good friends and a busy but less than wholly fulfilling life in West Dorset. I left the greyness of the English climate and the frustrations created by a Government I despised. I also left for health reasons.

The peace and tranquillity of Andalusia in general and Antequera in particular is an ideal background from which to gather together the strands of a life lived to the full whenever possible, although there is also much to be learnt from 'times out' when life seems to stand still, so in effect no time is really wasted.

Is it so small a thing
To have enjoyed the sun,
To have lived the light in the spring,
To have loved, to have thought, to have done;
To have advanced true friends and beat down baffling foes.

From the Hymn of Empedocles by Matthew Arnold

I

Early years
1931- 1949

Born on the 24th August 1931, my early years were spent in East Yorkshire, but apart from remembering the moment when my maternal step-grandmother told me in hushed and excited tones that I now had a brother, it wasn't until I was about five that the memories became more lucid. It was then one of the few times, I think, that we were all four living together as a family.

We moved from Yorkshire up to the town of Tain in Invernesshire. My father was in the Royal Air Force with Coastal Command and based at Invergordon. The year was 1936. My parents had a hectic social life, centred round the RAF Base and although they were out a lot in the evenings, it was a happy time for us all, apart, that is, for my brother, Chris, who suffered from rickets and was tied to a chair leg most of the time so that he wouldn't walk on his calcium-starved legs. Needless to say this filled him with anger and he hurled a new toy horse with moveable joints across the room and broke it; more fury. He also caught scarlet fever at the age of three and we went along to the local fever hospital to peer at him no closer than behind a glass screen. When he came out of hospital, Mummy asked him what he would most like as a present and also to eat. Without hesitation he lisped: "a thcarlet cap and minth and rithe pudding pleathe".

Outbreak of World War II - Yorkshire

When war broke out in 1939 we moved back to Yorkshire. To begin with we lived with my Great-Aunt Alice in a dark Victorian house in Bridlington. On the night that war broke out the sirens sounded to warn us of our first air raid and we left our beds and foregathered on the landing. Horror of horrors, there was Aunt Alice with no hair; we hadn't realised that she was completely bald and wore a wig during the daytime, so that the sight of her bald head was far more alarming, as it turned out, than that first air raid. Barbed wire fences went up on the beaches and we could no longer get to the sea. We then moved to another dark Victorian house on the edge of the Westwood in Beverley. Soon after that we shared an attractive cottage opposite the church in the nearby village of Bishop Burton with my paternal grandmother, my father's sister, Auntie Gee, and her son, our cousin, John Lineham.

Despite the war and the almost nightly air raids we were a happy little band. School was the village school and we had a lot of fun. We fished for tadpoles in the village pond and put them into the water butt in the garden from whence they hopped in their hundreds, as frogs, all over the place. The army had men billeted in the village and I used to knit socks and balaclavas for Geordie, the cook, in return for huge portions of army-type 'plum duff'. We all sang in the church choir and took it in turns to pump the organ.

My Family

At that time there was a very supportive family element living nearby. My maternal step-grandmother, Haldy, lived in Hull in a large house, but not dark like the earlier ones. It had a lovely garden with several apple trees and a secret woodland area, where the autumnal smells and general dampness made for wonderful well-remembered and magical intoxication. My grandfather, Luke Arthur Farthing, died well before I was born. He had married Haldy (my nickname for her, but otherwise known as Hylda) after his first wife Helen Craig Walker died. My real maternal grandmother was the mother of three daughters, known as the Three Farthings, and a son, Arthur. My grandfather and his business partner, Alan Wright, ran a flourishing timber business in Hull. They did a lot of business with Sweden, which is interesting, given that I spent nine years of my life in that country in my early twenties. Luke Arthur, judging from his Obituary, was a much-respected businessman in Hull and my mother adored him. She was, I think, only five when her mother died, which may well have contributed to her difficulties later in life. The family lived in great comfort in an attractive house called 'The Beeches' at Ferriby near Hull, complete with a tennis court, a housemaid and a chauffeur. Sadly, none of the family money filtered down to the next generation, and they all had to go off into the big wide world and earn their own livings.

Haldy was a great favourite of mine and staying with her was always a great treat. She took me to Hull Market where there was a stall selling rather big and sickly sweets, at which she always stopped to buy some for me. She also stopped at the stall selling horse-meat and innards, which she bought for the dog; not my favourite stop. In one of the guest rooms was a well-stocked bookcase full of such authors as Dornford Yates and I often read these rather pleasant novels well into the night by torchlight.

Two children were born in this marriage: a son, Uncle Reg, who was to me a heroic figure. He had been a reserve for the England Rugby Team and was at that time a Captain in one of the Yorkshire regiments. He used to throw me into the air and catch me just in time, his shiny uniform buttons scratching me as I fell. A jovial man who called me 'Tuppence', he took part in and survived the D-Day landings, but only just, as he was on the very last of the `little ships`, which rescued the men from the beaches at Dunkirk

His sister, Auntie Penny, was the youngest of the family. She was a rather superior person and a serious one who played, to my untutored ear, sombre pieces on the piano in the drawing room and had, at that time, a somewhat troublesome love life. She later married Geoffrey Siddle, a doctor, and they and their son and daughter, Nicholas and Hilary and their families are more-or-less my remaining close relatives. I have spent many happy times with them over the years, both in Poulton-le-Fylde in Lancashire where Geoffrey's surgery was and then in Chichester where they now live.

Auntie Norah, known as 'Nornie' was the eldest of the Three Farthings; she was by far my favourite relative. She and her husband lived in a house called 'Willowdene' overlooking the Westwood in Beverley. The house belonged to Nornie`s father-in-law, George Skinner, who was a wholesale grocer. At the back of the house was a huge warehouse from where the business was conducted and it was always a treat to venture into it and through to 'The Office' which had a couple of shiny mahogany Victorian sit-up-and-beg desks like something out of a Dickens novel. The air was dry and a clean, grainy smell pervaded the entire warehouse and into the kitchen area of the house where there was a large well-used mangle in the scullery. The front of the house was

3

light with picture windows looking out over the Westwood. The passages had highly polished floors and the stairs shiny brass stair rods and it was a haven of peace and comfort. In the early mornings one woke to the sound of horses clip-clopping along the back lane. They were from the local racing stables on their way to their morning exercise.

An alarming thing happened when I was staying at 'Willowdene'as a small child. One night I suddenly awoke to see, in the moonlight, what looked like a little gnome sitting on my bed. Terrified, I ran into the next bedroom crying: "Auntie there's a gnome on my bed." She came in to chase it away, only to discover that it was the point of the eiderdown that was sticking up in the air and closely resembling a pointed hat! Apart from that small incident, some of my happiest times ever as a child were spent in Nornie's company. Sadly she died on the 15th March 1969, from emphysema, after some years of indifferent health and worry. I was working in Venezuela at the time, so unhappily missed her funeral. She was a regular letter writer and I have kept many of her letters. She always referred to me as the daughter she had never had and when her husband, Uncle Kenneth, died in the 1980s he bequeathed all the family's china and glass to me, including some real treasures, which brought back and still bring back happy memories of 'Willowdene'.

Auntie Kath, the second of the Three Farthings, married a rather difficult man who ran a successful coal business in Nottingham. He made her unhappy when she was with him, but she was even unhappier away from him. I remember staying with them and all their conversations were conducted through their two sons, Michael and Keith, who later went to Sherborne School, where they were well away from the chilly atmosphere at home. Several years later Auntie Kath took her own life by hanging herself from the banisters. We more or less lost touch with them after their mother's tragic death. When she was alive and in happier days she was great fun and very amusing.

Of Uncle Arthur I know very little, except that he served with the Royal Flying Corps during the First World War and was a keen and expert photographer later in life. He lived with his wife Eva and daughter Elizabeth in Hull quite near Haldy and we often had scrumptious teas there. A much-coveted toy farmyard and set of farm animals were regularly brought out for us to play with before tea whilst Mummy and Auntie Eva talked their hearts out.

On my father's side Gran Barry ran Nornie a very close second in the popularity stakes. Her husband, my grandfather, died well before I was born. He had seriously considered becoming a Catholic priest as a young man, but went into show business instead. His name was Robert Thursby Hainstock, but took as his stage name Lennox Barry. My grandmother took the name Hainstock-Barry, as did I for a time, but I dropped the rather unwieldy Hainstock in due course. Grandfather was successful for some years, producing musicals and opening the first skating rink in Brussels. The couple spent interesting times, both `on the Continent' and in London. Gran used to recount tales of their travels, which involved a lot of hat boxes and trunks being off-loaded from trains and cross-Channel ferries. Names such as Augustus John and Lady Diana Cooper featured in these fascinating accounts of their social life. Sadly my grandfather took to drink and died after imbibing a bottle of brandy a day for too long.

Gran Barry then started up a fashion business in Hull, but I do not recall for how long and how successful it was. She herself was very elegant: tall and slim and blessed with a wonderful sense of humour, which saw her through many trials and tribulations. She had three sisters, the two older ones were spinsters. The youngest, Lydia, was sent out to relatives in Australia because her parents couldn't afford to keep her. She married there and had a large family, so there is a large contingent of cousins living in Australia, most of whom I have met up with over the years.

Family Connection to Captain James Cook

We have a common interest, in that the family is said to be directly descended from Captain James Cook, the famous explorer and navigator. There were three of his possessions in the family: a sea chest, an oil painting and a family Bible. The sea chest was in store in Hull and was lost when the firm holding it was bombed during the war. History doesn`t relate what happened to the oil painting, but the spinster aunts, Minnie and Lily, are said to have thrown away the Bible because it was rather tatty! However, my cousin, John Lineham, who saw it told us that it threw no light on the mystery of our relationship with Captain Cook.

I have spent many years researching Cook's life and have managed to get within one link, and the last important link is still proving very difficult. Based on my researches to date my conclusion is that Cook may have fathered a child, one Thomas Cook, out of wedlock before he met and married Elizabeth his wife. The couple had a number of children, none of whom had issue. The only offspring came from his sisters, Margaret and Christina. It is a record of Thomas Cook`s birth which is the sticking point. His marriage and death are fully documented, but not his birth. It is perhaps of significance that Cook asked that all his private papers should be burnt on his death. This I learnt from the Curator of the Cook Museum in Great Ayton, where he lived as a boy. Also, his Will is couched in odd terms, referring as it does to "my children" at one point and later on to "my child and children" which could highlight the fact that there was another child besides those born during his marriage to his wife, Elizabeth. It was one of Thomas Cook's daughters, Jane, who married a John Garbutt, one of my direct forebears on my paternal grandmother's side. I have not to date given up my researches.

My paternal grandmother, Gran Barry had a son, my father, Eric William, known as Bill and a daughter Marjorie whom I have mentioned earlier under the pet name I gave her of Auntie Gee. More of my father later. Auntie Gee was also my Godmother and when we were small we spent quite a lot of time with her family. John, her son, was the same age as we were. They had a lovely house in Hessle and one of the joys of staying there was that Auntie Gee wakened us up with a glass of orange juice every morning served in small glasses with blue and red stars on them.

John lived a rather charmed life as the only son and I rather envied him. His paternal grandmother, Granny Lineham, known as Big Gran (Gran Barry was known as Little Gran, but I'm not sure why) lived in what seemed to us a very big house, with a lovely garden complete with a fishpond. John had a nurse when he was very small who saw to it that we didn't tumble into it. Granny Lineham was a very intimidating person, but mellowed with age and when I visited her as an adult she always invited me to choose a book from her bookshelves. The last one I chose was an old, but not quite a first edition of Mrs Beeton's Cookery Book, which I still cherish. Cousin John was great fun and travelled across the world as an engineer in the Merchant Navy and eventually married his wife Jean. They had three personable sons, Andrew, Richard and Christopher. It was John who saw to it that I met our Australian cousins when they came over visiting.

I have deviated from my early saga in order to place myself in the context of my family, who were, after all, important in providing the background to my early life. They also provided the genes, which, for better or for worse have helped to make me who I am.

Wartime in Yorkshire

To go back a bit to Bishop Burton and the cottage we shared with some of the family; I think the lease must have run out because we then moved into part of North-End Farm, a stone's throw from the cottage. This we enjoyed, apart from the fact that we were always very cold there during the winter. Toasting pikelets over the fire at teatime was our favourite way of getting warm. The war was at a critical stage and we listened to the news on the wireless each night and also to Sir Winston Churchill's encouraging speeches. Every night there were sporadic or concentrated crumps of bombs falling on and around Hull and the sound of local anti-aircraft fire. When the bombs had been very close, we spent the night on mattresses downstairs or hid in the cupboard under the stairs. In the mornings we collected pieces of the German shells from the neighbouring fields. The local air-raid warden and fireman used to come round to the house when there was a raid and shout: "Buzzers a' blown" as if we hadn't heard the air-raid warning and that was a sign for Mummy to put the kettle on and make them a cup of tea.

One day, during the day when most men were at their work, a strange man knocked on the door and simply said "Water". He was despatched to the village pump round the corner and the local bobby was alerted as we believed the man to be either a German prisoner who had escaped from the local prisoner-of-war camp or else a German parachutist. This was not then as far-fetched as it seems now because the threat of a German invasion hung over us all at that time.

My father used to visit us from time to time on short leaves from wherever he was based. These visits were highlights in our young lives. He always brought a gift or two and I remember vividly a large Easter egg, a real luxury during the war, being eaten by the dog in a trice, much to my chagrin.

Billetted with us for a time was a young Army officer called Tony Wood, who it emerged had an aunt, Aunt Lorna, who ran a boarding school at Crowthorne in Berkshire called 'Woodlands School'. A plan was hatched for my brother, Chris, and me to go to this school. As well as giving us both a more rounded education it would also enable Mother to join my father, who was then stationed with Coastal Command at Dover.

Looking at the school brochure filled me with excitement and school uniforms were ordered. We waited anxiously for the postman to bring the parcels containing these uniforms, but they never came and off we went without them to our great disappointment. Another disappointment was when we queued for hours in the bitter cold outside the local cinema in Beverley which was showing 'The Great Dictator', an hilarious film about Adolf Hitler. Exactly as it came to our turn the cinema was pronounced full and we never got to see it. Tiny disappointments in the overall scheme of things, but at the time they were crushing.

First Serious Thoughts

Although Mummy had seen to it that we were regular churchgoers, I don't recall thinking very seriously about God as a small girl; but perhaps I did, because I do remember, when quite young, standing alone in a garden, it could have been Haldy's, and asking God to show himself, so that I could believe in Him. Of course he didn't appear, but I have often wondered if He did answer my appeal in His own way because I have always been blessed with a firm belief and faith in Him.

Woodlands School and Deanburn

Woodlands School had much to recommend it. The classes were smaller than at the village school in Bishop Burton and Latin and Literature lessons opened up a whole new world for me, as did piano lessons, which, alas, were only short-lived. And I seemed to do well in the school sports, which was an added fillip.

Bad news was just around the corner, however. Quite soon after we had begun to get used to this new life away from home, Mother broke it to us that my father had been taken a prisoner-of-war whilst serving with Coastal Command in one of the air sea rescue boats. This in itself was a shock, but so also was the news that Mother could no longer afford the school fees. In order for us to continue at the school, Auntie Lorna suggested that she might come and work at the school. Little did we know that the job the Headmistress had in mind was for Mother to help out in the Butler's Pantry under the eagle eye of a rather intimidating former butler. Mother agreed to this and although it was a heroic and well-meant gesture on her part she couldn't quite have envisaged how much we became rather second-class citizens in the eyes of our peers, having a mother working 'below stairs', so-to-speak. It can't have been much fun for her either and the arrangement lasted but a short time. Plans were then made for us to go and live at a private nursery school, Deanburn, in Crowthorne. It was run by two nursing sisters mostly for children whose parents were serving abroad.

The atmosphere there was deeply unhappy. The nurses were pathological bullies. Chris started to wet his bed and was beaten for it. I was forced to use my right hand when writing, although I was naturally left-handed. One little boy, aged about four, trembled with fear all the time. I wrote frantic letters to both parents, describing our misery and pleading for them to take us away. The letters to my father in a prisoner-of-war camp were opened by the two harridons and I was soundly punished. I remember forming up to the headmaster of the local school

8

we attended urging him to help us. Eventually mother came to remove us from this hell-hole. A letter I wrote to her just before she came to take us away said: "Please come and fetch us even if its raining?"

Reading

She did come, much to our great relief, and took us to Reading where she had arranged for us all to stay with an old gentleman, Mr Bowden, who had been a friend of my grandfather's in Yorkshire. He was a widower and had a housekeeper to look after him called Miss Ingells. Miss Ingells' features were not altogether kindly, nor was her disposition. But small wonder, having to cope with such a sudden influx of people into her household. Needless to say, relations between Mother and Miss Ingells became more and more strained and finally Miss Ingells went and Mother replaced her as housekeeper.

A relatively peaceful phase followed. Chris and I went to local schools and began to feel settled. By this time I had been to nine or ten different schools because of our itinerant life and my education had suffered from all these changes. I took and failed the School Certificate Exam and left school at the age of fifteen with no qualifications and a piece of paper which said: 'This is not a School Certificate'. However, the constant changes did teach me how to adjust and to make friends and to make good friends quickly. I joined the local Sea Rangers and also took riding lessons with the Pullein-Thompson family, two daughters of which, Diana and Josephine, were popular authors of horsey books, so beloved of teenage girls at that time. Partly as a result of this new interest, I toyed with the idea of working with horses when I left school, but a morning spent helping to muck out at a local stables rapidly disabused me of that as a possible career. I had to think again. Meanwhile life in Grosvenor Road, continued happily enough.

Mr Bowden had two married daughters and both families lived within visiting distance of their father. There was also a son who lived in a room above the garage and commuted to London each evening where he played the piano in a pub off the Kings Road . He wore a sort of waistcoat made of leather straps which it was believed came from train windows. These were covered in horse brasses. He had long black greasy hair, a beard and thick-lensed glasses. All these unattractive features shrank into insignificance when he played the piano. There was a baby grand piano in the main bedroom of the house on which he sometimes played and which he had painted a dull purple with floral decorations. We saw little of him, but I was curious to see what his room above the garage was like. So one day I plucked up courage and climbed up the stairs of the garage to have a look. The place was in chaos, with all sorts of odd pieces of furniture and jumble scattered around, including a rather beautiful harp. His bedroom was in one corner behind a curtain and into it I crept. The bed was unmade and the whole aspect was squalid in the extreme. To one teenage girl it was all utterly abhorrent and I fled aghast down the stairs and back into the welcome daylight. This was my first experience of the ugly and the beautiful residing in one man, and it was hard to believe, at that time in my life, that he was the son of such a gracious, civilised and kindly father as Mr Bowden senior.

The two daughters and their families were perfectly normal and we came to know them quite well and liked them. However Mr Bowden had left £100 to Mother in his Will on condition that she stayed with him until he died. It was not to be. One Sunday lunchtime, just as we were eating our gooseberry fool, Mr Bowden became unwell, turned a frightening shade of grey, his upper set of false teeth fell into his pudding, and to our horror his hands tried to retrieve them. He had suffered a stroke from which he never properly recovered. Mother nursed him, with the help of a District Nurse and although willing to go on doing so she was persuaded to leave by his daughters, so never got the money he had bequeathed to her and which she could so well have done with at that time.

My Father
Before this happened and whilst we were still happily ensconced there, Chris and I were in bed suffering from measles. A telegraph boy knocked on the door and delivered a telegram. Chris took it and refused to let me open it. As a way of getting him to release it, I said: "Look, it's got Daddy's number on it." It hadn't of course, but this ruse had the desired effect and we opened it together. Oddly enough it was from my father, who had been repatriated back to the UK and the telegram was to tell us this and to say he would be arriving with us at such and such a time.

He arrived in a pitiful state: skeletal, grey and suffering from serious asthma. Mother did what she could to rehabilitate him, but it was a long job and the two did not get on. Father went up to Yorkshire to stay with his mother, Gran Barry, and the marriage seemed to be virtually at an end. Mother broke the news to us the day he left, saying: "Daddy has left us; he doesn't love us any more." We were all very upset but after a time Mother went up to Yorkshire to try to bring him back. She did in fact succeed and by this time he was well enough to consider getting a job. He was not fit enough to return to the Royal

Airforce but went back to his first love, the Merchant Navy. When he was at sea his chronic asthma never worried him, which was an added incentive.

He went out to Hong Kong where he joined a ship, as First Officer, with a well known shipping firm called Mollers. The ship and father hit the headlines at the same time as the `Amethyst' did, but with less news coverage than the Amethyst, which became famous as `The Yangtze Incident'. However he navigated the ship down an undredged channel of the Yangtze River and they were fired on by Chinese Nationalist guards but managed to make their escape without injury. The newspapers reported it and Mother was interviewed along with "their two children, Angela and Christopher".

Not long after that my father's ship was hit by a typhoon and in trying to stabilize the wildly spinning wheel he threw an iron bar into the middle of it. This did the trick, but the impact hurled him across the deck and he suffered a broken collar bone. Whether it was this injury or an incipient predisposition, but my father then took to drink. His letters dried up and soon after Mother decided she had had enough and set in train divorce proceedings. I was very sad about it all and kept in touch with my grandmother about the whereabouts and condition of my father. He was someone to whom I could relate, probably because of his ridiculous sense of humour which more than made up for his shortcomings, as far as I was concerned. He was an unassuming man and very self-contained but wonderfully quick and witty. Mother always maintained that she had married him because he made her laugh – but not for long!

Gran Barry eventually managed to arrange for him to return to England. He was shipped home as a DBS (Distressed British Subject). Gran was advised by the British Consulate as to which ship he would be arriving on and when and I promised to try and intercept him when he arrived at Kings Cross Station to take a train up to stay with her. It was a cold and dank January day and I waited for hours, monitoring all the trains going to Hull, but in vain. Sadly, somehow I missed him. He had arrived home in a thin tropical suit and had nothing else with him. His mother and sister nursed him back to a reasonable state of health, although his asthma was still very bad. I used to go up to Yorkshire at intervals to see him and he seemed to appreciate these visits. We got on well and laughed a lot. He had made a concerted effort to give up drinking and eventually succeeded. His sister, Auntie Gee, arranged for him to see a chest specialist, but he died of a heart attack one night before seeing the specialist. Needless to say, I was deeply saddened by his untimely death at the age of 55 years, despite the fact that he had played such a small part in my life and upbringing. At the time he died I was living in Sweden and Gran Barry and Auntie Gee arranged his funeral and burial.

After leaving Mr Bowden's house, we went to live in furnished rooms nearby with a dear little person called Mary Owen, who was the sister of the World War I poet, Wilfred Owen. She was deeply religious but never tried to influence our own beliefs. I should add at this point that Mother had seen to it that we were brought up to be church-going Christians as she was. Chris sang in various church choirs and we were both Confirmed. My own beliefs have become stronger with the years and the Almighty has been ever-present in my life and a source of great strength and comfort.

Mary Owen talked to me a lot about her brother, who, sadly, was killed the day before Armistice Day. But his poetry lives on to remind us of the horrors of war. She gave me a little book of his collected poems, which she signed for me and which I cherish to this day. Otherwise it was not a particularly happy time within the family. Mummy had become nervy and bitter and I was struggling to become a person in my own right. We clashed continuously.

The local branch of the Sea Rangers became a great haven. We had two boats on the Thames and had a great deal of fun with these. On one occasion there was a gathering of all the Sea Rangers, countrywide, at the Royal Albert Hall, where Princess Margaret, our President, was the guest of honour. We were asked to be on parade at some unearthly hour of the morning at Wellington Barracks in London. It poured with rain relentlessly and we were thoroughly soaked through and the navy blue dye from our hats trickled down our faces long before the Princess was due to come and take the salute. But it was a memorable day and I was proud to be part of the Sea Ranger fraternity. There were two added bonuses of so being. One was to help sell programmes at classical music concerts at Reading Town hall. It was then that I developed a lifelong love of music; music of all sorts, with the exception of most operas, sadly.

The other bonus was to help out at weekends at Bisham Abbey, a residential sports centre run by the Central Council of Physical Recreation outside Marlow in Buckinghamshire. This was hard work but great fun. I met people from all walks of life among those who were on sports courses, their tutors and most of all among the other helpers.

Most of the helpers were former pupils from Queen Anne's School in

Caversham. I had seen the girls sweeping along in their scarlet cloaks and wished I might have been one of them. Now I was, somehow, during those happy weekends at Bisham Abbey. One of them, Jo Watson (nee Preston), became a long-standing friend until her sad and premature death in the 1980s, as did Synolda Butler (known as Bin), another Sea Ranger, who lived nearby, and who remains a friend to this day. We met originally when I was practising for the school sports by running round the block before school each morning and Bin was running, always running, to catch the bus at the end of her road, the first part of her journey to St James's Secretarial College in London. The Queen Anne's girls were marking time before going on to university or other training, like Jo who went on to St Thomas's Hospital to train as a physiotherapist.

II

Bisham Abbey, Marlow

I so much enjoyed those weekends that, when I left school with no qualifications except for School Certificate credits in Art, English Literature and English Grammar and a pass in Maths, and was asked by Miss Merman, the Warden at Bisham Abbey, whether I would like to join their permanent staff, I leapt at the idea. I spent a year there and friend Din was on the permanent staff too as secretary to the Warden. There was also a girl called Molly Chilton. She was extremely pretty so she rather put my nose out of joint as far as the men were concerned. However I had one or two boyfriends whilst I was there. The first was a sweet and kind young man with red hair and another a golden-haired Adonis for whom I used to make cakes well into the future. I suppose Mother had told me that the way to a man's heart was through his stomach. But this time it wasn't!

The sports courses were full of all sorts and conditions of men and women and were great fun. The teaching staff changed with each course, dependant upon which sports were programmed. They were all great characters and a conversation that took place between two of them at breakfast one morning as long ago as in 1948, sticks in my mind: it was about the depth of frustration and irritation inanimate objects can cause to the smooth-running of one's life. Now that I am slowing down, this discussion seems to be pretty apposite. Inanimate objects get in the way, keep falling and very often breaking and more often than not getting lost. The leaflet in every packet of pills always contrives to stop you putting the pills back into the packet. Maddening! But I digress.

During the 1948 Olympics, we had a number of competitors staying at the Abbey. Several of them were Olympic canoeists and their coach, John Dudderidge, took time off to instruct Molly and me in the art of turning the canoe over in a somersault and back to the surface again. It was tricky. He also arranged for us to follow the races in a launch on the Thames. One of the teaching staff, Joe Jagger, was the father of the leader of the 'Rolling Stones', Mick Jagger. He was a charming man with an equally charming wife. Various well-known sports personalities came whilst I was there. Dan Maskell, the champion tennis player of that time actually signed my own tennis racquet, which I proudly showed everyone until it was `past its sell-by date' and I sold it to a friend for the price of a bottle of gin. One's priorities tend to change over the years.

Bisham Abbey is a beautiful Elizabethan house on the banks of the River Thames near Marlow. It was at that time rented to the Central Council of Physical Recreation (CCPR) by a Miss Vansittart-Neale, the owner, for one peppercorn per annum, the lowest legal tender. Queen Elizabeth the First was said to have stayed there in what in my time was the lovely bay-windowed drawing room. Most of the public rooms were still furnished in keeping with the house and were not used during the courses, except for the Great Hall, which was the dining room. During the summer the Abbey was alive with the ping of tennis balls on racquets and the cries and laughter of the students. It was very quiet during the winter, although a number of sports bodies used it for conferences. One of these was the Football Association, led by Sir Walter Winterbotham, who was then Director of Coaching and Manager of the England Team. He was later to become General Secretary of the CCPR from 1963-1972. Another was the Weightlifter's Association. Needless to say these conferences had their lighter sides for us. One morning as I was getting dressed in my bedroom up in the old tower, there was a knock at the door. As I was in the very initial stages of dressing, I leapt into another part of the room, unseen from the door, and before I could deter him, one of the weightlifters had crept into the room to hook an old bell onto the springs under my bed. I must have caught sight of his face, so as he came in to breakfast I said to him: "Is it usual for you to come into a lady`s bedroom, whilst she is dressing and attach a bell under her bed?" Of course the poor man was flabbergasted as he hadn`t realised

I had had a bolthole and thought I was standing unclothed in the main part of the bedroom watching him. A great roar of laughter ensued from his colleagues and he was soundly teased. They were all great fun and we enjoyed their visits.

As I said, it was very quiet during the winter and between conferences there were only four or five of us there. We worked hard during the day keeping the place shipshape, but it could get a bit spooky during the nights. The Abbey was said to be haunted by Lady Hoby the wife of Sir Thomas Hoby, an early owner of the house. They had a son who kept blotting his copybook, literally. He was said to have been soundly beaten and died as a result. Some blotted schoolbooks were found behind a wall in what was called the Stone Room and however many times the wall behind which they were found was repaired it always collapsed again afterwards. Lady Hoby was said to wander about the house in anguish wringing her hands. She had been seen by a number of people over the years and the haunting was the subject of a long article in the Picture Post magazine in the 1940s with a ghostly figure, said to be Lady Hoby, on the front page.

I caught a glimpse of her several times and, more frighteningly, felt her presence on two occasions. The first was when I woke up one night in my tower bedroom to see a very pale woman's face looking down at me. It disappeared in a trice and I don't think it was imagination. The second time was when I had been into Reading on the bus to see Mother, who was suffering from nervous debility. On my return journey the bus stopped in Bisham Village and this entailed a good few minutes walk to the Abbey's drive and then on down to the house. It was very dark and I called in at the local pub to ring the Warden who agreed to turn on the house lights to guide me down the drive. As I approached the house, it was in darkness, and standing in the moonlight on the basketball pitch was a white figure. I was terrified, but as I got nearer to the house saw, much to my relief, that it was just the basketball post. Severely shaken I let myself in through a side door and went into the butler's pantry to get a drink of water. It was very still and there appeared to be no draught coming from anywhere, yet some tea-towels hanging on a line were swinging slowly backwards and forwards. Even more uneasy, I began the tortuous walk up to the tower: up the main staircase, through the drawing room, through the ballroom and up the final spiral staircase to my room. The door had a latch which was broken and one had to secure it properly once inside. This I did. I undressed and climbed into bed, turned on my radio full blast to give myself courage and began to read with my back to the door. Although hearing no sound something compelled me to turn round and to my astonishment the door was wide open. I saw what I can only describe as a white mist, which I was able to follow with my eyes round the room. It then disappeared and I got out of bed, shut the bedroom door and literally shook with fright all night. Miss Merman insisted that she had put on the house lights and couldn't understand why they weren't on as I approached the house. No-one scoffed at my frightening experience during the night as the ghost was a well-respected phenomenon and part of the house. There had been many such incidents over the years when many guests sleeping in one particular room had experienced the presence of Lady Hoby.

Another rather alarming experience there was when I woke up one night to hear blood-curdling cries. I had no idea what it could possibly be, but was far too frightened to go and investigate. It eventually stopped and in the morning we learnt that the Head of the CCPR, who was presiding over their Annual General Meeting at Bisham, and who was a diabetic, had been unable to reach her insulin and so was trying desperately to attract someone's attention. Fortunately she succeeded and she was none the worse for this alarming episode. Bisham Abbey remains a well-known sports centre to this day, despite its ghost.

III

Selling Books

Heelas, Reading

Whether it was because of that experience, or Mothers nervous debility, I returned home after about a year at Bisham and found a job at Heelas department store in Reading in the Book Department. Mother worked in the Fashion Department and probably played a part in landing me the job. The manager of the department was a keen but rather serious man who belonged to the Salvation Army. The other assistant besides me was a very young, good-looking and serious lad who was also a Salvationist. I loved the work and being surrounded by books and as we became busier another assistant joined us. Before very long she and the young lad sometimes read the Bible together in the stockroom. It wasn't very long before she too joined the Salvation Army and came in and showed me her new uniform bonnet with great excitement. Each to his own, I thought.

Life at home had become very difficult indeed and I knew that I had to get away. This couldn't happen in the twinkling of an eye and in the meantime there were some fun occasions to mitigate the difficult times. Diana Bull, a friend who lived nearby, arranged for a few of us to go to the annual Tea Dance at Phyllis Court on the banks of the Thames at Henley on the Sunday before the start of the annual Henley Regatta. We had the opportunity of meeting crews from all over the world and then became cheer-leaders for the team we most liked the look of, and vice versa of course; and at the end of the week one of Diana's friends who lived in Henley gave a lunch party for this crew. The lunch was more relaxed than the tea dance, of course. One year Anthony Armstrong-Jones, who later married Princess Margaret, happened to be the cox of the crew we had decided to support and he was a lot of fun. We followed his boat during Henley Week and met up with the crew for the final evening celebrations. Just before the fireworks began at the finale, I needed to find a loo. As my escort and I were in the middle of milling crowds on the river bank this proved difficult and the need became a must. We eventually got to the big tent, but I couldn't find what I wanted and in desperation relieved myself outside the tent, but within its enclosure. There was no-one there, but imagine my horror, when gleeful cries arose from above. It just happened that the Big Wheel in the Fairground was directly above, and each couple who came within sight of me, exclaimed with delight. But I doubt that I was recognisable from that position and distance.

Hatchards, Piccadilly

Eventually, I got a lovely job lined-up in London and, through a friend of Mother's, a room in the home of her sister . This was a basement flat, albeit a very nice and commodious one in Sussex Gardens near Paddington. When Gran Barry heard where it was she cried with horror: "Darling, you can't live there, it's an awful district." But I did and nothing untoward happened, nor was I conscious of any 'ladies of the night' operating there. The job was as a bookseller's assistant at Hatchards in Piccadilly. Now I really had reached the centre of the great wide world. It was an exciting move.

All sorts of celebrities and, even more thrilling, members of the Royal Family came to buy their books at Hatchards. I recall Queen Mary arriving and by some breakdown of communication she came in unannounced. She stood just inside the front door glowering because the usual welcoming and escorting manager and assistant manager were not there. They very soon were and Queen Mary and attendants were able to wend their way round the shop.

On one occasion she paid a visit to the Children's Department, where I happened to be working at the time. The lady I was assisting was, it turned out, oblivious to Queen Mary's presence and kept getting too close for comfort behind her. As I had feared, Queen Mary suddenly turned round and my customer was so surprised and indeed shocked, that the upper set of her teeth fell with a clatter to the floor. Luckily the Head of the Department, Diana Rhodes, managed to steer The Queen away and I rushed to retrieve the offending upper set.

Another amusing memory was when a Dutch girl who was working there came up to me to ask what books I had on horses. Her face was contorted in an effort to tell me that the customer standing behind her was something special. I looked to see the immensely good-looking and smiling face of the actor David Niven. I very nearly swooned, but showed him what books on horses I had and then sent him upstairs to the secondhand department for more. As he came downstairs afterwards on his way out of the shop, he graced me with another dazzling smile, which made my days for some time to come.

Marina, Duchess of Kent came into the shop quite frequently and was very elegant and charming. So did Sir Richard Attenborough, who at that time was plain mister and a jolly and chatty person he was too. One day after a late night out, I said rather gracelessly to a man who suddenly came in and appeared to be looking for someone in the Children's Department: "Do you want anything?" and then realised to my embarrassment that it was The Duke of Gloucester. Yes, respect was paramount in those days and I had failed on that occasion.

My fellow assistants were an interesting group of people and the two senior lady assistants took great pleasure in teasing me, in the nicest way, but always went out of their way to help me whenever they could. One day a tall man came to me asking for books on duck farming. As I tried to think what we had and where such books would be, Mrs Doubleday the senior assistant started gesticulating to me behind the man. When he had gone, she told me excitedly that he was none other than ex-King Peter of Yugoslavia who was living in England.

She overstepped the mark one day, after she had sold a huge pile of books to one man. Before leaving the shop he asked to speak to one of the other assistants by name. The two exchanged a few words and after he left the shop, Mrs Doubleday said to the girl: "Do you know him?" and before waiting for an answer confided that he was Mr So-and-So and the books he was buying were for his mistress who lived in Mayfair. It turned out that the man was the girl's father. Mrs Doubleday was of course full of remorse and the girl kindly told her that the family knew of the affair, but she wondered how much was known to the staff of Hatchards. To this day, whenever I make an ill-judged remark and afterwards regret it, I counsel myself that it wasn't quite as bad as that one – so far so good.

Romance

Two people who worked at Hatchards became important people in my life. One was Dick Butterworth, who worked in the Order Department. He was not as attractive as David Niven, but was great fun. Several of his school friends from Rugby School popped in to see him and the ones I thought to be attractive, he would invite to a theatre and supper party so that I could get to know them better. After a while Dick and I used to pretend that we were about to marry, and had make-believe conversations in front of the others about how many ironing boards and other wedding presents had been duplicated or even triplicated. The joke almost became reality, but not quite. However, we were `an item' as they say, for quite some time and we had some splendid times together. Dick was a wealthy man and in due course Mummy never forgave me for not accepting his marriage proposal. Not, I think, because of his wealth although this was an added draw, but because he was such a kind man and this was something that was of paramount importance in a marriage in her view, about which I wouldn't quibble. However, the missing factor, love, didn't quite seem to be part of the equation on my part. He took me to all the first nights at the theatre and to the ballet. We enjoyed some wonderful performances by such actors as Laurence Olivier, Paul Schofield, Vivian Leigh, Cicely Courtenidge and a host of others who were playing in the late forties and early fifties. We dined often at The Café de Paris where on one wonderful occasion Noel Coward was performing. We also sat at the next table to him and a `friend' at The Ivy restaurant one evening, so I was able to see him properly. One evening when the band from the Café de Paris was playing at The Savoy Hotel, the bandleader saw us come in and immediately got the band to play 'our tune'. I can't recall what it was now, but I certainly appreciated the compliment.

Dick's home was near Rochdale in Lancashire and I went there on a number of occasions for the week-end and, I think, got on well with his widowed mother. She used to pay a couple of visits a year to London and always gave a large luncheon party at Claridges for family members and friends who lived in or around London. They were a bit intimidating to begin with, but hugely enjoyable after a time.

Before Dick came on the scene, I was rather keen on a man called Stanley Gill, also from the north, who was about to become a barrister. He was something of an intellectual and our great mutual interests were books and music. He had many friends of some standing in the music world, like the conductor John Pritchard, the soprano April Cantelope and also Anthony Hopkins. One memorable afternoon we went to John Pritchard's home in Anthony Hopkins' very old car, so old that mushrooms were growing in the back seat. There we listened in this august musical company to a recording of Balakirev's First Symphony while having tea on a cold and misty November afternoon.

Some 45 years later Anthony Hopkins gave a wonderfully amusing performance at Bridport in Dorset to which I went and had the opportunity of reminding him of this occasion. He remembered the car, but not the occasion. Stanley was duly called to the Bar, but we went our separate ways and only his amusing but rather formal letters remain, penned in splendid copperplate writing, together with a copy of John Aubrey's 'Brief Lives'.

Flat Sharing

The other person who became a good friend and was at Hatchards at that time was Winifred Shanks (known as Winfy), whose family name has graced baths, basins and loos thoughout the world for many years. A Scot, she had been an assistant stage manager at Windsor Rep, the well-known theatre company at Windsor in Berkshire, before becoming engaged to a fellow Scot who was a Reserve for the Scottish Rugby team. She had broken off the engagement at the eleventh hour and was in a sorry state when she came to Hatchards. She recovered from this blip and asked me to join her and another Scots girl, Mary Rutherford, in renting a delightful flat in De Vere Gardens in Kensington.

At this time my life changed for the better in so many ways. We did all the things young unmarried girls did in those days, short of sleeping around, and enjoyed a highly entertaining social life, combined with quieter times in the flat. But around the time of the annual England versus Scotland rugger match we were invaded and entertained by various members of the Scottish team and after one particularly hilarious evening dining at the Café de Paris we ended up having toothpaste squirted over us by these huge and fairly inebriated men.

The one downside to all this fun was that Hatchards paid a very meagre wage, something like £4.15.6d a week. As I paid a rent of £2.15.0d each week there wasn't a lot over for food, travel, clothes and so on. The others were, I think, subsidised to some extent by their families. One managed somehow, but whenever I was invited out to dinner and the theatre it was usually in borrowed clothes. The others were always kind and understanding and when we threw drinks parties I paid less and invited fewer of my friends and it seemed to work happily enough.

One day one or other of us arrived home from work to find a great hole in the front door and the bottle of milk on our top step had been opened and half of it consumed. Burglars, we thought, and the police were sent for. In those days the police arrived pretty promptly. They looked into one of the bedrooms which was strewn about with clothes and all the drawers open. "They've obviously been in here," exclaimed the police constable. "No, it sometimes looks like this," was the reply. As luck would have it the burglar or burglars hadn't got into the flat after all. They must have been disturbed or thirsty for more than half a bottle of milk. We were so lucky.

We had a merry time but although we lived it up with parties, theatres and the like, very often just the three of us enjoyed quieter times in the comfort of the flat, usually on Sunday evenings listening to 'Songs of Praise' on the radio and choosing which hymns we would have at our weddings. I still listen, but have changed the choice from wedding to funeral hymns. Time passes inexorably.

Mother's Remarriage

When I spent weekends with Mother I invariably came back weeping because of some altercation or another, so it was a comfort to return to my friends, and get on with this new life. I should mention here that a wonderful thing came about to make Mother's life happier. She met and was keenly courted by a widower, Dick Henderson, whose wife she had known in her younger days in Yorkshire. Once the decree absolute came through following her divorce from my father, they were married in Reading. Dick was a wonderful and a kind husband and they had some very happy times together for nigh on 34 years, when sadly he died.

Dick had a daughter, Janet, who was 13 years old when her mother died, so Mother helped complete her upbringing, but with fairly predictable difficulties, being a step-mother. Once she came of age Janet soon got married to John Morley and they had three super children, who in time gave her six grandchildren.

Chris, my brother, who left home even before Mother remarried and then did his National Service, married his wife, Sheila, at the tender age of 18 years and a happier couple it would be hard to find. They had two daughters, Julia and Jane, who in their turn married and have children of their own.

So Mother was well looked after and well-loved, until her death at the age of

91 years. Her final years, as a widow, were not happy ones and she eventually lost her sight completely. She had always been a very active person, doing voluntary work of various kinds and sitting on Red Cross and local Conservative Committees, so she found her forced immobility acutely frustrating. Nonetheless she mellowed as she got older and relations between us were easier and happier; but it remains one of the great sadnesses of my life that nothing I could do to try and please her really seemed to succeed in getting rid of whatever it was about me that she appeared to disapprove of so continuously. Perhaps it was simply that I reminded her of my father.

But, as I have said, I got great support from my two flatmates. Winfy was and still is a great champion of the underdog. She clearly detected that I was a bit of a waif and tended to jolly me along with great kindness and affection. This support was of immense value and continued well after we all went our separate ways and then again in recent years.

The Book Society

During this time my health became something of a bore and I realised that financial anxieties, being on my feet all day at Hatchards and a fairly active social life were having a detrimental effect. Much as I enjoyed working at Hatchards, I had to find a more sedentary means of earning a living.

My next job, still with books, was as a clerk at The World Book Club, a subsidiary of The Book Society. The office was beautifully situated in Dean's Yard, just behind Westminster Abbey. Our view was over Westminster School's playing fields and watching the little chaps doing rugby tackles and the like was a welcome diversion from typing addresses onto envelopes. But everything has a good side and here it was being able to read proof copies of all the best-selling books which appealed. Otherwise it wasn't much fun there and I had to think hard what to do next.

During this time I had to have a cartilage removed from my right knee, following a kick during an evening of country dancing at Bisham Abbey. After an initial consultation, the orthopaedic surgeon told me that they would have to operate and would give a ring when a bed became free. That very night I had a dream in which I was in a hospital bed out in the country, with the sun shining through the trees around me. Later I was in a ward and coming towards me were Dick, Winfy and Mary, bearing white flowers and goodies. Exactly one week later all this actually happened. What I hadn't realised was that the Royal

National Orthopaedic Hospital, which I had visited in Portland Place, had a second hospital at Stanmore in Middlesex and this was were the operation was done. After it was done, my bed was wheeled out onto a balcony into the sunshine. Later Dick, Winfy and Mary did indeed arrive and walk down the ward bearing white flowers and goodies. All very strange.

I celebrated my 21st Birthday in some style. Mother and Dick came up to the flat bearing gifts and a birthday cake and a small black doll which they said they had found on their doorstep. Humour apart, this doll still has pride of place on my dressing table and has just had a new set of clothes made very expertly by Chris's wife, Sheila. Her other clothes were attacked by mites, white ants or moths while I was living in Singapore.

On the eve of the birthday Dick Butterworth took me to dine at The Savoy and at midnight as the band played "Happy Birthday to You" he gave me a gold signet ring with a bloodstone and a copy of 'Katharine Mansfields' Letters to John Middleton Murray. He knew that I admired Katharine Mansfield's work a lot at that time.

IV

Two Big Decisions

It was clear that I had to make a decision about whether or not to marry Dick – and soon. I had always hankered after going abroad, but Mother had stipulated that until I came of age that was out of the question. She had wanted me to get a job as a librarian at Reading Library. This was not something that appealed to me. An American friend who was visiting Europe at that time sent me a post card from Norway. That is where I must go, I decided. Somewhere quiet and clean, where I could make up my mind in peace. As it happened, I found a friend with a contact in Sweden rather than Norway who knew of a family anxious for an English girl to live with them for three months, talk English to their two daughters aged, respectively, 12 and 10 years and help with the ironing and mending. This was the answer and also something of a watershed in my life.

It must be remembered that a lot of unsettling things had happened in a short space of time: my parent's marriage had broken up; Mother had a new husband and so I felt less than at home in their joint home; Dick Butterworth's marriage proposals needed to be answered; I had no money to speak of and my health was far from robust. On the other hand, great support was always at hand from my two flatmates and I had a widening circle of good friends. One of these was Jo Preston who had married Bun Watson and was living quite close by in Nevern Square. So too was friend Bin, both friends from Bisham days. Shortly before my departure for Sweden, dear Jo presented me with a cheque for £25, saying: "Just pay me back when you can; no hurry at all," and I was able to buy myself a much-needed and rather smart camel-hair coat. Was it really sensible to leave them all and go out into the great unknown? The decision to grasp this nettle was helped by the fact that for reasons I cannot recall, Mary, Winfy and I had just given up the flat in De Vere Gardens and each found other accommodation. Although we kept very much in touch with each other, I was on my own again and Sweden beckoned.

After an emotional last evening, which took in a drinks party for many of my friends, dinner at The Arts Theatre Club and finally a rather alcoholic finale with my closest friends on a houseboat on the Thames at Chelsea belonging to one, John Grinter, an occasional escort of mine. I went back home the next day to pack, helped by Mother, who greatly admired the new camel-hair coat and seemed quite proud of me. She, Dick and Janet took me to the boat train at St Pancras Station where we were joined by Winfy and Mary and after the usual awkward chat and farewells amid laughter and tears, I was off on the great adventure.

V

Sweden

My destination was a small town called Munkfors in Värmland, an area of lakes and forests, roughly half way between Stockholm and Oslo and the home of the Köhncke family: Märtha, Rolf, Irene and Katrin. I took a train from Gothenburg to a place called Deje and when I alighted from the train, the smell of the place was quite awful. This, I discovered later, was the smell of paper pulp, and my fear that the whole of Sweden smelt like this was unfounded.

Märtha met me off the train. It was January and pretty cold and snow was piled up on the sides of the roads. What I should mention now is that Märtha had asked me to send a photograph of myself before accepting me. It emerged much later that she had shown it to a friend for her opinion. The friend had commented: "Well she doesn't look very intelligent, but she looks kind!" So I was accepted.

History doesn't relate what her first impressions were on meeting me. We drove to their home in semi-darkness, and what a home it was. A largeish timber house full of beautiful furniture, some modern and some quite heavy pieces which had come from Rolf's home in Germany. Magnificent paintings filled the walls, including a Braque and a Miró, as well as a lot of Delft ceramics. The floors were covered with splendid oriental rugs, one of Rolf's weaknesses – or rather strengths; and the house was wonderfully warm. My bedroom had the most beautiful French wallpaper, depicting nymphs and shepherds, and it was a lovely light room.

As I started nervously to unpack, the two girls arrived home from school and came in to meet me. It wasn't a good moment because, fearing that there might not be any English tea, I had brought some along with me together with a tiny tin teapot and somehow the tea packet had split and the girls caught me on my knees wondering how to clear it up. An awkward moment ensued, particularly as I had come to teach them English and at that point we weren't able to communicate. Meeting Rolf Köhncke was the easiest of all. He was a large, genial man with tremendously kind brown eyes and bade me a warm welcome.

The first weeks and months were not easy, adjusting to the strangeness of it all and coping with the moods of each member of the family, including a round, red-faced little maid. I gave an English lesson to the girls each day, but had never been trained as a teacher and so had to feel my way along whilst the two girls, often with pencils stuck up their noses, challenged me at every turn. Even in the evenings, when the whole family was together they were all avid to learn about England and the English and I was constantly being asked what various plants and trees were called in English. "Oh", I used to say "we don't have them in England". When it became obvious that the English countryside and the gardens were almost barren, I had to admit that I didn't know what these things were called in English. Also their knowledge of English history was far greater than mine. However, with all these challenges my sense of humour came into play and so did theirs and at last there was a break-through.

I was rather nervous of Märtha at first. She tended to be a bit prickly at times and on the day of Queen Elizabeth II's Coronation, when, with her permission, I listened to the ceremony from start to finish on the radio, the atmosphere was very tense indeed. It was only when some time later I received an ultimatum from Dick Butterworth asking me to come home for Easter so that we could become engaged, that I felt able to talk over my problem with her and we became firm friends from then on. I was thus able to write and tell Dick that, sadly, I couldn't marry him. In the event he married someone else quite soon after I had turned him down and his daughter's coming-of-age photograph was in 'Country Life' some 20-odd years later.

Märtha's own love life had not been straightforward and when we came to know each other better she told me what proved to be a fascinating story. By the time

I met them both, Rolf Köhncke was an engineer with Uddeholms AB, a large Swedish company comprising in steel, timber, chemical products, mines and railways. It had sales offices throughout the world and Munkfors was where their steel cold-rolling works were situated and where Rolf worked in an executive capacity.

The family had a summer house called 'Trakten' on a lake called Lakene surrounded by pine forests about half-an-hour's drive from Munkfors. We often spent weekends there and longer in the summer. It was idyllic and to sit watching the light changing over the lake and the hills beyond filled me with a great longing to be in love and to experience this beauty with someone dear to me. It was not to be, but we certainly had some happy times there. Rolf had wire recordings – there were no tapes or CDs in those days – of much of my favourite music which we often sat listening to over many glasses of wine in front of a roaring log fire. Rolf was a great connoisseur of wine and had a large well-stocked wine cellar. Coming from Germany his preferred wine was Mosel, which didn't agree with me one bit and I had some nasty bouts of sickness before realising what was causing them. On rainy days he would get up at dawn and potter in the garden looking exactly like something that lived in the forests, clad in an extraordinary array of old clothes and a sou'wester. Märtha was a very special person and fascinating to listen to and to talk to, and the girls and I had great fun too, so life had begun to look up.

Märtha and her elder sister, Elsa, were the daughters of Gustav Jansson, a former Managing Director of Uddeholm's Works in Munkfors. When Märtha was a young girl, she told me, she fell in love with Rolf, a German engineer who often came over to Munkfors on business. Her mother wasn't happy about this liaison so she intercepted Rolf's letters and thinking that he no longer cared for her, Märtha married a well known Swedish writer and publisher, Carl Björkman, by whom she had a daughter, Annika. As members of the PEN Club, Carl Björkman and Märtha met a whole host of literary figures of the day, including Thomas Mann. But the marriage was not a happy one. While Märtha was on holiday with a friend in Travemunde some years later, she met Rolf again, quite by accident. By that time he too was married and had a family. To cut a long story short they realised that they still loved each other and moved heaven and earth to be together again. Märtha divorced Carl Björkman, who later married a girl younger than his own daughter.

Märtha explained to me that, when World War II broke out, Rolf had had to enlist in the German Army so a permit to marry had to be obtained and signed by Adolf Hitler. Prior to this they were lying on the beach together one day at Travemunde when a Nazi soldier came by, gave the Heil Hitler salute and said: "Make good German children." They were appalled at this of course. But a permit from Hitler was secured and the couple duly married. Rolf was serving in Germany and was not sympathetic to Adolf Hitler and nor was Märtha. She managed to find someone, who, at a price, was willing to smuggle Rolf out of Germany and get him to Sweden; in other words to defect. One night she had a telephone call from her contact in Germany who told her to go to a rendezvous deep in the forests of Värmland where Rolf would be waiting for her. Transport during the war was difficult, few people were allowed to run cars, but her father was one of the few who was and she drove off into the night to the rendezvous. It was pitch black and suddenly Rolf's voice said "Ten minutes late as usual!" It was an extremely happy moment for them, but there were two less happy sequels to this saga.

Living in Stockholm during the war were anti-Nazi Germans and pro-Nazi Germans. Clearly Rolf was one of the former and was keeping a fairly low profile. One day when he and Märtha were planning a dinner party they were approached by one of their guests who asked them to invite a particular German along. Märtha didn't like the man he suggested and declined to invite him. They learnt afterwards that plans were afoot to murder this man at their dinner party. It wasn't long after this that there was a knock at the door of their apartment. A hefty German stood there and asked to speak to "Herr Köhncke". Suspecting trouble, Märtha replied that he wasn't at home, at which the man put his foot in the door and said that he was an emissary from no less than Field Marshal Hermann Goering and that Goering had given his assurances that if Herr Köhncke would return to Germany no harm would come to him. Rolf, who had been listening from inside the apartment, climbed out of a back window and Märtha eventually persuaded the man that Rolf was not at home and he went away. For safety's sake the Köhnckes moved down to their house in Värmland where he was well out of harm's way. He was later given a job with Uddeholms AB in Munkfors, for which he was more than suited.

At the end of the war Rolf, as with all German males, was sent back to Germany, and in Rolf's case, it was to Lübeck, from whence he had come. But when he entered the country he was arrested by the British as his name appeared on a 'wanted' list. He was then interned by the British military authorities. Märtha went over to try and get him released. Speaking fluent

German, she took on the role of a German journalist and with the help of Count Bernadotte and a British Army officer succeeded in doing so. Rolf returned to Sweden and in due course became a Swedish citizen.

Many years later when Märtha celebrated her 50th Birthday with a grand dinner party at her mother's large mansion in Stockholm, I was invited and sat well below the salt. It was a splendid and an emotional occasion and when Rolf rose to give a speech to his dearly-loved wife and came to the time of his incarceration at the hands of the British, he turned towards me and gave a little bow saying "And for a short time I was a guest of His Majesty King George VI". It was said humorously and with no sign of any resentment and we all laughed.

Because my decision not to marry Dick had been made, there was no hurry for me to return to England when my three months were up and I was persuaded by the family to stay on until Christmas while awaiting a work permit to take up a job at a hotel in the ski resort of Abisko on the Swedish-Norwegian border, which Märtha had kindly instigated through a friend. Märtha and Rolf had planned to motor down to Hamburg to celebrate the 50th Birthday of Rolf's brother, Carl, just before Christmas and they thought it would be nice for me to drive down with them, thus seeing a bit more of Europe.

In principle it was a lovely idea, but in practice it turned out to be a bit of a nightmare. Somewhere in Germany their English Morris shuddered to a halt and had to be towed to a garage. I was booked onto a train leaving Hamburg for London later that evening so somehow a means had to be found to get me to Hamburg in time for that train. All went well and I bade a sad farewell to them on a cold and blustery station and climbed onto a little local train bound for Hamburg. Even then I only caught the boat-train by the skin of my teeth as I somehow got locked in the Station 'Ladies', but was released just in time.

During my time with the Köhncke family, I met fairly frequently the Herlenius family, Märtha's sister Elsa, her husband Jonas and their children Malcolm, Irma and Göran. Malcolm and Irma were more or less my contemporaries and Göran was 12 yrs old. I spent an action-packed weekend with them during the summer when the Köhncke family were away on holiday on the island of Sylt. We played tennis and swam in Råda Lake from their jetty below the house and it was all a lot of fun.

A curious thing happened at Trakten just after the family left for Sylt. I spent the first night in the house by myself before going on to the Herlenius family the following day. In the middle of the night the bedroom door opened and in came the family's elkhound. It was slightly unnerving that she had opened the door by herself. I looked out of the window and to my astonishment there was a little circle of lights bobbing about in the field nearby. I watched them for quite a long time and came to the conclusion that they were dancing trolls. You may laugh at this and can be forgiven if you think: 'There she goes again.' However, it was said that the farmer next door had a white horse which the trolls didn't like and they were said to make this horse's life a misery at nights. Who knows........? But I was glad to be going to stay with the Herlenius family the following day.

During the autumn Märtha took me to Stockholm to stay with her daughter Annika and family, and showed me round that beautiful city and other places of interest on the way home, like Gripsholm Castle and Uppsala, the university town. By this time I felt completely at home with the family and Sweden in general and it was with a heavy heart that I left them all and returned to London not quite knowing when I would be back. The working permit for Abisko still hadn't come through and somehow I had to find a job to tide me over as I arrived home with only five shillings in my pocket.

VI

Short Spell in London

Friend Jo suggested I get a job as a waitress until the working permit came through. She knew of an up-market restaurant where all the waitresses were debutantes and so-called 'Sloane Rangers' so I went along to try my luck. I think it was actually in Sloane Street. Rain was pouring down and it was evening and I was tired after the long journey from Sweden. Sadly they had no need of another waitress, so I had a coffee and as I went to pay, the rather grand cashier suggested I might try my luck at a restaurant in South Kensington called 'The Green Lizard'.

This I did and got a job starting the following day. It was quite fun until I was asked to go and work at their other branch just off Oxford Circus. This was hectic in the extreme and I had nightmares for months afterwards as a result of the frantic situations I had to contend with. The other girls were experienced waitresses and were forever pinching my customers' 'welsh rarebits' or whatever for their own customers, leaving my people baying for food which then took a long time coming. I survived, but when a letter came from Elsa Herlenius in Sweden asking me if I could come over the following week and look after the house and their youngest son, Göran, because she and Jonas were going skiing in Switzerland, I leapt at the idea. As I mentioned earlier, I had seen quite a lot of the Herlenius family, and felt that there was an instant rapport between us all, so I was very happy to be seeing everyone again.

VII

Long Spell in Sweden

A week later, almost a year to the day of my first foray to Sweden, I was on another Swedish Lloyd ferry heading there again. The Herlenius family lived in a large timber house on Råda Lake, on the other side of which was Uddeholms AB Head Office. Like the Köhncke's house in Munkfors a few miles away, it was gracefully furnished, and had a long open veranda overlooking the lake. It was a relaxed and comfortable house and I ended up living there for some eight years in all. Eight years which changed my life and my approach to life in a host of different ways. The work permit for the job in Abisko never did materialise, and this turned out to be a blessing in disguise.

It was good to be back and also to see the Köhncke family again, of whom I had become very fond. When I had left them just before Christmas, my luggage was full of thoughtful little Christmas gifts from Irene and Katrin, complete with affectionate verses and a lovely book on Värmland from Märtha.

Nothing untoward happened whilst Elsa and Jonas were away in Switzerland and on their return I settled down to a happy existence. Irma, who was 22 years, just a year younger than I was, already spoke good English, but Göran needed lessons. This was a slow business because, although no-one realised at the time, he was dyslexic and all my exasperation and irritation over the fact that he couldn't grasp the simplest points of grammar, were manifestly unfair, but he never seemed unduly worried about it. He was very much his own person, even as a boy, and grew into a wonderful man despite, or perhaps because of continuous ill health of one sort or another. He loved horses and had a truculent pony called Blaker, which only he could keep under control. Göran always came in to meals wearing two brown and yellow check shirts and exuding a strong smell of stable. Charged to some extent with keeping him in order, I was forever telling him to take his elbows off the table. Many many years later when he was an adult, he said to me in the middle of a dinner party: "Take your elbows off the table, Angela." We were quits at last.

Irma and I became very good friends and had a lot of fun together. She was always a very natural and in many ways an unsophisticated girl, which added to her charm; and she didn't mind in the least being teased. At that time she was very much in love with Christer Borlind, who later became her husband. When she was being sent to do a French Course at The Sorbonne, she tried every argument she could muster to stay in Sweden to be near her best beloved, but to no avail. On her return, her English had improved no end because she had been talking to and consorting with English students instead of speaking French, although she did in fact master French too.

Malcolm, who, like his father, was an engineer, was working with Uddeholms AB in Brussels at that time. He came home fairly often and I loved his visits. His sense of humour exactly mirrored mine and thus a lifelong rapport built up between us. Actually all the family were blessed with a good sense of humour, which may go some way to explaining how they all came to accept me into their family as they did. And not only the immediate family, but aunts and uncles and cousins too.

Netten, (Antoinette) the wife of Jonas' brother Ivar was a case in point. She was a warm, but quiet and self-contained person whom I saw quite a lot of later when I lived in Stockholm quite near to their home. I recall spending one or two very happy Easters with them both. When I left Stockholm, Netten's letters, which continued very nearly until her death at the age of 99 years, were a great source of warmth and friendship and very much reflected what a very kind and cultivated person she was. Norwegian by birth, her English, both spoken and written, were well-nigh perfect, although she had never been to England. Her daughter, Stella, brought up in much the same vein, also has a remarkable knack of writing marvellously colloquial and amusing English and remains a firm friend to this day. The close friendships I formed within the family were and still are almost beyond my comprehension.

Elsa was a warm, wise and immensely positive person but as with most larger-than-life people she could often be quite maddening. Whenever family members got together, they always had great fun regaling each other with memories of some of her more bizzare exploits, which I was well able to contribute to. But she was held in great affection by everyone. She wielded a great influence over me in so many ways and I have every reason to think of her as "my Swedish Mum". She taught me a lot, as did Märtha, for like most Swedish women of their standing and generation, they were well versed in the arts, literature and history. They also spoke very good English, French, German and in Elsa's case, quite good Italian. Jonas, in contrast, was shy, formal and very self-contained; he was almost a nobleman, rather than just a gentleman and if rather hesitant, a good friend. When he did let his hair down at family gatherings it was a joy to see. I loved them all.

In the summer life was idyllic. We swam and played tennis and I got to know all their friends in Uddeholm, many of whom were fellow directors' families. They all had beautiful homes round Råda Lake and entertained a lot.

Uddeholm's agents from all over the world paid regular visits to their Head Office and were entertained to lunch or dinner by Elsa and Jonas. I loved these occasions particularly because English tended to be the main language, unlike the times when their friends came and everyone spoke Swedish, except when talking directly to me. Towards the end of such evenings my smile began to wane a little. As my Swedish started to improve, the wife of one of the directors asked me to family lunches on a regular basis and by talking only Swedish to me slowly and carefully they were able to coax me into speaking more and better Swedish.

I should mention before going any further that soon after my return to Sweden, both Elsa and Märtha persuaded me that I needed to have some sort of training in order to make a proper career for myself. They both suggested that I learn shorthand and typing, which they assured me would open the way to all sorts of opportunities. Much as the idea appalled me, I saw their logic and sent off for a Pitmans shorthand correspondence course and a handbook on typing. A typewriter was lent by the office and I set about learning both skills. On one of Malcolm's home visits, I remember him peering over my shoulder as I wrestled slowly and laboriously with the shorthand outlines and saying: "Funny, I thought that was supposed to be a speedy way of writing!" But I persevered and eventually got a job in the Hot Rolled Steel Sales Department as an

'English correspondent'. Elsa and Jonas were happy for me to go on living with them and I am eternally grateful for their kind and generous gesture.

By this time Irma had left home to do a domestic science course in Stockholm, so I think they were probably quite glad, apart from anything else, to have me keeping an eye on the house and giving Göran a chance to go on practising his English. They both travelled widely, both on Uddeholm's business and for pleasure and it was difficult to get reliable staff in the house.

At one time we had a shell-shocked German widow, who I felt unsure about, and two German maids, who were quite nice but who didn't stay very long, probably because of the dreaded Frau. I remember being ill in bed one day whilst the family was away and in the evening there was a terrible storm and all the lights fused. I heard her slow footsteps coming up the stairs and must confess to having been rather frightened as she was so unpredictable. All was well; she was only bringing up a candle for me. But she eventually became a real liability and Elsa had to ask her to go. The day she went Elsa was away and I was charged with seeing that her suitcases weren't full of things she had pinched. I had a chance to look whilst she was out of the way and to my horror Elsa's fears were realised. But as she had taken mostly linen and nothing more valuable I couldn't bring myself to confront her.

She was replaced by another unstable character; a Swedish woman of uncertain age who had found a boyfriend through an advertisement. He used to visit her at the house, but sadly they weren't allowed to marry because of her mental state. She too had to go quite soon. Then a younger, rather mute girl came but she was wont to go into Jonas's bedroom as he was dressing or into Elsa's when she was sunbathing on her terrace in her birthday suit and just stand and stare. So I think my rather more stable presence in the house gave Elsa and Jonas the confidence to go off on their trips and Göran and I managed to keep things on a reasonably even keel.

But he too could have his moments. On one occasion he had a friend to stay and they spent much of the time riding and tending a very fine military horse, which Elsa had arranged for him to exercise. One evening they came to tell me rather sheepishly that they had failed to secure the door of the inner stable and the horse had helped himself to a quantity of oats, which could have had disastrous results. I got Eriksson, the chauffeur, to come up to the house and he walked the horse round to try and get rid of the wind that was building up inside its stomach. But it wasn't sufficient and we got the vet in. He wanted to feed a rubber hose up the horse's nostrils and down into its stomach. The horse of course took great exception to this and started to buck wildly. The vet himself was terrified and so Eriksson and I had to do our best to hold it still, fortunately successfully and we all survived, including the horse.

One of the reasons Elsa was able to arrange for Göran to look after this military horse was because she was a senior officer in the 'Bilkår', the Swedish women's army corps, whose members drove cars and lorries for the Swedish Army. At that time National Service was mandatory, even for married women, and many of the more robust of them joined this corps. It was one of Elsa's paramount interests and she spent a lot of time driving lorries through snow-laden forests and sleeping under canvas as well as attending camps and committees and fighting the women's corner with various Army officers, including the Generals. In fact she was eventually awarded one of Sweden's most prestigious medals for her efforts, the Vasa Order. Jonas too held this Order. They both excelled themselves in different ways and were warmly respected, both as a couple and individually.

In August each year the crayfishing season started. This is one of Sweden's most popular traditions. The Uddeholm Company allotted each family a stretch of river in which they were allowed to fish the crayfish as soon as the season started officially. The office closed early on that day so that everyone could get off to their allotted spot in time to put down their nets. They then had a picnic on the river bank, downing a fair amount of schnapps in the process. The nets were then collected and everyone drove home at twilight in order to cook the crayfish immediately they got home. The Herlenius family was no exception and even writing this evokes the wonderful smell of crayfish cooking in lots of crown dill.

The following evening most families held a crayfish party. It is difficult to describe what fun it all was. One of the best parties was held at a fishing club, high in the hills and in the depths of the pine forests. The members of this Club, Lapptjärn, were mostly directors and former directors and managing directors of the Uddeholm company, who went up to fish for trout throughout the year in the lake there. They came with their families and dogs for the annual crayfish party which was always a splendid occasion, with speeches and then the wholesale devouring of as many crayfish as one could manage. As the shells had to be removed and the crayfish then sucked in a ritualistic sort of way, with the juice running down one's wrists in the process, the ladies usually removed their jewellery and put it in little heaps on the table beside them. The tradition is said to be that a glass of schnapps be drunk with each fish tail. As a lot of the men could eat up to 40-odd crayfishes in one sitting this amount of schnapps would have resulted in certain death, but a fair amount was downed by those who didn't have to do the driving home. All this was interspersed with drinking songs and the atmosphere and the volume of chat and general high spirits was something one needed to have seen to have believed.

When all the crayfish were finished, everyone went outside to rinse their hands in a huge wooden tub of cold water full of lemon slices. Dogs were exercised, the crayfish remains disposed of whilst the ladies organised the second part of the meal, which was a gallimaufry of dishes provided by each family. Göran told me recently that on one occasion as people were tucking into the dinner after the crayfish, Elsa suddenly cried: "Who has taken my dog food?" A rather red-faced lady emerged from the kitchen to admit that she had taken it as she thought it was part of the main course, which everyone was in the process of eating. The wife of the Managing Director, true to her calling, was heard to remark: "Well if this is dog food I'd be happy to have more of it!" I shall never forget what fun it all was and I still look back on these happy occasions each August wherever I happen to be.

Christmas was usually the next occasion for making merry in traditional style. Jonas's brother Ivar and his wife Netten, their daughter Stella and her family and Hans-August, their son, very often joined the immediate family, who began arriving in dribs and drabs from about the 22nd December. On the 23rd December we dressed the Christmas tree in the elegant salon and afterwards had a splendid supper at which the main dish tended to be fresh lobster. Everyone had a lot of news to catch up on and the party spirit began to filter through, regardless of how difficult the journey there had been. Stella kept us all laughing with her wit and her genius for recounting wonderfully evocative anecdotes. Her father, Ivar, ran her a close second with his Värmland stories all told in faultless dialect, at which he was a past master. It became a tradition for the same stories to be told year after year.

Elsa usually spent most of that morning visiting and bearing gifts to old family retainers who lived in the area. I often accompanied her and our last call was to her mother's grave in the churchyard at Ransäter. Her family is related to the famous Swedish poet Erik Gustaf Geijer and the family home, Geijersgården, is nearby. In the Ransäter Hembygdsmuseum there is now a sculpted head of Elsa and one or two other things of historical interest given by the Herlenius family.

On Christmas Eve morning everyone foregathered in the hall after breakfast to prepare for a ski trip planned by Jonas, who knew which routes to take like the back of his hand. Ivar, his brother, was notorious for wanting to start at the crack of dawn, but after a spat or two with Elsa about what time breakfast would be served he accepted the inevitably later start.

By this time a wonderful cook had been found and the odd collection of staff became a thing of the past and best forgotten. The new cook was called Fröken Finqvist, a dear person, who besides being an excellent cook, was a very nice woman. She was big and always wore a white overall reaching almost to her ankles which were huge and seemed to overlap her big and sturdy black shoes. On her head she wore a white cotton head-piece and one could never imagine her dressed otherwise. But she was strict with Göran and his friends, who teased her a bit.

One morning at breakfast well after Christmas, Elsa summoned Fröken Finqvist from the kitchen to ask where the Christmas Cake had got to. This cake was made from an English recipe and was totally delicious. Fröken Finqvist replied without hesitation: "Miss Barry has eaten it up." Said like that it sounded as if I had wolfed it down in one go and I turned a bright shade of pink, much to everyone's amusement. In fact it was put out at breakfast times from Christmas onwards and, not surprisingly, no-one wanted to eat it after healthy platefulls of bacon and eggs. I, on the other hand, often had a slice in the afternoons with my cup of tea over several weeks, so, in effect, I had eaten it up!

The ski trips could be totally exhausting, for me at least, who had not been brought up to ski. We slogged up hills and through the forests for what seemed like hours in varying temperatures. It was sometimes so cold that our sweaty anoraks froze on our backs. And if it wasn't cold, the snow built up on the bottoms of my skis, making it even heavier going. Jonas usually helped me wax my skis, but usually not until we had reached whichever summit we were aiming for. Flying back down through the forest tracks always filled me with terror as there were always boulders or loops of tree branches to be avoided, which at speed I found difficult to do. Once I landed on what looked to be a friendly mound of snow which turned out to be a boulder with a thin coating of snow.

That time I cracked my coccyx and couldn't sit down for weeks. Another time one foot went into the centre of a looped branch and I ended up in a muddle from which it was difficult to extricate myself. By this time the others were well ahead and I feared I would freeze to death in a hole. Not so, there was always one kind soul, usually Malcolm, who would come back to help.

Needless to say, after returning home and enjoying a sauna downstairs in the cellar, we were more than ready for the main Christmas Dinner. In Sweden, this consisted of various sorts of marinated herring, home-made sausages and Swedish rye bread and cheese, accompanied by ice-cold schnapps and a special Christmas beer (Julål). Christmas drinking songs were called for with each new glass of schnapps and we all became merrier and merrier. This was followed by delicious ham on the bone, spinach and small potatoes and also Jansson's Frästelse (Johnson's Temptation), which was a mixture of anchovies and strips of onion and potato, baked in butter and it really was totally delicious. To follow came something to help the digestion in the form of a special fish (lutfisk), marinated in lye (lut), which is, I'm told, an alkaline solution, from which it emerged grey and slimy. It was eaten with a white sauce, petit pois and melted butter and most Swedish children avoided eating it at any cost. For pudding there were mountain raspberries, which also grow in Scotland, and little tartlets filled with strawberry jam and clotted cream.

Present giving followed. Jonas was in charge and as many of the gifts came with an apt little verse penned by the giver, this went on for a long time, interspersed with long intervals when we repaired again to the dining room for fruit, nuts, water and a wonderful home-made Punch, which Hans-August provided. He was a medical student and could easily get pure spirit to make it with. The bottle usually sat outside immersed in the snow until we were ready to taste it. This all took place on Christmas Eve.

On Christmas Day those who wanted to got up at some unearthly hour and staggered through the snow to the little church in the village. On the whole the Swedes are not regular churchgoers, but on Christmas morning the churches are packed. There were lighted candles on all the windowsills and as the aroma of alcohol consumed by everyone the night before filled the church it got very hot. The priest took this opportunity to chastise the congregation for coming only on Christmas Day, so what with that and the heat and the fumes we were glad to emerge into the snow again and home to a huge breakfast of bacon and eggs and the aforementioned Christmas cake.

Afterwards there was usually another ski trip, from which we returned just as it was getting dark. After a sauna and a rest we all foregathered, the men in black tie, the ladies in pretty dresses, for turkey and all the trimmings and Christmas Pudding. At 3 p.m GMT I was usually to be found crouched over the radio in an effort to hear The Queen's Speech through an inhibiting amount of atmospherics.

After Christmas Dinner one year, when Elsa suggested playing bridge, I protested loudly, no doubt influenced by the generous amounts of alcohol consumed during the meal. I said it would be kinder if we could play a game that everyone could join in. There was something of a deathly hush and Elsa's anger was fairly palpable. I fled to my bedroom and burst into tears. Elsa followed and in measured but kindly tones said that it was time I learnt to play bridge. All was well and of course the suggestion was a good one, which I followed with the family's help and have never regretted.

Irma's wedding to Christer Borlind took place in mid-winter after some very heavy falls of snow. A nightmare scenario ensued with the arrival of the large numbers of guests, all of whom had to be accommodated once their long and fairly hairy journeys had been successfully completed. This had all been planned in meticulous detail and in the end I think everyone eventually arrived. Poor Malcolm was not met at the station and had to wade knee-deep through the snow arriving unheralded in the middle of the night.

On the day of the wedding, Eriksson, the chauffeur, took Jonas to the office in the morning but got stuck in a snowdrift on the way home. He was still there when Jonas wanted to return home. Jonas rang the house time and time again with gathering impatience and no-one could tell him what had happened, but he was eventually picked up. Meanwhile Elsa had given herself a face-pack with the 'fango' mud from Italy and when the official photographers arrived to photograph the happy couple at home before the wedding ceremony; she opened the door to them complete with black face, which gave them a bit of a fright.

The wedding took place in the little village church and when we drew up as near to the door as the cars could take us, Hans-August took upon himself the task of carrying all the girls one by one over the snow and into the church. We were all dressed in long evening dresses and the men in white tie. After the marriage ceremony we continued through the snow to Uddeholms Herrgård for the reception. This was a large and imposing timber manor house, where Jonas' father, a former managing director of the company, had lived and where Jonas was brought up. It was subsequently used as the company's guest house.

The wedding dinner was a huge success and even though a waiter spilt a glass of claret down my dress, the dress happened to be claret-coloured so no stain was left. Christer, the bridegroom, who was studying law, was the son of Ove Borlind, a Hovmarskalk (member of the Royal Court) and ADC to Prince Bertil of Sweden, and Elizabeth Borlind (known as Bethan). The guests included a fair number in military or naval formal dress uniforms and members of the Swedish Diplomatic Corps, so it was a distinguished and colourful gathering. Irma made a wonderfully pretty, happy and smiling bride as the couple walked down the aisle at the end of the wedding ceremony.

To give an idea of how unaffected she was, an amusing anecdote springs to mind. Her parents-in-law gave a little dinner for her to meet Prince Bertil and Princess Lilian formally shortly before the wedding. During the course of the meal, Irma drained her schnapps glass and then poured the final drops into her beer glass. She suddenly noticed that all eyes were trained on her. Completely unabashed she looked at them all and said: "Well Papa always does it," and the laughter which ensued showed how much she was appreciated.

In 1956 HM The Queen and The Duke of Edinburgh paid an official visit to Stockholm. As I had registered with the British Consulate soon after my arrival in Sweden, I automatically received an invitation to a Reception for British Residents to meet the Royal pair. It meant taking the train to Stockholm and staying a night in the Herlenius' flat at Tystagatan 7. It was all very exciting for a committed royalist and although I wasn't lucky enough to meet either of them I was able to see and appreciate them at close quarters for the first time. Another bonus was that I happened to turn round at one point to find Lord Mountbatten standing right behind me.

Bethan and Ove Borlind, Christer's parents, gave a drinks party in their 'grace and favour' apartment next to the Royal Palace. As all the roads in the area had been closed to traffic, Christer came to pick me up in a large black car bearing a royal crown. He was dressed in a navy suit and as he held open the back door for me he hissed: "I'm your chauffeur, get in." I did as I was told and rather enjoyed being peered at by the waiting crowds and even chanced a discreet royal wave or two, unseen by my 'chauffeur'. Once there, we were able to watch the

Royal couple arrive by boat at the jetty below the Palace. As Hovmarskalk and ADC to Prince Bertil Ove had been invited to the official dinner party at the Palace He looked very grand in his, I suppose, Number One uniform and tricorn hat as he set off and he was able to give us a blow by blow account of the occasion on his return; all great fun.

I have made no mention of my work with the company; suffice it to say that although it was immensely boring I worked with some very nice people and had quite a busy social life in my own right apart from the family. One day a group of us went up to Dalarna to ski the Vasaloppet. This was the route King Gustav Vasa took on skis in 1521 when fleeing from the marauding Danes. Every year people gather there to do as much or as little of the route as they are able. After our varyingly modest attempts we watched an ice-hockey match, became frozen stiff and travelled back to Värmland. But I enjoyed taking part in such an historic tradition.

One of the early highlights when living in Sweden was learning to drive a car, which I did with a little local firm in Hagfors, the nearest town to Uddeholm. My fellow learner-drivers all seemed to be local youths dressed from head to toe in black leather. They got immense pleasure from listening to my attempts to answer questions about the car and road safety in halting Swedish. But I actually passed first time and like other members of the family before and after me always offered to do the driving when we went out in the evenings. It meant that I couldn't drink alcohol, but it was well worth foregoing this to do the driving.

One weekend when there were no staff in the house, Walther Sommerlath and his wife were coming to dinner. He was the company's German director who headed the office in Dusseldorf. His daughter, Sylvia, later married Prince Carl Gustav and eventually became Queen of Sweden. We youngsters all helped with getting the meal ready and clearing it away. I had put the family Volkswagen away in the garage earlier in the day and in doing so had badly scraped one of the wings. During the times we were in the kitchen whilst clearing the table, we hatched a plot as to how to explain away the damage. Immediately after dinner, we said we were going off to see if we could see any elks as it was just beginning to get dark and we knew that this was the time when they would be out feeding. We came back saying that an elk had leapt out of the woods and hit the car, something that tended to happen quite often. A naughty white lie, and I don't think the truth was ever discovered. Worse was to come, however, at a later date.

VIII

Uddeholm's Office in London

Much as I loved the life I was leading, I had been thinking for some time that perhaps I ought to go back to England. The house had become rather empty: Malcolm was working in Mexico where he had met and married a Mexican wife, Elenita. Irma and Christer were living in the north of Sweden and Göran was away at a special school at which it was hoped his dyslexia could be dealt with more effectively than was the case at his local school. Elsa was often away on her Army duties and Jonas too on business. I applied for a job with the Swedish Institute in London, but before committing myself I was offered a job in a newly-opened London office selling Uddeholm tool and drilling steel. This was the idea of Cecil Robinson, the Director of Uddeholm's main office in the UK in Birmingham. I had got to know him quite well, liked and much respected him and the offer seemed too good not to be seriously considered. Steel had not hitherto been high on my list of interests, but in the event I took the job.

The Manager was a former miner who had been writing for various associated journals and knew that particular world better than most people. He was kindness itself, but a fairly rough diamond who had no idea how to run an office let alone keep his papers in any sort of order. The whole thing became a nightmare and although I persuaded him that we needed another secretary, which certainly helped, I knew that this wasn't what I wanted in life. There were some light-hearted moments when the sales representatives called, but other than that there was little to recommend it. Cecil and his wife Margaret were kindness itself and I spent some happy week-ends with them in their lovely old farmhouse in Kings Norton, complete with dogs and children.

I was living in a flat in Earl's Court during this time. It was owned by an ex-Sherborne girl, Carol, who shared her sitting room with me, but the other two flatmates had their own bedsitting rooms. We all shared the kitchen and bathroom, but the whole set-up was slightly uneasy-making. I liked them all but Carol had a strange boyfriend, Neville, who was a barrister. He used to arrive late at night and whilst waiting for him Carol would brew supper for him, comprised always, it seemed, mainly of boiled onions. The smell was all-pervading. Neville was seldom seen and when we did happen to bump into him he scuttled away, apparently terrified, back into Carol's room. At weekends when he came he spent most of the day under the bonnet of his very old Rolls Royce outside the front door. There was one colossal drama when he found out that Carol had another boyfriend and he arrived one evening consumed with anger. Carol daren't let him in and he spent the entire night on the stairs shouting and banging on the door, much to the neighbours' and our own discomfort. Carol eventually married a charming ex-Naval officer and I spent one or two very enjoyable week-ends with them in the country.

During the time I was back in London, Winfy Shanks married Jim Spicer, an officer in the 1st Bn The Parachute Regt, whom she had met at a friend's wedding. Mary Rutherford and I, her ex-flatmates, were two of her bridesmaids and the wedding was held in the Chapel of the Tower of London, St Peter ad Vincula, close to Jim's Regimental Headquarters where the Reception was held.

During our days in the flat she had always said she would have the hymn 'O Perfect Love' at her wedding and she did. Mary and I who were facing each other near the altar caught each other's eyes and dissolved into discreet tears. Photographs were taken outside in a bit of a blizzard and I have never been so cold. A lovely photograph later appeared in 'The Tatler' and behind Winfy's windblown veil a tiny shimmer of a face could be seen. It was me and this was the one and only time I appeared in 'The Tatler'. But it was a happy occasion and Winfy and Jim joined us in the evening at Hatchetts in Piccadilly where we bridesmaids and the ushers were dining.

IX

Uddeholm's Head Office in Sweden

After not much more than a year in London I decided to emigrate to Canada. It had the advantage of being an important member of the British Commonwealth and had a climate rather like that of Sweden. I had been made to feel a bit guilty about living abroad, when one of the immigration officials remarked to me the previous time I had gone to Sweden: "Leaving us again Miss Barry?"

Before going firm on this idea, however, I decided to spend some time in Sweden again to make quite sure that I didn't want to live there permanently. After all there was a welcoming family and many good friends awaiting me. Elsa and Jonas seemed delighted at the idea and proposed that I should accompany them on a sort of Grand Tour of Italy soon after I returned. My former boss agreed to give me back my earlier job and raised no objections at all to my going on the Grand Tour. In all honesty it would have been difficult for him to do so as I was going as a guest of his boss.

X

The Grand Tour

So that is what happened and a few weeks after returning to Sweden the three of us set off on what was to be a magnificent trip. We went by car the whole way with Elsa and Jonas sharing the driving. Their car was at that time a Ford Mercury and huge. It had all the Italians in the smaller towns pointing at it and crying excitedly: "The little house!" We drove through Germany, visiting Würtzburg, where we saw its wonderful castle and sampled some delicious local wines. In Rothenburg we watched as the little puppet men emerged on the hour from the clock-tower of the Town Hall and appeared to take a draught of beer from their raised tankards. From there we went into the lovely church blessed with a most exquisite altarpiece carved by Reimenschneider, the famous medieval wood sculptor. Celle and Hannover were our next stops and I was fascinated to see the museum given over to the forebears of our own Royal family.

A Swedish Army officer called Hugo Bärnbeck, whom Elsa had worked with in the Bilkår, came with us for part of the trip. He was a married man with three children, in his forties, who had suddenly developed leukaemia. Elsa had heard of a Dr Issels who ran a clinic near Munich and who claimed to have had some successes in his treatment of the disease.

We stayed in Zurich for a night with Margrith Hürlimann and her husband, a successful Swiss banker. Margrith was the sister of Hans Kohler, Uddeholm's Swiss director, who had recently died. She spent a whole day showing me round Zurich, another first in my travel itinerary. The whole trip was my first real taste of foreign travel and I was fascinated, especially as I had such knowledgeable guides. We continued on to Bavaria, to the little town of Rottach on the lake of Tegernsee. Apart from the rather serious nature of our detour to Bavaria, the countryside was so beautiful and Rottach itself such a picturesque little town that I was more than glad to have an opportunity of seeing something of it.

Dr Issels` prognosis was not as encouraging as had been hoped. Hugo was left with making the decision of either giving the doctor a chance to prolong his life, but in doing so losing precious time and money away from his family, or simply returning home and letting the disease take its course. When we reached Milan, Elsa and Jonas stayed with Max Künzli, the Italian director of Uddeholm's office in Italy, and his wife and Hugo and I at The Hotel Rosa just behind the very imposing cathedral. I spent the evening trying to help Hugo make his very difficult decision, before he flew back to Sweden the following day. In the event, he decided to go to the clinic for Dr Issels' treatment. He spent six months there and on returning home to his family, sadly, lived for only a further six months.

I spent the next day on my own sightseeing in Milan and went up onto the roof of the beautiful Duomo marvelling at the marble roof and the view over the city. This Duomo must be quite one of the most sumptious and beautiful cathedrals in the world. From there I took a bus to the Monastery of Santa Maria delle Grazie to marvel at Leonardo Da Vinci's mural of The Last Supper. Despite its suffering from the depredations of age and damp, seeing it was a wonderful experience. That evening we all dined at a fabulous old and famous restaurant, Gianinos. Going through the memorabilia of this trip recently, I re-lived the excitement of it all and it still remains one of the great highlights of my life. I was part of a family who were keen to show me as much as ever possible and to meet their friends. The greater part of my subsequent travels have been done mostly on my own, which is never quite the same, however interesting.

After Milan we headed south to the little spa town of Abano, famous for its healing waters and the 'fango' mud from numerous hot springs throughout the area. On the way there, after a long day's drive, a motorcyclist suddenly drove out of a side road and into our car. It was a glancing blow, but the man lay on the roadside groaning. In the twinkling of an eye we were surrounded by a hostile crowd and the police were sent for. By this time the injured motorcyclist was standing up and not too badly the worse for wear. But we were detained for about an hour and our passports scrutinized by the police. Suddenly they decided to let us continue on our way and Jonas gave the motorcyclist money to repair his motorcycle.

Tired and not a little shocked we arrived at The Grand Hotel Orologio, where we were greeted with obsequious enthusiasm by the Manager, looking very much the part in tailcoat and striped trousers. Elsa and Jonas were known to him from previous visits so were able to negotiate a small room at a reasonable price for me. The room was close to the huge swimming pool full of healing waters. I had a rather snazzy navy and white swimsuit and being unable to boast a reasonably-sized bust, I had bought a pair of 'falsies' made of sponge rubber, enveloped in white covers. The poolside was full of the rich of the world, some of whom had come from as far afield as Argentina to take the waters and treatment. As I crept rather nervously down the steps into the pool, I was afraid that many eyes were upon me as I set off down the pool in a steady crawl. As I surfaced, shock and horror greeted me because my buoyant falsies had come adrift and were floating on the surface of the pool. Not a happy moment and I grabbed them and fled the pool, not daring to see how many people had noticed. If they had they were courteous enough not to roar with laughter.

Treatments began at the crack of dawn in the basement of the hotel, overseen by the resident doctor, and when it was finished and after the statutory rest Elsa and Jonas were free to spend the rest of the day sightseeing.

We saw a lot of Padua, which I loved, particularly the church of St Anthony, to whom one prays when losing or mislaying something (and it usually works). In one of the little old goldsmiths shops I bought a gold watchstrap for the gold watch the Herlenius family had given me for my 25th birthday, a bracelet and a little finger ring; my first venture into the world of gold jewellery. Elsa bought two rings, one for her niece Stella and one for me. Mine was an amethyst in an old white gold setting and I have worn these Padua rings every day ever since. The bracelet was valued at £335 when last I had it valued for insurance purposes in 1990 and it cost me only £9.

During our stay in Abano we did lots of trips to the surrounding areas, one of which was to the home of the great thinker and writer, Pertrach. Another day we went to the little village of Asola, to see the graveyard where Sarah Berhardt is buried; most of the graves are graced with little photographs of the dead taken during younger and happier times.

I got to know a very nice girl at the hotel, Carola Wolff, who was there with her three year old daughter and nanny. She belonged to the German Wolff family, the makers of drills and other tools. She had smashed one of her legs badly in a skiing accident, but after 10 days treatment and constant exercising in the pool, she was able to accompany me sightseeing in Venice one day on foot, which said a lot for the efficacy of her treatment.

Elsa and Jonas had taken me to Venice several times during that visit. The first time we came to St Mark's Square and gazed upon the magnificent church of that name with its famous bronze horses above the door and the teeming life around the square and in the outdoor cafés, Jonas looked at me and murmured: "Well say something," but I just stood transfixed, marvelling at it all.

Positano was to be our next stop, after taking in Ravenna, complete with the wonderful mosaics in the church of Sant'Apollinare in Classe, Ferrara, Bergamo, Rimini, Ancona and Urbino, to name only a few of the places we visited on the way south. We were by then quite ready to relax at the seaside and just lie in the sun. In the evenings we all went down to the tavern on the beach, the Bucca di Baccha, for coffee and a Sambucca (still my favourite liqueur) and mingled with the fishermen, townspeople and the other tourists. It was before the days of tattooes, nose rings and lager louts and the atmosphere was one of fun and bonhomie. We spent ten days there and were joined by Märtha, Rolf and Katrin Köhncke, together with a young cousin, Sigrid, who hated being there because she was madly in love with her boyfriend back home in Stockholm.

The girls and I visited the Blue Grotto at Capri and then the museum of San Michele, the home of Axel Munthe, physician to Queen Victoria of Sweden and a philanthropist in the slums of Italy. His book, 'The Story of San Michele', a magical and compelling book, part memoir, was published in 1929 and became a best seller in 25 languages.

As we wandered round Capri later we also caught a glimpse of Gracie Fields' house. The sun shone on us all all the time and I think it was probably one of the happiest holidays I have ever spent. It certainly opened my eyes to the world of art and beauty, not to mention the sunshine, the wonderful hallmark of the Mediterranean countries, which seriously appealed to me.

After that idyllic break, we wended our way to Rome, but only for a day and a night. We met Jonas's nephew, Torgil, son of Jonas's sister Karin (Kaja) and her husband Helge Magnuson, who took us to a restaurant for dinner situated on the spot where Brutus slew Caesar. Torgil, a professor, later became a Vice-Director of The Swedish Institute in Rome. He wrote several travel books on Italy and Europe in general, but his magnum opus: 'Rome in the Age of Bernini' has become a widely read authority on the City for academics across the world. More recently he has written a similarly erudite book: 'The Urban Transformation of Medieval Rome'. He always travelled everywhere by motorcycle, but on reaching his eighties has recently had to give this up.

That night our car was broken into, probably because I had unthinkingly left an empty but very elegant crocodile handbag, which Jonas had brought me back from Brazil, well in sight for the marauders to covet. This was not popular as Jonas had been keen to make an early start that morning. However, he was somewhat mollified when he heard that a large number of parked cars had been painted scarlet during the night, so we really came off fairly lightly.

While the car was being repaired, Sigrid and I decided we still had time to go to St Peter's Basilica for, sadly, only a quick look round and to join the crowds visiting the resting place of Pope Pius XII, who had just died. Having done this, we tried to leave, but whenever we saw a door it was closely guarded by a Swiss guard, complete with halberd. By this time we were in danger of being late for our rendezvous and departure with Elsa and Jonas. It was a nasty moment, but it had one plus factor. When taking a taxi from our hotel to St Peter's, the driver had demanded a large fee, which we refused to pay, offering him the amount we knew to be right. He became very angry and refused to take anything. As soon as he had driven off, Sigrid realised she had left her umbrella in the taxi. When at last we emerged from St Peter's frantic for a taxi, there was 'our' taximan, complete with umbrella and a wide smile. He got us to our meeting place in double quick time, so we gave him what he felt was his due and we all parted very amicably. A tiny insight into one of the Italians' unpredictabilities and charm. As we drove out of the city, white smoke had begun to emerge from the chimney of the Sistine Chapel signifying that the Cardinals had chosen the next Pontiff, Pope John I.

Florence was our next stop and we stayed right in the centre at the smart, but very noisy Hotel Berchielli. Elsa took me to the Pitti and Uffizi Galleries, where among so many wonderful works of art, the Flemish painter, Hugo Van der

Goes' (1482) triptych of the Portinari family, called 'The Adoration of the Shepherds', still remains one of my favourite paintings. Lorenzo Ghiberti's magnificent bronze doors of the Baptistry, described by Michelangelo as worthy to be the gates of Paradise and Giotto's Campanile are still firmly embedded in my mind as things of the utmost beauty. Although having had strict instructions from my mentor to go and look at the Michelangelo statues in the Medici Chapel, I got sidetracked on the Ponte Vecchio, full of tempting stalls to empty the purses of tourists, mine included, and the Chapel was closed when I eventually got there. I was soundly berated for my utter stupidity, but I did get there on a visit to Florence some 20 years later.

XI

Back to Uddeholm

Once back from the Grand Tour I began work again at Uddeholm's Head Office. It was no less boring, although my colleagues were fun and the job fairly undemanding and, after all, I was there to make up my mind whether or not to emigrate to Canada. This option fell by the wayside when I had a serious car accident and by the time I had recovered, emigration to Canada seemed to be a step too far.

It was St Lucia's Day, 15 December, and I had accompanied Elsa and Jonas to a lovely Santa Lucia dinner in Karlstad. Elsa had driven all the way back from Stockholm that day to attend this party and Jonas wanted to enjoy it to the full, which, if he was to drive home, meant that he could only drink a couple of glasses of wine. So I was quite happy to drive us all home. The huge Ford Mercury had gears, but also an overdrive, which was not recommended for use on roads covered in snow. However, I didn't realise that the overdrive was switched on and we set off for home on roads that were fairly lethal as the temperature had risen thus making the snow and ice unpredictable. As we came into a bend with seemingly no end, the car began to skid and I couldn't get control of it. As I saw it, the best option was to find a gap in the pine forest where I might safely bring the car to a halt. But as the skid gathered momentum, we came to a railway tunnel with concrete walls. I took the car up a rise just before the tunnel, which actually saved us from a nastier crash, but in doing so caught my forehead on the metal part of the sun visor and my head then hit the windscreen. We all climbed out safely, but I got back in to turn off the engine as smoke was issuing from under the bonnet.

Elsa and Jonas appeared to be unscathed, apart from being pretty shocked, but blood was streaming from a gash in my forehead, which added to their shock. As luck would have it, and we certainly needed it, a taxi was passing and stopped to help. He drove me to Karlstad Hospital, while Elsa and Jonas got help with the car. The lady doctor who treated me had the most awful cold and really didn't do her stuff. I was sent home without having my head X-rayed, although she did stitch the large gash in my forehead just above my left eye. The doctor at home was no better, and after examining me the next day, left some headache pills and advised me to stay in bed until the headache had gone, just in case I had concussion. Well, I had actually fractured two layers of my skull, apart from being badly concussed. After a fortnight at home feeling dreadful with a skull which felt like a block of wood, I spent two weeks in hospital having various tests, but nothing could be done except to rest as much as possible. It was a very long time before I got rid of the ill effects, and I think it left me with a very low flash point, which still rears its ugly head if I get too tired or stressed; although it passes in a trice it tends, not surprisingly, to upset those friends of mine who have witnessed it. The poor car took six months to be put right, but never once did the family intimate that I was culpable. Indeed, the particular curve which was my undoing had been an accident spot for a long time and shortly after my accident much-needed alterations were made to the road.

The social life in and around Uddeholm was good and when Elsa and Jonas were away on their travels, they were very happy for me to entertain my friends and left out ample wine and spirits to enable me to do so. Bridge suppers were the order of the day.

What of men? Well, there were a number of young men working in the company, Swedish, French, Swiss and German and I actually lost my virginity to a young and personable Swiss chap, who was also an incipient alcoholic. After an evening out with him he pleaded with me to go to bed with him, saying that if I didn't he would drink himself silly, or words to that effect. Silly me fell for this approach and needless to say, I didn't enjoy it one bit; an ignominious and unromantic first try.

Another unsuccessful relationship followed with a Swede I met at a rather splendid birthday party in Stockholm, although this time I didn't make the same mistake. Hans was an old friend of Märtha's daughter, Annika, whose birthday party it was. As he lived in Stockholm, it wasn't easy for us to meet very often, but he came up to Råda once and I went down to his parents' summer house outside Stockholm several times. His parents were separated and his father had a mistress who looked just like a younger version of his wife. We all stayed together in the summer house and it was strictly above board with no-one sleeping with anyone and oddly enough we all had a lot of fun. Hans's mother was half Russian and a warm and wise person. His father was a film director and certainly looked the part, appearing at breakfast in a blue silk spotted dressing gown and holding an elegant cigarette holder, both slightly out of place in the fairly primitive, but cosy wooden summer house. Hans, although very attractive to look at was a complete misogynist, which became slightly wearing after a time. One morning he and I went out fishing in a little rowing boat on the lake beside their house. Hans didn't catch anything and I asked him to let me try. To his utter fury, I managed to catch quite a good-sized fish and as I got up to let him have another try, he jolted the boat so that I lost my balance and fell into the lake. This was no joke as it was autumn and I had on a duffle coat, so swimming to the shore was difficult. As I was struggling, with Hans just looking on, his mother appeared and asked where was I: "Oh she caught a fish and fell in," he said scathingly. Of course his mother was properly concerned and as I finally reached the shore bore me away to be dried and cossetted. What angered me most was that my watch, a twentyfirst birthday present, was waterlogged and ruined.

The atmosphere at supper was tense to say the least, particularly when Hans refused to eat the fish I had caught, settling for a smaller one he had succeeded in catching later. So, unsurprisingly, that was pretty much that. I met up with him again quite by chance when I moved into a flat across the road from his in Stockholm a year or two later. He had had a brief and unsuccessful marriage and, on his own again, he was suffering from Hodgkin's Disease, from which he died quite soon afterwards.

Talking of rowing boats, one summer I bought a small flat-bottomed boat, smartened it up with red and white paint and flew a tiny Union Jack hoisted onto half a ski stick and with the help of a contentious little outboard motor used it, among other things, to commute across to the office in Uddeholm. It was called 'Mon Oncle' after the Jacques Tatti film about Monsieur Hulot, which I had recently seen and thought hilariously funny. The Råda lake below the house was several miles long and quite wide and when the wind got up it could get quite choppy. Rather than be tossed out of it on such days, I used to jump out into the lake and swim home, towing the boat behind me. It felt safer that way.

In the winter it was possible to cross the heavily frozen lake on something called a 'spark'. This was rather like a scooter but with steel runners like a toboggan. It was a very quick way of getting across the lake, but it needed to be as the winter temperatures could be far below freezing. It had the distinct advantage, though, of getting one home from parties when one had been drinking above the legal limit. This was very low indeed even at that time in Sweden.

At one point, Mother made a surprise decision to come out for a short stay. Elsa and Jonas were going away and were happy for her to come and they put their Volkswagen at my disposal so that we could make a trip to Stockholm. The house belonging to Elsa's mother in Stockholm had been sold on her death to Broms School, a private school which the Crown Prince, Carl Gustav, attended. The family had retained a flat in the house as a pied-a-terre, so Mother and I were able to stay there whilst in Stockholm. I relate this solely to make the point that, when leaving the flat one morning, a small boy held open the main door for us. It was the future King of Sweden.

I was anxious about the visit and wanted it to be a success, but on the way to Stockholm I succeeded in skidding on a minor gravel road – I expect I'd lost the way and was becoming even more anxious. The car went into a ditch, the passenger door flew open and Mother fell into the ditch. Very, very fortunately the car door stuck into the side of the ditch which stopped the car from falling on her and she scrambled out, shocked, but none the worse for wear. We both banged our foreheads on the windscreen and a suitcase parked on the back seat flew forward and knocked it out into a field. I cannot understand to this day how the suitcase didn't hit me on the back of the head, or perhaps it did! Mother, bless her heart, was in the safety of the ditch at that point. I cannot now recall how we got the car to a garage and completed the journey to Stockholm, but we did.

The next day we managed to see quite a lot of the town and met up with Stella and her two small children who showed us round Skansen, famous for its zoo and old Swedish cottages in natural settings. Reading letters from Mother quite recently, written soon after her return to England, she seemed, amazingly, to have enjoyed the visit. Perhaps it was her innate stoicism, although she did mention coming out in a rash, which she put down to delayed shock.

Elsa and Jonas, although initially upset about the whole incident, were rather pleased because they got, through their motor insurance, a brand new Volkswagen. I should add that, although the two car accidents I had in Sweden appear rather close together in this account, several years did elapse between them. But the more serious one had the effect of making it impossible for me to get into a car and drive it for some four years. More of this later on.

XII

British Embassy, Stockholm

As time went on and I began to feel stronger, I decided to look for a job in Stockholm. This took time, but I was eventually offered the job as interpreter in the Visa Section of the Canadian Embassy. By this time my Swedish would have been up to it, but they wanted someone immediately and that I couldn't do as my contract with Uddeholm specified a 3 month's notice. Back to the drawing board and I finally joined the British Embassy as a clerical officer.

Landing the job turned out to be a touch and go event. I'd come down by train from Värmland for the day for the interview with the Commercial Counsellor. All seemed to go well until he said he had better test my shorthand. This filled me with horror and I asked could we do it quickly as I was in danger of missing my train back to Värmland and the trains were few and far between. "Certainly" he said and proceeded to dictate at a fair speed. Needless to say, I missed a lot of what he was dictating and suddenly found myself staring at a typewriter in the next room with a mind which had gone completely blank. Suddenly an older lady, his secretary, wandered into the room, introduced herself and asked how did I spell the name Barry as her name was Berg and pronounced in almost the same way as Barry. This was not the sort of exchange I welcomed at this moment in time, but it had the effect of removing the paralysis from my brain and I was then able to get on with interpreting my inadequate and self-taught shorthand as best I could. The Commercial Counsellor looked at the piece carefully and then said that he would consider me for a job and would write to me. This was a blow and I told him that I really needed to know immediately as I had been offered a job with the Canadian Embassy and of course would much rather work for the British Embassy. He thought for a moment and then said that the job was mine. I almost hugged him but instead smiled gratefully and asked him if he could please get me a taxi. He also smiled, got me a taxi and I caught the train, as with the job, by the skin of my teeth.

Naturally leaving the Herlenius family and my job with Uddeholm was a great wrench, but I knew that it was right at that time to launch myself once again into the great wide world. Mind you, it wasn't too unfamiliar as several members of the Herlenius family lived in Stockholm and Irma and Christer had a lovely villa in Djursholm, an attractive and sought after area some twenty minutes out of town. Both Stella and Annika and their families were in town and Elsa had negotiated a room for me in the home of a friend right in the nicest part of town, just off Strandvägen and the water which surrounds this beautiful city. So there was a ready made social circle and of course the Embassy was a hub of social activity, although it took a little time before this new and rather lowly member of staff began to be included in the social round.

Being locally-employed rather than London-based made a great difference in terms of status. I worked in the typing pool of the Commercial Department along with some four other locally engaged-typists. We typed out drafts prepared by four marketing officers and it was all pretty boring stuff. Sometimes one was called upon to do some typing for the Commercial First Secretary, one Donald Murray, who some years later returned to Stockholm as Ambassador. He was a keen and a jovial man who had lost a leg during the war and the tapping of his artificial leg down the corridor made his approach fairly obvious and filled me with alarm as he sometimes wanted to dictate, but luckily not too often as most of his work was classified. As a locally-engaged typist, I was not privy to any classified material.

One day he needed an unclassified Aide Memoire typed to take along to the Swedish Ministry for Foreign Affairs and it had to be done in double-quick time. I was the only person available to do it and with him breathing down my neck and in a hurry I became flustered and had to begin again several times. I can still hear him shrieking at me: "You've done it again you silly monkey!" Luckily such occasions were few and far between and he was in reality a very nice man. He and his wife Marjorie had a number of children looked after by an elderly lady known to everyone as 'Nurse'. It was said that their last child had been conceived in order to retain Nurse in the family!

In the cellar of the Embassy there was a sort of tea-room where everyone congregated for elevenses and afternoon tea. This was mainly where I gradually got to know everyone. The Head of Chancery was a most engaging character called Sidney Hebblethwaite. He wore red braces and suede shoes and made it his business to circulate and get to know us all. Although a bit of a tease he had a certain presence and was treated with due respect by all.

I once had to beard him in his rather grand office in the smarter part of the Embassy to ask whether there was any chance of my taking over a little flatlet which was being vacated by one of the London-based girls. When I put my request to him rather nervously, he said quite firmly "No: it will be needed for her replacement." For some reason or other I thought it possible to have another try some time later. When I knocked and came into his room he didn't look up, but simply said "Yes?" I asked him whether he had meant what he said about the flat and he said "What did I say?" I repeated his negative response and still without looking up said, "Yes you can have it," and then looked up and smiled. I was a firm fan of his for ever afterwards.

The flat was tiny with a bed which folded into the wall and with a minute kitchenette and bathroom, but it was mine. Life began to look up again and also one or two embossed invitations began to arrive for parties given by the diplomatic staff, including the Service Attachés, who in those days could be counted upon to give very good parties.

Walking along the water's edge one day on the way to a ladies' lunch, a group of us came upon the Ambassador's Secretary, newly arrived from Zimbabwe, sitting rather dejectedly on a rock looking frozen. She reminded me of Frances Cornford's poem: 'Oh fat white woman who nobody loves, why do you walk through fields in gloves, missing so much and so much'. She was not particularly fat, but did have gloves on and turned out to be a real 'ball of fire' who was loved by all. She and I became long-lasting friends. She was called Dorothy Laing, Dotty to all her friends except for me. I just couldn't bring myself to say it and called her 'D' instead. She had a small blue car and we had great fun going places together, particularly to the Embassy's week-end cottage in the country. It was fairly rough and ready, but big enough to accommodate the Embassy's largest family – the Murrays – and made for some hilarious week-ends.

Naval Visits to Stockholm, of which there were many, were always highlights, especially the party on board which the Captain always gave for the local Diplomatic Corps and business community. It was during one of these that I met a most attractive Swede called Anders Skiöldebrand. Sheena, his wife, was English and great fun and remains a good friend to this day. They were long-standing members of the Embassy's social circle and knew everyone. Andy had been charged with looking after a motor fishing vessel (MFV) called 'Foresight' belonging to Captain Ryder, VC, who had helped to blow up the St Nazaire Docks during the war, for which he was awarded his VC.

I never met Captain Ryder on his rare visits to Stockholm, but some 15 years later when spending a weekend with Andy and Sheena at their house in West Byfleet, they suddenly came upon the idea of asking him over to Sunday lunch. However it was summertime and they decided that it was rather short notice and he would in all probability be out sailing. On my way back home that evening, I switched on the car radio to hear the news. The newscaster began by saying that Captain Ryder, VC, of St Nazaire fame had died whilst out sailing that very day. Of such coincidences the world we know not of makes glancing blows upon our lives.

The Skiöldebrands tended to take a party of friends out sailing in Stockholm's Archipelago almost every weekend and suddenly I found myself included on these hilarious trips. We drank copious amounts of alcohol, swam naked – girls to one side and the chaps on another side - and never the twain did meet. Regularly included on these trips was a wonderful raconteur called Alan Tapsell, a translator at the American and British Embassies, who had us all falling about with mirth for hours on end. So there were at least two very good reasons for being grateful to the good Captain Ryder, VC.

Another colourful character was a tall and very good-looking Austrian diplomat, Ferdinand von Stollberg, who was, I believe, a grandson of the Austrian Emperor Franz Josef I. At diplomatic parties he stood looking very grand, but rarely saying very much simply because he was so tall and could never hear what anyone was saying to him. On 'Foresight' he tended to be more relaxed and smiley. Some forty-five years later when I was living in Dorset, I was invited to a dinner party given by the Austrian Ambassador to the Knights of St John, who with his wife had a beautiful home there. The only Austrian I knew was Ferdinand, so I dropped his name tentatively into the conversation at one point.

There was an immediate and electric reaction. My modest presence became the focus of attention and I was brought up to date on the gorgeous Ferdinand, who by this time had become an Ambassador.

As time went by I realised that diplomatic life might be the answer to my lack of a real career and I discussed the possibility with friend 'D'. She thought it a distinct possibility too, as did one of the other secretaries who offered to send for an Application Form on my behalf. Typing endless screeds on the European Free Trade Area (EFTA), however important at that time, failed to inspire me. The thought of joining the Foreign & Commonwealth Office (FCO) and travelling to other countries certainly did inspire me and my Application Form went on its merry way. I gave up my job in the Commercial Department and returned once more to London in anticipation of being granted an interview at the FCO.

XIII

The Foreign & Commonwealth Office, London

I have to confess that, despite plenty of practice, both in Uddeholm and Stockholm, my shorthand skills were below par. This was very evident when tested during the all important interview at the FCO. Nerves played their part of course and in the end I simply couldn't keep up with the dictation and laid down my pencil. During the final interview with the all-powerful Personnel lady, I felt a distinct failure. Tru Trubody, as she was known, had a formidable presence, although her voice was low and unsteady, rather as if she were the nervous one. But, as I came to know, this was part of her success and her charm. She chastised me for my poor showing and said in quavering tones: "You should have done better, Angela." 'Oh help,' I thought, that must be that. But it wasn't and a Letter of Acceptance reached me shortly afterwards.

Many years later, when I used to organise golfing matches between past and present lady members of the Service against the men, Tru was a regular member of our team. She lived in Dorset and when I lived there on retirement, she came to lunch one day and was able to tell me that, although my shorthand hadn't been up to much, she had written on my file: 'Take this one.' Yet another 'skin of teeth' scenario. I certainly had Tru to thank for her far-reaching decision, which paved the way to some 27 rewarding years working for the FCO.

I ought to make clear at this point that my work with the FCO was more important to me than it appears to be in this account, which tends to err on the merrier side of my life. It would be quite wrong, though, to infer that there were no fun moments in the office; there were many. Suffice it to say that some of the work was very interesting, sometimes exciting, but it very often entailed a good hard slog of fairly mundane tasks. It was, however, of paramount importance, particularly when serving overseas, and one's private life usually took second place. We worked within a close-knit society and one of the mitigating features was the calibre of the people one worked alongside, from the most senior to the most junior. The common denominator most in evidence seemed to be a sense of humour, which often saw one through the most testing situations, but not always. The fun one had during the time spent out of the Office was a very necessary antidote to the pressures within it. I therefore make no apology for the frivolous nature of much that appears in this account of my life.

During my first year in the Office in London I had to have an operation to remove an ovarian tumour at the very excellent Westminster Hospital. After the op Mother and Dick came to take me back to Wokingham, where they then lived, to recuperate. It was a complete disaster, with Mother showing little understanding of my obvious weakness. Her doctor was called and pronounced that to stay there would seriously hamper my recovery, so amid huge tensions Dick drove me back to the flat in London. My flatmates did all they could to help but I was keen to get back to my new job, went back too early and had a relapse.

As I was a newcomer to the Foreign Office, and hence did not qualify for much paid sick leave, I had to present myself at the Social Security Office at Charles House in Kensington to sign on for the dole. I sat among old-timers who strongly urged me not to tell the truth: "Oive bin cummin 'ere for years, luv and never tell 'em the truth." The Interviewing Officer asked for my details and then for my rent book. Needless to say I had no rent book, living as I did in a flat with friends. He then asked me where I worked and when I said "The Foreign Office", he couldn't contain his amusement and sent me off home to get a rent book. When I was fit enough to return to the Office, I recounted all this to my boss. He was appalled and strode off to Personnel Department to put my case and they were able to change the rules concerning sick pay to newcomers. The thing that impressed me most at this early stage of my career and beyond, was just how helpful everyone was, thoughout the Office. As in most organisations there were exceptions, a few of which I encountered over the years, but on the whole the 'goodies' prevailed both at home and abroad.

XIV

Foreign Postings

British Embassy, Copenhangen

In early 1963 I was on my way by train to the Embassy in Copenhagen and my first posting abroad. It made good sense in principal because I knew Scandinavia and the Swedish language at least. But I found Copenhagen a gloomy place and preferred the Swedes to the Danes. In general the Danes had little time for the Swedes, but the Swedes liked the Danes, although they very often spoke English when visiting Denmark. Whether this was because of the difficulty in interpreting the noises produced by the glottal stop, or whether they felt they would be made more welcome speaking English, I never really discovered. Stupidly I imagined that, with my Swedish, I could sail through the Danish language exam and qualify for a language allowance, but I failed miserably because many words, although almost identical, mean something totally different. I had taken lessons in London before leaving, but never did master that language.

Work was hard and my colleagues worked all the hours that God gave them as if it was the most natural thing in the world, hardly stopping for lunch at all and working late most evenings. I joined them in this, but found it hard-going.

I managed to find a nice little flat in Hellerup in the house of a Danish schoolteacher, just behind the Tuborg Brewery and some gasworks. It was also a stone's throw from the seafront, so the air was filled with three alternating whiffs, depending on the direction of the wind. Hellerup is a rather nice suburb of Copenhagen and the vast Deer Park is situated there. I cycled everywhere because there are cycle paths almost everywhere so it is a cyclist's paradise.

Outside the office one enjoyed the gastronomic delights of the many excellent restaurants, particularly at Tivoli. Also, there were some magnificent dancers at The Danish Ballet. At one performance, during the interval, I spotted a rather scrawny man with wispy hair, rather like Worzel Gummidge. He had on very distinctive pointed shoes. I can see him now standing chatting at the top of the theatre's grand staircase. It was Rudolf Nureyev, a very new defector from the USSR. The next time I saw him was when he gave a magificent performance of Swan Lake, with Margot Fonteyn in Berlin, a year or two later.

One evening one of the First Secretaries asked me to accompany him to an evening of classical music at a private house in another suburb of Copenhagen. "I've no idea what it will be like," he said. "The Ambassador has asked me to go in his stead. The dress is white tie, so it must be something rather special."

Dressed up to the nines, we arrived at the gate of a fairly typical suburban house and joined the rest of what turned out to be most of the senior members of the Diplomatic Corps in Copenhagen. We were greeted by our Danish host, complete in white tie, and given a drink in his garden. There were large bird cages all round the garden containing a variety of species of birds. Eventually we were shown into a wooden auditorium in the garden. As we settled into our seats there was an earth-shattering roar from the loudspeakers followed by equally loud bird song and then some music. A rather sinister voice said: "We have now arrived by plane at my house for this concert." He added: "We have had the volume of sound checked by experts and are assured that it is within the limits of what the human ear can stand." After some more deafening music, the voice intoned: "It is now midnight and anyone who is afraid of ghosts should leave now." By this time the audience was beginning to become slightly bewildered and not to say uneasy. I for one whispered to my companion that I intended to leave that minute. He protested that there were several Ambassadors present so we really couldn't leave. Undeterred by protocol, I got up to leave. As we emerged into the garden, our host caught us up, asking angrily why we were leaving. I explained that I had only come out for some air as I was feeling faint and would return shortly. The man looked fairly demented and gone were his jacket and white tie. "Come into the house and I'll give you an injection."

By this time my escort was finally convinced that we should leave and insisted that the garden gate, which had been locked, be opened so that we could be on our way. Somewhat shaken we enjoyed a quiet dinner in town.

Not surprisingly, I was full of the story when I came into the office the following morning and wanted to tell my boss about it. A senior secretary advised me not to do so "until the Bag has gone." This was the weekly Diplomatic Bag to London, which we all bust a gut to catch, typing furiously up until the last possible moment. During this ugly rush my boss had been called out and he returned looking grim. He called me into his room and then embarked on a sort of third degree interrogation about the night before. He said that The Ambassador had had an official complaint from our Danish host about the British representatives rudely leaving in the middle of his concert and the Ambassador knowing nothing of the circumstances was angry. Needless to say we were exonerated when the awfulness of the occasion emerged. In fact at the very next diplomatic gathering I was besieged by many of those who had been there and who had wished they too had left when we did. The madman, on his return from 'seeing us off', had locked the door so that no-one else could leave. Naturally the Ambassador was concerned that so many members of the Diplomatic Corps could have been duped into accepting the man's invitation in the first place.

In due course things improved both in and out of the office. A new First Secretary and his wife gave a drinks party soon after their arrival and at one point during the party our host was showing a lovely Russian painting to some of his guests, two of whom were known to be Russian Intelligence Officers. I was admiring it too and suddenly one of the Russians turned to me and asked if I liked it: "Oh very much," I replied. "I'll get one for you," he said. "Oh please don't," I replied ungraciously and we all began to laugh, as he realised I was thinking it might turn out to be a sinister bribe. During the interval at a concert I went to some weeks later with a friend, I thought to myself that this was just the sort of occasion when the Russian might appear again. He did, some minutes later, and we exchanged pleasantries. I introduced him to my friend and soon after off he went and I never saw him again, thank goodness.

One of the good things about Copenhagen was its proximity to Sweden, which meant that many of my Swedish friends could visit and also I could spend week-ends and holidays with the Herlenius family. Irma and Christer had moved permanently to their summer house at Haverdal which was by the sea near the attractive little town of Halmstad, just north of Gothenburg. The house was one of two with views overlooking the sea. Christer's parents lived in the other one and we had many happy and relaxed dinner parties in both houses.

The office was a disappointment, though, mainly due to a bossy senior secretary, who spent her time needling me and who had been sitting on work that I should have been dealing with, which had had some serious consequences. She had been in the FCO for 22 years and as I was a newcomer, the cards, unfortunately, were stacked against me to begin with. Thankfully this righted itself in the end, but it played havoc with my confidence and wellbeing and I had asked for a move. Instead of being posted home as I had expected, I was cross-posted to West Berlin to finish my tour there.

Further Serious Thoughts

An antidote to my unhappiness in the office was to give more thought to the perennial questions about the meaning of life. I was helped in this by a colleague who introduced me to a highly esoteric book called 'The Wisdom of the Overself ' by Dr Paul Bruton. It was an amalgam of Comparative Religion, Mysticism and Philosophy and proved both interesting and helpful and channelled my thoughts away from the immediate problems in the office and towards something less ephemeral in the overall scheme of things.

British Military Government (BMG), Berlin

When a senior secretary met me off the plane at Templehof Airport, one of my first questions was to ask how long she had been in Berlin so that I could then work out how much longer she would have to serve there. I needn't have worried. She was a most splendid and humorous Scot and we became firm friends. We were all part of the British Military Government at the head of which presided a Major General and under him was the Foreign Office civilian presence headed by Peter Hayman, with the rank of Minister and Deputy Commandant.

Berlin was a completely different ball-game after the gloom of Copenhagen. The well-known 'Berliner luft' was a fact of life and made for a stimulating atmosphere, both in summer and in winter. Also, it was exciting to feel that one was in the middle of the Cold War with the Berlin Wall appearing, sometimes quite suddenly, when one went for walks in the Grünewald forest. Over the Wall there were viewing towers, manned by heavily-armed East German soldiers and some rather nasty-looking Alsatian dogs. Sometimes the Wall passed through the middle of a house and even a church so one was in no doubt that they all meant business.

The large Allied military presence, British, American and French, must have seemed equally daunting seen from the other side. Spandau Prison, which was in the British Sector, still held a couple of important prisoners and the Four Powers, which included the Russians, of course, took it in turns to preside over the prison for a month. At the end of each month the presiding Power gave an official lunch at the Prison to which a selection of officers, both military and civilian were invited. I once had the luck to be invited and was placed next to the Russian Commandant. A Russian-speaking officer in the British Military Government interpreted our conversation. Two points stuck in my memory: one was the fact that the Commandant told me that his wife was away, which made for an amusing exchange, via our interpreter, and the other was that he introduced me to the wonderfully piquant Tabasco sauce which I have been using in food ever since. The whole occasion was a unique experience one way and another.

Many of us were not allowed into the Russian Sector for security reasons, which was a pity because there were many fine performances at the Opera House in East Berlin and also the famous Pergamon Museum. However, the lovely and beautifully presented Dahlem Museum was in the British Sector and I spent many happy hours there. When one needed to pass through the Russian Sector in the car, those of us who were not allowed into the East had to take the British Military Train to Helmstedt, the French train to Strasbourg or the American train to Frankfurt, depending in which direction we were heading. Our cars were driven to these points by a member of the British Military Police and we continued on our way by car. Sometimes we took the French train to Strasbourg just for the fun of it, because the train was an enormously comfortable wagonlit and of course the town itself was worth seeing and the restaurants served delicious food. It made a nice break from the restrictive atmosphere of Berlin. But I felt happy in Berlin and was able to go to some wonderful concerts in the splendid Concert Hall, the architecture of which alone was well worth seeing. And the town boasted many fine restaurants to suit all pockets.

Socially, Berlin was a great place to be, especially for a single girl, surrounded as we were by so many attractive single men from the various and ever-changing regiments stationed there. We each had an Army quarter, which for the secretarial staff comprised a commodious one-bedroomed apartment in

Churchill House. Churchill House was in Charlottenburg and close to the centre of West Berlin and the shops. It had been given the name 'Kinsey Corner' by some wag, after the well-known Kinsey Report on Sex. At the time I was there it didn't seem to be a den of iniquity, but rather a starting point for a number of courtships ending in marriage. One of these marriages was that of Rosemary Norden, an FCO secretary who worked for the Head of Chancery, to David Manger, an officer in the Royal Military Police. He proposed to her the second time he met her and eventually, after a short posting to Moscow, she accepted him. Rosemary was the staunchest of friends and remains so to this day. The couple had two children, Andrew and Alison (now known as Alice) and Andrew is my Godson. He is now happily married to Helen and they have an entrancing little daughter, Catherine. Sadly Rosemary and David's marriage broke down and the couple divorced in 1991.

The first great social experience for me was The Brigade Ball. It was held in the Olympic Stadium, which Adolf Hitler had built for the 1932 Olympics. The Stadium also boasted a theatre-in-the round, of which more later. As I hadn't been in Berlin very long, a kind colleague who knew the ropes and one of the organising officers, set about finding an escort for me. I had a choice of about three and chose a French officer who was on attachment to the Brigade. We were in a group hosted by the Brigade Major, George Rochfort-Rae, a Grenadier, who invited us for drinks before the Ball. When eventually we were comfortably seated at dinner our host, the Brigade Commander, Brigadier Allan Taylor strode in to take his place at the top table. His arrival caused a frisson among the assembled company and I realised that here was someone of great significance. He was unbelievably good-looking and had a very evident charisma. The ball was great fun and heralded the start of a continuing round of entertaining occasions.

In due course, I became the Secretary of The British Players, a theatre group, comprising a gallimaufrey of talent from within The Brigade. Although my paternal grandfather had been deeply involved in the theatre in his time, I had no talent in this direction but enjoyed being on the organising side. We put on a number of plays, including George Bernard Shaw's 'Pygmalion' with the Brigadier's daughter, Jackie, playing the part of Eliza Doolittle. She had a lot of talent and the play was a great success.

This prompted a young subaltern by the name of Michael Parker to seek the Brigadier's permission to put on a hugely ambitious performance of

Shakespeare's 'Richard III' in which he would play Richard and Jackie would be the leading lady. It would be shown in the theatre-in-the round in the Olympic Stadium and the costumes would be hired from Nathans in London. The Brigadier gave his hundred percent support and the show eventually took place amid great excitement. I was charged with arranging an area where the German and British dignitaries could have drinks together during the interval. I arranged for enlarged and framed photographs of the players to be hung on the walls in this area and the Brigadier delegated 12 soldiers to me to clean the windows and generally spruce the place up and arrange pots of plants in strategic positions. Everything was set for a succesful evening, but in the days prior to the opening, Michael developed laryngitis and could hardly speak. Somehow or other disaster was averted and he managed to regain his voice in time. We had good Press coverage both in Berlin and in the UK.

Michael Parker left the Army soon after to run an antiques business in Pimlico, but the General Officer Commanding, General John Nelson, asked him to come back to arrange the Annual Berlin Military Tattoo, which he did. The final event to round off the Tattoo was a helicopter pulling a 144 x 80 ft Union Jack (probably the biggest in living memory) above and across the Olympic Stadium. Unfortunately it wasn't properly secured and hurtled down into the Stadium on top of some of the audience, causing mayhem and serious injury to some of them.

Michael was awarded an MBE and went on to become a showmaster of the highest order, in particular organising spectacular events for important Royal occasions. The one celebrating the Queen Mother's 100th Birthday in 2000 was probably one of the most spectacular and successful, after which he was well-deservedly knighted, becoming a KCVO on top of his CVO and MBE. Its theme, which highlighted magnificently the events which had taken place in the country during her lifetime, was enacted by means of a long procession of ordinary British people in costume, representing each decade, to the accompaniment of the stirring music of those times. It enshrined the British character at its most attractive, sturdy, gentle and humorous and everyone loved it.

One of his, not quite so successful, events was a firework display in Hyde Park the night before the wedding of Prince Charles to Lady Diana Spencer. I went to Hyde Park with a group from the Office and was one of thousands. Most of the Crowned Heads of Europe were there and were ferried to their seats in a large coach. The crowds were so massive that it was quite difficult actually to see the fireworks, but the atmosphere was good and everyone was in a party mood and on their best behaviour. They needed to be because at the end we were all kept waiting for well over an hour to allow the coach bearing the Kings and Queens of Europe to make its way to the exit. The authorities had closed all but one exit, which was at Hyde Park Corner.

We as a group managed eventually to jump over a fence into Knightsbridge, but as we headed for Grosvenor Place we were stopped in our tracks by some young policemen, who clearly were not entirely versed in crowd control. The pressure from the thousands behind us mounted and suddenly I realised that we were in danger of being crushed to death. It became difficult to breathe and it was clear from the look of horror on the faces of those who had climbed up onto a railing above the crowd, that they could see the full awfulness of what was about to happen. Fortunately the policemen at last realised this danger and let us through, but not before time. It was a frightening moment.

The streets round Hyde Park Corner were littered with abandoned cars and buses, which looked as though they had been dropped from the sky as their owners had despaired of sitting in immovable traffic jams and just left them. It was difficult to believe that the roads would be cleared for the big day ahead, but somehow they were.

During my time in Berlin, some of the men and women who had been imprisoned as British secret agents on the testimony of the treasonable George Blake started to emerge from prison. Quite naturally, they sought compensation from the British Government. It was a sad business. Many years later, well after I had retired from the FCO, I read in the newspapers that George Blake had written his Memoirs and had had the temerity to have them published in the UK by an English publisher. As is well known, he had been sentenced at The Old Bailey to 42 years' imprisonment for treason but had escaped with the help of two Irishmen and was living comfortably in Soviet Russia as a hero.

I wrote an indignant letter saying how wrong this was as the man had forfeited any rights he had in the UK by his betrayals. I sent it to my local MP, Sir James Spicer (Winfy's husband) who forwarded a copy each to the Lord Chancellor and the Attorney General. There had been a court case over whether or not Blake should receive the royalties on his book. The case was presided over by

Lord Justice Scott who had also presided over the famous 'Arms to Iraq' case and the outcome was that Blake should be allowed to receive the royalties. However there was an Appeal and I read, also in the newspapers in connection with another court case, that, in the end, George Blake had been denied the royalties on his book as "it was not in the Public's Interest" for him to receive them. I like to think that my letter might have played a part in this final decision. Who knows? However, in September 2006 it was reported that Blake had appealed to the European Court of Human Rights and the outcome was that the British Government was ordered to pay him £5000 in compensation. So much for the sanctity of British justice.

Romance

At the end of one of the many drinks parties, I was introduced to the Brigade Commmander, Allan Taylor. On hearing that I was in the Foreign & Commonwealth part of the BMG (British Military Government) he launched into a spirited criticism of the length of FCO telegrams. Of course I had to mount a defence, although I rather agreed with him. The following day I had a phonecall from his secretary inviting me to a dinner party at his home. I donned 'the little black dress' for the occasion and on arrival found that it was quite a small and select affair consisting of a visiting Major General, the Judge from the Supreme Restitution Court, Judge Stephen Henry and his French wife, Helene and the Anglican Chaplain of the Brigade, Jimmy Kelly and his wife Joan. It was all a bit daunting, but our host soon made us feel relaxed and I began to enjoy myself.

After dinner we ladies left the men to their port and chat and did our chatting outside by the swimming pool. After a very long time, by any standards, we began to get restive and I suddenly decided to have a swim. Not surprisingly, none of the other ladies joined me, but kept watch to warn me when the men were approaching. They arrived rather quickly and I was hard put to leap out of the pool and into the little black dress before the Brigadier arrived at the pool's edge, exclaiming: "Angela – you haven't got a towel!" We looked at each other and the world suddenly stood quite still. I had fallen instantly in love with him! The rest of the evening passed in a haze and little did I realise that I had embarked on what turned out to be the best part of a lifetime's preoccupation which was in turns life-enhancing and heartbreaking.

After the party I heard nothing more from him, despite many prayers to the Almighty. However, I hatched a little plan to give a drinks party and invite him to come along. He replied that he would love to come, but that he had to go to a Dinner Night afterwards so couldn't stay very long. This was better than nothing and he duly came and went, looking marvellous in scarlet mess kit. At the end of my party a group of us repaired to the Officers' Club to have dinner. To my amazement Allan was there playing roulette with his hosts, officers of The Queen's Own Hussars.

When we had finished dinner Brigadier Kerry Harding, one of my party, suggested that we all go on to 'The Black Bottom', a well-known nightclub in the town, and he urged me to invite Allan to join us. After some persuading, I did so and Allan promised to make his way there once the roulette had finished. Needless to say, once at the night club, my eyes were on the door all the time and my escort remarked: "He'll never come you know." "I think he will," I replied and he did, in the company of the Officer Commanding the QOH Squadron, another colourful character who a year or two later disgraced himself and had to forfeit his commission and leave the Army.

After some preliminary chat Allan invited me to dance and again the world stood still. When it was time to go home, he offered to take me home and invited me to drive his Mercedes. What an honour and what an excitement. I don't believe he even came in for a nightcap, but it was clear that there was a colossal spark between us.

We subsequently had a lot of fun together and dined out and danced a lot. One evening he asked me what I would most like to do and I replied: "Go out in a boat." He looked a bit surprised but said "Done: you are with about the only man in Berlin who can grant you that wish because I have the key to the GOC's (General Officer Commanding) boathouse." We drove to the Villa Lemm, on the banks of the Havel Lake, and in no time were heading out in the General's motorboat well away from the shore. As the East German border ran through the centre of the Havel Lake, I began to panic a bit and said rather nervously: "Allan, I'm not allowed into the East." "I'll have you know neither am I," he said. So all was well. He had radioed the Military Police earlier to tell them where he was. It was all very romantic, but suddenly we noticed a lot of bobbing lights along the shore and he decided to investigate. To our horror, it seemed that the whole of the German Police Force was out, complete with Alsatian dogs, to see who was out in the boat. Allan headed for the shore, manoeuvred the boat back into the boathouse in double quick time and we raced to his car. Once inside the car Allan drove off at top speed avoiding the police, who had to leap swiftly aside to avoid being mown down. The British Military Police had clearly failed to alert the German Police as to who was out on the Havel in the GOC's boat. Of course there was an immediate enquiry and I suppose Allan was hauled over the coals, but he never mentioned it afterwards nor did he appear to be chastened by it. As Brigade Commander he was immensely well-liked and respected by all ranks. Perhaps there was a bit of a wobble in the early hours of some mornings by officers detailed to sit up with him when he was reluctant to leave a party; he was an inveterate insomniac.

One Easter a German spy plane, a new model, crashed into the Havel in the British Sector. This was a great coup for us, but the Russians did everything they lawfully could to stop us taking possession of the wreckage of the plane. This included sending the platoon of Russian soldiers whose job it usually was to guard the Russian War Memorial in our Sector, to encamp on the banks of the lake to oversee the salvaging of the wreckage, having been informed that, as it had crashed in our sector, we should be responsible for salvaging it. This was a sensitive matter and had all the hallmarks of developing into a serious political incident. The GOC was away so Allan was the senior military officer in charge of the operation, in tandem with our Minister, Peter Hayman, on the political side. It was a tense time for all and Easter celebrations became non-events. We all spent most of the Easter holiday in the office, dealing with the ripples that were continually emerging from the situation.

After some deft and nifty technical work on the part of the Royal Army Service Corps (RASC) and some equally deft work on the political side, we managed to extract the information we wanted from the wreckage, without Russian tanks rolling down the Kufurstendam. The wreckage was then to be handed over to the Russians.

There was a rather amusing ending to the whole saga. A well-known British journalist had prepared a piece on the handing back of the plane to the Russians, couching his description on the lines of Tennyson's poem 'Morte d'Arthur': "The barge she sat in etc. etc." It was destined for the Sunday papers, but the actual handover kept being delayed. Finally on the Saturday evening he thought he'd better check that it had been handed back and went to telephone, but finding he had no change, he took the chance and the piece duly appeared in the Sunday papers, but there had been a further delay and his piece, though splendidly written, had jumped the gun.

Although the Office had posted me to Berlin to finish my two-and-a- half-year posting to Copenhagen, my boss wrote asking that I be allowed to do a full posting in Berlin. I was overjoyed but the euphoria became slightly lessened when the annual Confidential Report time came. I was told that my probation period had been extended for a further year, presumably on account of the problems in Copenhagen, which I considered had not been my fault. However, the whole episode had played havoc with my self-confidence, and perhaps that was the reason for the extension. Happily at the end of the year I was accepted as a full member of the Service to my huge relief.

During my time in Berlin the whole grandeur of military display took place for an official visit by HM The Queen and The Duke of Edinburgh. The Brigade Commander, Allan Taylor, mounted on a fine chestnut horse, presented the Berlin Brigade to Their Majesties. The Queen and the Duke then inspected the assembled Brigade from an open Army car. As they began their tour The Queen was seen to remove a raincoat from one of the seats, left inadvertantly, it was said, by a security officer who had been inspecting the vehicle before the parade started; a minor blot on the otherwise immaculately organised Royal event.

Another special occasion which, besides the military, included many senior civilian figures and many German dignitaries, was the Memorial Service for Sir Winston Churchill held in the Olympic Stadium. It was, understandably, an emotive experience for all to witness the British and their Allies together with a large German representation headed by The Mayor of Berlin, Willy Brandt, coming together to honour the man who had very largely masterminded the defeat of Hitler's Germany in 1945.

When eventually my tour in Berlin came to an end, I was very sad indeed. My boss threw a farewell party for me and that morning I had a phonecall from the GOC's ADC asking me to dinner at The Villa Lemm that very evening. The ADC apologised for the short notice and the fact that it was the night of my farewell party, which the GOC and Lady Nelson were hoping to attend, but I was given a special dispensation to arrive a little later. As it was more-or-less a Royal Command my boss was happy for me to accept and off I went a little nervously, but having thoroughly enjoyed my own farewell drinks party.

On arrival our host greeted me with the words: "Angela, I'm afraid I can't say that you are our guest of honour this evening, as we have the Governor-General of Tasmania, Lord de Lisle, coming, but until he does you are certainly our guest of honour. This made me feel particularly happy because on arrival, one of our senior diplomats had said:"Hello Angela, who are you coming instead of?" I assured him that I was there in my own right this time. And later, before going in to dinner, his wife, a pretty and ebullient character, came up to me and said with some surprise: "Angela you have been placed higher than me," to which I replied: "Well I'm a bit older than you, Alexandra." Such was the enormous importance given to status in those days. But I can't say it didn't give me a bit of a thrill, particularly when I realised I was sitting next to the visiting Head of the Civil Service at dinner. So it was a good note to bow out on.

Serious Thoughts

I have to say that any serious thoughts I had whilst in Berlin were not about the meaning of life, but about the meaning of love. And most of my nightly prayers and then some were to do with my relationship with Allan. It all seemed to me to feel so Right.

Sailing Holiday, Denmark

My next posting was to be Caracas, but I had to spend some time in London first. This was fun and an opportunity to catch up with friends. It also had the added bonus of my being able to join some army friends sailing round the Danish coast from the Army Yacht Club at Kiel. There were eight of us: Ian and Anne Greenlees and their 12-year old daughter Diana, Philip Haslett, Peter Dryland, all officers from the Berlin Brigade and an Irish Corporal, Paddy, who was in training at The Yacht Club. He was our Skipper.

As we sailed out from the club on the first day, we came into the thrall of a Force 6 gale almost immediately. Paddy did his best to keep us on an even a keel, but it was clear that he wasn't about to succeed. Ian, who was our First Mate and an experienced sailor, took command and we were soon safe and sound again. It was an inauspicious start for Paddy, but he took it well and redeemed himself some days later. We tended to spend each night moored in some picturesque Danish harbour and one morning we sailed off into a strong gale with Ian at the helm. He had great difficulty in taking us out of the harbour, but eventually succeeded. Paddy, with a tiny hint of triumphalism shouted: "I've never seen anyone make such a pig's ear of it - Ssirr"!

We had a wonderful trip, but it was a fairly chilly one, which wasn't always assuaged by a noggin or two of the hard stuff. One night I retired early feeling particularly cold. Just as I was falling asleep I heard a repeated and monotonous cry from outside. As it didn't sound like 'Abandon ship' or 'All hands on deck' I decided to stay where I was. During one of my nightly trips to 'the heads' when I had to go through the main cabin, housing Philip and Peter, I was amazed to see that, unlike all other nights, when Peter lay in his bunk wide awake and with arms folded saying "Good-morning", as I passed through it was Philip who greeted me in the same way. Peter was fast asleep. It transpired that when he returned to the boat from his ablutions ashore he fell between the boat and the harbour wall and was hanging on by his fingers to the side of the boat. As the wind got up he was being buffeted about a bit, hence his repeated cries for help. It was a particularly dirty harbour and in the morning we looked with horror at his dirty jeans which were standing up by themselves. But Peter was none the worse for wear and one of the first to laugh it off in the morning.

Another drama took place one gloriously sunny afternoon when most of us were sunning ourselves and snoozing on deck, except for Ian who was fishing for our supper. He suddenly shouted: "Where's Diana?" We searched the boat from top to bottom and could find no sign of her. Ian turned the boat round and headed back in the direction we had come, using the motor for the sake of speed. It was a tense and worrying time looking for a tiny head bobbing about in the waves. However, after a further search on board she was eventually found right at the end of one of the forward bunks covered by a blanket.

These dramas apart we thoroughly enjoyed both the sailing and the sightseeing in between, not to mention each other's cheery company. And I have to say that the Danes we met en route were very much jollier than those I had encountered when en poste in Copenhagen.

Before accepting the posting to Caracas, I needed to know if an absence of two-and-a-half years would make any difference to Allan's oftimes stated decision never to marry again. His previous marriage had ended in divorce some years before I met him. By this time he was attending the Course for senior officers at The Imperial Defence College in London. He had also been promoted Major General. But it was clear when we met that he wasn't going to change his mind, and I set off to Venezuela with a very heavy heart. I remember buying my first new car, a little white Sunbeam, which should have been a rather exciting experience, but even this failed to raise my spirits.

British Embassy, Caracas
On the way out to Caracas, the plane suddenly plunged about 500 feet. We were

in the middle of dinner at the time and when the plane stabilized again I had the remains of my chicken casserole in my shoes and the coffee I had been drinking had flown into the face of the man sitting next to me. He had mentioned to me earlier that he was an expert on leprosy and he appeared quite unphased by the whole incident. We had an English football team on board and they made light of the very frightening experience and in no time calm was restored; luckily there were no casualties. We were flying around the area of the Bermuda Triangle, so we were probably fortunate not to have disappeared altogether.

It was a relief when we landed safely in Caracas. The sky was a brilliant blue and the sun hot and strong. I was met at the airport and greeted with the dramatic news that there had just been a strong earthquake, the epicentre of which had been very close to the flat of the secretary I was to replace . In fact she had watched in terror as her block of flats swayed dangerously towards the ground, but then luckily righted itself. She was naturally in a state of shock, so our handover was fairly chaotic as a result.

I was put into a high-rise service flatlet, which was unscathed by the earthquake, but surrounded by wrecked buildings. Many of the Embassy staff had frightening tales to tell. Our Ambassador, Sir Anthony Lincoln and his Anglo-Argentinian wife, Lisette, had been staying the weekend at an hotel on the coast. As the earthquake struck they both tried to dive under a bed, but the beds were divans and there was no room for them to shelter beneath them. Happily they survived.

About a week after my arrival it was my birthday and Anne Glendinning, the Ambassdor's PA, had arranged a surprise dinner party to celebrate. It was a splendidly warm gesture to a newcomer which I appreciated no end and typical of her kindness and thoughtfulness, traits which she has carried with her to the present day.

Life in the rather clinical service flatlet was not ideal and with the help of my boss, who spoke fluent Spanish, the search began for a suitable flat. While viewing the first one, the landlady, who took us to be a married couple, sized us up and said: "You're going to need a bigger bed". Tim, my boss, had a rather endearing habit of clearing his throat and hitching up his trousers when he was embarrassed. This was one such occasion.

Eventually I found a delightful one-bedroomed flat in a smart part of town surrounded by grand villas. The villa immediately below was said to belong to a 'Rum King'. Six guard dogs roamed round the garden. When the paperman came each morning at 5 a.m. the dogs set up a cacophony of unwelcome barking. My landlady told me that the last occupant of my flat had shot two of them from the balcony. I asked our Information Counsellor how I should deal with this noise problem and when I told him how my predecessor had dealt with it he said: "Well there you are, Angela, that's your solution." "But there are six of them, Leslie." "Well get a six-shooter," he replied! In fact I invested in a free-standing air-conditioner which drowned the early morning cacophony and also kept the bedroom cool.

Caracas was actually quite a dangerous place in which to live and one was lucky not to have had any bad experiences there. The only time I opened the front door without first looking through the spyhole, it was to a man clutching sharp knives in both hands. Luckily he was only a knife-grinder, but I never did it again. The wife of an American diplomat was accosted in the street one day in broad daylight by a robber who demanded all her jewellry. To save her diamond engagement ring she swallowed it and the man shot her through the throat. The diplomatic world was rife with such stories.

There was only one strong earth tremor during my time in Caracas and I woke to find my bed shaking. What to do? Should I go downstairs and sit in my car, which is what people used to do? But what if it was just my imagination; I'd feel a bit silly all on my own, so I turned over and went to sleep.. It turned out that everyone else went down and sat in their cars until they felt safe again.

As each weekend came along, Anne and I would take off to a beach club on the coast, taking a plentiful supply of gin and tonics and plenty of ice. The sand and the sea were absolutely glorious and after a paella at the club restaurant we slept happily in the sun until we heard the unmistakable sound of the BOAC plane from London arriving at the airport nearby. This meant that our letters from home would be ready to pick up at the Embassy in the time it took us to dress, pack up and drive back to town . This was of course one of the highlights of each week. Allan kept in touch sporadically, so there was always the chance that a letter from him might be 'in the bag', so-to-speak.

Occasionally a group of us would drive further afield to another beach club. The final part of the journey was slightly dicey in that one had to drive the car onto a small raft which was then hauled across a stretch of water by local Venezuelan

Indians. One then drove through mudflats surrounded by water in which lurked crocodiles. It was a popular place in which to hunt them and the agile young men who did so would stand on the long noses of the beasts and spear them; and timing was everything. I have to say that I wasn't inclined to go anywhere near them.

The beach club consisted of small, rather insalubrious chalets and it was fairly common to throw back the bedclothes before getting into bed and find the odd cockroach sheltering there. And there were colonies of tiny crabs which used to climb the walls and sidle their way across the ceiling, which made sleeping a rather hit and miss affair. But the sun and the sand and the rum punches and local food were all worth the downsides.

The beaches were in a sheltered cove, so there was no fear of sharks, although at another beach club Anne and I did almost come face to face with one. We were enjoying an evening swim and suddenly became aware of a large fin moving about 10 feet from us. All we wanted to do was to swim for the shore as quickly as possible. It reminded me of those nightmares one sometimes has of running away from something and not making any progress. Anne kept uttering little squeaks and when we were safely ashore, I asked her what those little squeaks were about. "Oh they were shark-frightening noises," she replied. Well, undoubtedly they worked and we were glad to have escaped with limbs intact. But we found it difficult to convince an English girl who obviously knew the club well, that she should not venture into the sea. "Its only a dolphin," she insisted. But seeing the paleness of our faces she double-checked and came back to tell us that "Yes, it was a 6ft shark and thank you for the warning".

I came to enjoy Venezuela. Personalities in the Embassy had gradually changed for the better and it was a comfortable place in which to live and work, although there was a lot of real poverty. Driving up from the coast we passed a huge rubbish tip which was always full of poor people scavenging along with the vultures. The copious amounts of oil which were being pumped out of Venezuelan land had made it suddenly a very rich country – for the few – and the centre of the town was a mixture of the old and the very new. There were fabulous shopping centres and smart shops were springing up everywhere. But the contrast of wealth and poverty made for an uneasy society and as I mentioned above, serious robbery was rampant. The countryside was beautiful and of course the constant warmth and sunshine helped. When it rained it did so with a vengeance and afterwards there were delicious curry-like smells, particularly in the forests, as the sun dried out the trees and the vegetation. Most of the cars in the city were large American limousines and the Venezuelan ladies used to drive with their left arm trailing languidly outside the car window, their hands and wrists full of jewellry. How they dared, I simply don't know. It was said that Venezuelan wives used to boast about their husband's affaires because it made the menfolk more 'macho' – an all-important part of the male psyche there.

A group of us drove south to the Orinoco River and Ciudad Bolivar, which had been the old capital of Venezuela and also where they make angostura bitters. We visited the nearby guacharo caves, the home of the guacharo birds. They are also called oilybirds and are only to be found in South America and Trinidad. They are rather like a cross between an owl and a hawk to look at and never come out in the daylight, but when night falls they fly out to the Orinoco river. The caves are full of their droppings, which make for a pleasantly soft carpet throughout the deeper, drier caves.

We were met at the entrance by a very old man carrying a lantern. He led us in and we waded through quite deep pools of water and clambered over rocks. At one point he took my hand to help me over some rocks and I saw that one of his fingers was heavily bandaged. Panic stations! I thought I'd catch some dire disease from the contact. He also shone his lantern onto the walls of the caves which were full of creepy crawlies and then he showed us some rats running round about us. The birds swooped and flew around us as we traversed the caves. Having always been a bit sensitive to such things, the whole adventure began to feel just very slightly threatening. As we went deeper into the caves we came upon some really spectacular stalactites and stalagmites and they were wondrous to behold, but I was quite glad when we emerged into the sunlight again.

As an unwelcome sequel to this, I had to leave the table feeling violently ill at a rather grand dinner party given by the Swedish Ambassador and his wife the day after we got back from this trip. It passed as these things do, but I did ask the doctor, rather tentatively, if I might be getting psittacosis from all those birds. He didn't think so and of course he was right.

Another interesting trip, which I did with Anne, was to drive up into the Andes as far as the town of Merida, where we saw the huge and imposing statue of the Virgin of the Snows. It was quite a hairy drive, but fun passing through the Indian villages and seeing and even buying some of the villagers' handicrafts.

The worst thing to befall us was as victims of a well known sport indulged in by the young. They waited in groups by the roadside and as we drove past with windows wide open they threw in plastic bags full of water. The joke was that I spotted a group on Anne's side of the road and was able to warn her to shut her window. I hadn't noticed a group on my side and they scored a real bullseye, catching me right in the face. But it was pleasantly cool and wasn't urine, which some of them were wont to put into their plastic bags. We saw a lot of cretinous folk, the product of families who lived cheek by jowl, so-to-speak, in caves in the mountains.

Elsa and Jonas Herlenius stopped over in Caracas for a couple of days on their way to join a Russian tour ship passing through the Panama Canal and back to Sweden. As luck would have it, my landlady was Secretary of a country club on the outskirts of Caracas, and gave me free tickets so that they could spend a day there playing golf and swimming. I had intended to leave them there for the day whilst I cooked a large turkey and generally got ready for a little dinner party in their honour that evening. However, Jonas would have none of that and wanted me to spend the day with them. I therefore got onto the phone and ordered the dinner from a catering firm.

The three of us spent a beautifully relaxing day at the Club and I looked forward to introducing them to my friends over dinner. It was a pouring wet evening and the guests arrived safely, albeit dripping wet, but no food arrived. Imagine my chagrin and dilemma! However, after we'd all had a couple of drinks and I'd made a frantic phonecall or two, a couple of drenched 'hombres' arrived with a series of trays, much to our amusement and relief and a good time was had by all.

There was one particularly fun Naval Visit and at the Captain's Cocktail Party on board one of the ships, I met a delightful, amusing and laid-back Lieutenant Commander, who invited me out to dinner after the party. It was great fun and the following day the ships made an early start to carry out night exercises on their way to their next port of call which was the island of Curacao, part of the Netherland Antilles. Meanwhile, back at the Embassy, the Naval Attache, Chipps Selby-Bennett, was alerted to the fact that a mailbag had arrived late for one of the ships and someone would have to be detailed to fly down with it to Curacao. I made one or two keen noises and was given this task, much to my delight.

My amusing naval officer met me off the plane, looking extremely tired after the naval exercises the night before. I'm sure that the last thing he wanted at that moment in time was to be meeting a little-known female off a plane rather than catching up on sleep. However, true to form, he escorted me to the Captain's Cocktail Party on board that evening and I enjoyed it all no end, as I think he did. He was happily married and I had no interest in anyone other than Allan, so it was all very chaste and a lot of fun. I followed his subsequent career with interest and was happy and suitably impressed to see that he became an Admiral and commanded the aircraft carrier 'Invincible' during the Gulf War. He retired after a very successful career with a KCMG. Naval company apart, what I saw of the picturesque port with its rows of Dutch houses and buildings also contributed to making the visit well worthwhile.

Holidaying in Barbados

As Barbados was so close, I spent some of my local leave there. Anne, who was on her way back to the UK, joined me for a few days and we shared a chalet in the grounds of a lovely hotel on the sea-shore. The first night I had a terrible nightmare about a huge West Indian coming in through the chalet door. I got up and started looking behind all the doors and under the bed. Anne stirred a little and muttered "What's the matter?" "I've got the heebyjeebies," I replied. "Where are they?" she asked sleepily. "I don't know, I'm just looking for them," I answered her and she drifted off to sleep again.

As I walked alone down the beach to the next hotel a day or two afterwards, a huge West Indian, who had been lurking in the trees came out and asked if we might swim together. I explained that my husband was about to appear and went on my less than merry way. He had been pressing enough for me to be nervous of walking back on my own, so I joined a family for the walk back. He was still lurking in the trees, so I was glad not to have been on my own. When the High Commissioner in Barbados paid a private visit to Caracas some time later I met him and told him my story. "You have to blame some of the air-hostesses, who are such fair game that the poor local men have come to expect that all Western women are like-minded," was his answer.

That experience apart, Barbados was a wonderful place to spend a holiday and we hired a car and traversed the island and did the sights, like the famous cricket club in the capital Bridgetown. On Sunday I took myself to a local church. I was the only white person there and the church was packed with beautifully dressed families, with children of all ages, who processed round the aisles singing happily and heartily and really entering into the spirit of the service.

I contracted two of the most common illnesses during my tour in Caracas. One was amoebic dysentary, which was treated in a rather draconian way with arsenic and made one feel wretched for weeks, but which did the trick. The other was dengue fever. This was cured in my case by dint of a fortuitous episode. I was nearing the end of my tour and anxious to sell my little Sunbeam car. Someone living in the same block of flats as I did answered my advertisement and I duly called on him to show him the car. He turned out to be a Venezuelan naval doctor and realised during my sales pitch that I wasn't feeling too well. He handed me an ampoule containing dengue-defying fluid and told me to go to the nearest chemist and get them to inject it into my posterior. The chemist showed me into a little alcove behind a curtain at the rear of the shop and did just that. I was better in no time, having languished in bed with a fever for about three weeks beforehand. I think one would be slightly chary of trusting a strange syringe like that nowadays, but it was common practice there at that time.

So my tour in Caracas drew to an end. Stupidly, I had given up my Spanish lessons at an early stage, which of course I deeply regret at this time of my life in Spain, but I did make some long-lasting British friends there. Apart from Anne, the Director of The British Council, George de Sausmarez and his wife Mouse were wonderfully good, kind and amusing friends with whom I spent may happy hours and also Christmas Days. They had two daughters and a son, Jeremy, who was fifteen and who came out for the Christmas holidays from Sherborne School, along with his sisters. He confided to me during one holiday that he loved me and would definitely marry me one day. He had the most amazing sense of humour, but in this case he seemed to be in deadly earnest. We all laughed about it; in fact we laughed a great deal of the time and I have so many happy memories of those times together. We kept in touch and visited each other fairly often when we had all returned to the UK and were living in the West Country. Apart from the first few months in Caracas, when I was missing Berlin and all the wonderful things which had happened to me there, I very much enjoyed this posting. South America was a sunny and exciting part of the world which I would have enjoyed exploring more extensively.

XV

Journeying back to the UK

Mexico

One of the advantages of serving further afield was that, time and leave permitting, one could explore other places on the way home. It was thus my good fortune that Malcolm Herlenius and his wife Elenita lived on the outskirts of Mexico City, so I was able to call on them on my way back to the UK.

There was a slight mishap on my arrival as they weren't at the airport to meet me, as arranged. I waited a fair amount of time and then took a taxi to their home. There was no sign of life there and not knowing quite what to do next and with a pile of luggage at my feet, I rang the door bell of the house next door. A dear old man answered the door and eventually grasped my plight. He invited me into his rather dark and austere house to wait for my hosts to return. He was anxious to entertain me and as we couldn't converse because of my meagre Spanish, he put some records on a wind-up gramophone. It was all tango dance music and thankfully he didn't invite me to dance. I often laugh when I imagine Malcolm and Elenita arriving to find me bent double in a tango posture in the arms of their elderly neighbour!

Malcolm was working for the Swedish steel firm, ASSAB, (Associated Swedish Steels AB), a group of several Swedish steel companies. The family lived in a quiet and peaceful area on the outskirts of this heavily polluted and very crowded capital city. At the time I visited them they were renting a holiday villa in Cuernavaca with their two small children Gustav and Louise. Malcolm commuted to his job in Mexico City during the week, returning at the weekend to relax. It was lovely to spend time with them and be shown round both places. I particularly remember being very impressed indeed with the Museum of Modern Art in Mexico City, to which I was taken by the children who can only have been quite small at that time. And I loved the colour and the verve of Mexico, to which I was to return many years later and see so much more of this vibrant country.

Spain

A Foreign Office colleague who was working at our Embassy in Madrid had invited me to visit her there for a few days. It rained a lot of the time and I found Madrid rather a gloomy place, as I did too the Prado Museum, except of course for the superb paintings of Velazquez, El Greco, Goya and Zurbaran. It seemed that one had to wade through endless rooms of less captivating works to discover them.

One day we drove in pouring rain to Toledo. I have only a hazy memory of what we saw, but well remember buying a replica of Don Quixote's sword, which I later had mounted into a stone to give to Allan as a door-stop (The Excalibur legend has always fascinated me and I had recently read T.H. White's 'The Sword in the Stone').

Switzerland

Irene Köhncke was living and working in Geneva at that time and she too invited me for a couple of days and it was fun to catch up again with someone I had given English lessons to as a child and who was now an attractive and sophisticated young lady with an American Master of Arts degree. She and the family owned a villa in Villars, to which they repaired each winter for skiing. After showing me round Geneva and wandering round the shops a bit, Irene drove us up to Villars and we spent the rest of the day with some of her friends, including Marino Marin, her husband to be. He was an attractive Italian political journalist and they live in Rome to this day.

I visited them there in 1989 when I was in the throes of buying a house in Italy shortly after I retired, a project which in the event never came to fruition. Katrin, her sister, went to live in America, where she practised law and married an American lawyer, John Hatherley. They have lived in Los Angeles most of their married life and to date still do, although Katrin owns the Köhncke family house, Trakten, at Lakene in Sweden, which she visits now and again when catching up with friends and family in Europe. In this context, I have to record my hope that the basic English I taught the girls in Sweden might have helped them in their subsequent careers. On one occasion many years later when Katrin visited me in London, I said I was so happy that she always laughed at my jokes: "I was weaned on them," she replied with a wide grin.

Stockholm

Back in London in the autumn of 1969, I was posted for a brief spell to Stockholm to cover someone's temporary absence. This was a welcome posting, although pretty hard work getting to grips with what was going on and becoming familiar with the various systems in the 'twinkling of an eye'.

Of course I thoroughly enjoyed catching up with my Swedish 'families' and many Swedish friends and I had a lovely holiday with Irma and Christer at their home by the sea in Haverdal. By this time Christer was a Judge at the Court in nearby Halmstad and they had two small children, Christian and Birgitta. On one of my visits The Landshövding (Lord Lieutenant) of Halland gave a large and rather exclusive party at his castle at Halmstad, a charming little town along the coast from Haverdal. I was invited along too and it really was a grand affair. Most of the guests were landowners with titles and large estates in the area . The guest of honour was Princess Margaretha of Sweden.

Otherwise holidays spent with Irma and Christer were very relaxed affairs, with crayfish parties, golf, lots of sea bathing and sunshine and plenty of laughter and good food. I have to record that I had the honour of being introduced by Irma to Princess Lilian, the Consort of Prince Bertil, on the golf course at Tylösand one day. The Prince himself was on a neighbouring fairway at the time so, sadly, I didn't have the pleasure of meeting him as well.

Gran Barry with my father and his sister

My mother at an early age

The author when small

A happy beach day at Bridlington just before the war with my mother and her sister Nornie. Chris, my brother and I are in the middle of the row of children

My father at sea

Leaving party for me at the British Embassy, Stockholm, in 1961 with Fred Everson, Commercial Counsellor; and Donald Murray, First Secretary Commercial

My Mother with Chris and me in Mr Bowden's garden

With my father in Granny Lineham's garden at Hessle, Yorks

Märtha and Rolf Köhncke at home in Munkfors, Sweden

Aboard 'Mon Oncle' on Råda Lake, Värmland, Sweden

Aboard 'Foresight' with Andy and Sheena Skiöldebrand
and Rutger von Seth

Jacqueline Taylor and Michael Parker in Michael's production of Richard III
with the Berlin Brigade in the Olympic Stadium's
theatre-in-the-round, Berlin in 1966

Sailing holiday in Denmark

Heulyn at home outside her new plant nursery – 2008

XVI

More Foreign Postings

British Embassy, Kuwait

My next posting was to Kuwait early in 1970 and my first impression on arrival was the wonderfully clear and sparkling air, the blue skies and the golden tinge to everything as the sun went down. I found the inhabitants friendly and courteous in general, although some exceptions were to emerge in due course.

The British Embassy was housed in an old villa near the sea. It had clearly been an attractive house in its hayday and with an attractive garden. It fulfilled its role as an Embassy and was sandwiched between the American and Russian Embassies. It was cool in the summer and boasted a reasonably-sized swimming pool. In contrast our office was pokey and gloomy. When a new Ambassador, Sam Falle, arrived with his Danish wife, they had a number of alterations made to their official Residence which was on the upper floors of the house. Unfortunately their new bathroom was immediately above our office and the loo had been resited. Fine in principle, but an irresponsible builder had managed to re-instal it so that leaks came through our ceiling, and the resulting stench had to be experienced to be believed. We put bottles of air freshener all round the office and were greatly relieved when the builders eventually put things right.

I moved straight into the flat of my predecessor, which was less than salubrious.

It was on the main road into town; small and gloomy it had a wash-basin in the front hall. More I do not remember, but knew that I needed to find something more comfortable as soon as possible. An added incentive to this was that early on I woke up in the night thinking I saw an Arab standing by the door and although it turned out to be my dressing gown hanging on the door, the experience was unpleasant and rather stayed with me. The flat was well situated, however, to hear the wonderful tones of the muezzin issuing from a nearby mosque in the early morning and as I got up to look out of the window the sky was a magnificent profusion of varying shades of red, heralding the sunrise. It was indescribably beautiful.

I found a better flat quite soon. It had no sumptious views and looked out onto a fairly bare and scruffy bit of land, but it was spacious and modern and comfortable. We were guarded day and night by two young men who sat in a little hut by the front entrance watching for marauders. The flat was a new Embassy hiring and until new Ministry of Works' furniture arrived I had to furnish it as best I could with discarded furniture stored in the Embassy cellars. The good thing was that I had a say in the colour scheme of the new furniture and curtains and when they eventually came, after many months, it was well worth the wait.

At that time Kuwait was classified as a 'difficult' posting, which meant that the tour was reduced from the usual two and a half years to eighteen months. The heat was excessive and we worked from 7 a.m. through until 1.30 p.m. or thereabouts, after which we lunched, took a siesta or at any rate hid indoors from the relentless heat. Bottled water was delivered, but sometimes delivery was delayed and if one was clean out of water life was tough.

My flat was situated just within the bounds required to get me into the Embassy, if needed, at any hour of the day or night in about ten minutes. I recall having to go in at some unearthly hour in the middle of the night and when I got home I couldn't for the life of me remember having closed all the combination locks which guarded the inner sanctuaries. Back I drove only to find that my fears were unfounded. It took some time to fall sleep once I got into bed again.

Another time I had to go in one Saturday morning. A telegram needed to be actioned by my boss who came in and drafted a reply on the back of the copy of the incoming telegram, which I then inadvertantly put through the shredding machine before typing out the reply. Chagrin all round as the boss had to be recalled to draft it again. But the Embassy was a happy one under the Ambassador, Sam Falle and the Head of Chancery, Alan Goodison, a clever and colourful character with a charming wife, Rosemary. It mattered terribly for the well-being of the staff what manner of man or woman presided over us all, especially in a difficult post.

Romance

Attached to the Embassy was a British Army Colonel who was commanding the Kuwait Liaison Team. This team comprised detachments of the British Army and Air Force who were there to help instruct their Kuwaiti counterparts in the essential elements needed to become efficient fighting forces. They wore the uniforms of the Kuwaiti Army and Air Forces and their Commander-in-Chief was General Mubarak, a member of the ruling Al Sabah family.

The Colonel was an immense help in my efforts to become settled in this new post and among other things lent me his Land Rover until my own car arrived by ship some months later. He certainly eased the way for me and we became great friends. At weekends we took off into the desert and to the seaside where we barbecued delicious morsels for our lunch, drank copiously of both water and wine and swam a lot.

The relationship deepened and although Allan was still firmly ensconced in my heart and mind as the man I still wanted most in my life, this had begun to seem an unrealistic hope. Mike was married, although the couple had not lived together for many years. It was a sad situation as his wife had had a brain tumour removed, but not entirely satisfactorily so that her mental faculties were impaired. It was essential, therefore, that our relationship showed no obvious signs of impropriety. I recall that my air-conditioning unit broke down one day and the heat in the apartment was unbearable. Mike invited me to stay the night at his house. The following morning I reported the fact that I had gone to Mike's house for the night and the reason why. My boss laughed and said: "When my father lived in India there was no air-conditioning in those days so he had to wrap himself up in a damp sheet each night". "What did he die of?" I asked. "He's still alive," he said. Oh, how we laughed.

Mike had a wonderful man to look after him. His name was Ali and he was Iranian. He was small of stature, had bow legs and wore a black beret to cover his bald head. He also sported a huge black moustache and having looked after

Mike and his predecessors for many years he spoke English like an English colonel. And his manners were impeccable. The other important member of Mike's household was Ilsa, a large boxer bitch. Mike and Ilsa were devoted to each other and she did not take kindly to my presence in Mike's life. The feeling was mutual. One day Mike asked me if I would kindly move into the back of the Landrover as he wanted to take some photographs of Ilsa. Not in itself something I should resent, but Ilsa had a way of showing somehow that she knew she had scored a point over me.

She was also a past master at being sick just as we were sitting down to a romantic little dinner. She also sensed when a row was brewing and removed herself to the farthest corner of the room to be out of reach of whatever missiles we might decide to hurl at each other. It was a stormy relationship, but in his calmer moments Mike was kindness and consideration itself.

Meeting General Mubarak

On one occasion Mike was invited to lunch by General Mubarak and his wife at their beach house. Knowing that as soon as lunch was over he would be expected to leave, which was the custom, he got the General's ADC, a large Palestinian called Nizzar, to escort me and a colleague from the Embassy to a nearby beach where we had our own picnic lunch.

As expected, Mike was able to join us for the afternoon, and Nizzar took his leave. As we were packing up to go home, I spotted a man in grey flannels, a white shirt and a sombrero making his way down the beach towards us closely protected by a man in Arab dress and wearing a small skullcap. The visitor was no less than the General and his bodyguard who had come to greet us and to hope that we had had a happy afternoon on the beach.

He and his non-English-speaking wife once gave a lunch party at their palace for the officers of the KLT and their wives and Mrs Violet Dickson, of whom more later. I was lucky enough to be invited too. Sadly, a heavy dust storm was blowing, so that their plan to have lunch outside was thwarted and we ate inside sitting at little trestle tables, each bearing a vase of artifical flowers and dishes groaning with roast lamb. There were no sheeps eyes, thankgoodness.

We had been welcomed initially into a magnificent reception room where we sat on throne-like seats round the perimeter of the room while our hosts came round to greet each one of us. Apart from being served with only soft drinks it was all very grand and therefore a bit of an anti-climax to eat in less auspicious surroundings because of the dust storm. Immediately after lunch the party broke up but Mike and I were invited into a private room, reminiscent of the Arabian Nights, where we drank coffee with our hosts. At one point I visited their private bathroom, which sported a pair of adjoining gold baths and I felt I had seen something of the way the Arab hierarchy lived. It was an experience to be remembered.

Soon after this occasion, Nizzar suggested that I give a lunch party for "ten of your best friends" and he promised to bring some special roast lamb for us to eat. It was all great fun and Nizzar did indeed bring an enormous dish of juicy lamb, surrounded by joints of chicken in a bed of delicious saffron rice, a gift to the General from the Indian Ambassador. We ate with our fingers, sitting cross-legged on the floor in true Arab style. However, Nizzar took great exception to my eating with my left hand (the unclean hand) and roared: "Angela, if you were a Bedu (Bedouin) I would kill you". To which I replied "Well I'm not a Bedu, Nizzar, and I'm left-handed"; luckily he accepted my obvious explanation in good part. But it was a sensitive point which I should have respected and one which I bore in mind for future occasions.

After the party a great deal of lamb remained, so I decided to make a present of it to Hussain, the man who did my cleaning, and his little family. Hussain was a friend of Mike's factotum, Ali, and like Ali he too was Iranian. He was also the Head of State's tea-maker and spent most of his time at the Royal Palace on hand to make tea for the endless streams of Kuwaitis who arrived to pay court to their leader and pour out their concerns to him. Hussain was a quiet and modest man who discarded his shoes before entering my flat and who somehow got rid of the dust from the floors using his hands rather than a dustpan and brush.

He lived in a grace-and-favour house with his family behind the Royal Palace. Although sparsely furnished it was fairly spacious and comfortable. It housed his wife and their daughter, who proudly told me she was learning English at school, and their two-year old son. They were all thrilled with the lamb, of course and it was a happy visit. When my posting came to an end, Hussain brought them along to my flat to say farewell and to present me with a lovely bone picture frame containing a miniature bone painting of a typical Iranian scene. Written on the back of the frame, in pencil were the words: 'from Mrs Hussain'. It was a moving occasion but ended in laughter when the small son, overcome with emotion, started to wet his pants and was born away dripping to the hole-in-the-floor loo off the kitchen.

Cornered by a Would-be Rapist

A less enjoyable occasion developed when I had to visit my doctor's surgery one Friday (the Muslim Sabbath). My Indian doctor, who had trained in Newcastle, had asked me for some English stamps to stamp and address an envelope bound for Newcastle. As expected, the surgery was closed and I was in the process of writing a little note to pop under his door with the stamps when the door opposite opened. An Arab dressed in Western dress stood there and invited me into his office to make writing a little easier. I demurred, but he insisted and anxious not to appear impolite I went in. He promptly locked the door after us. I pretended not to notice and sat at a desk in what seemed to be an open-plan office with small plaques and gravestones on chairs ranged round the room.

As I was about to get up and go the man threw his very strong arms about me and said: "Give me a kiss!" "Don't be so silly," I said and tried to break free from him. Easier said than done and he began to drag me towards a small room where I saw that there was a bed. In an effort to create a diversion, I tried to pull a typewriter off a desk as we struggled past, but only succeeded in cutting one of my fingers. As he pushed me onto the bed, I roared "Let me go!" Surprisingly, he did so. I think my anger rather than fear had completely nonplussed him and he muttered: "Please go"! I needed no further bidding, but first I had to retrieve my car keys and earrings, which had become separated from me in the struggle. As I searched for them I picked up a pair of women's long cotton knickers and realised that I was not the first woman to be seized upon in this way. We walked in silence to the door, which he unlocked and remembering to put Dr Sahni's stamps under his surgery door I left the building as calmly as I could.

I alerted my boss to what had happened and the outcome was that I had to accompany an English Special Branch Officer, on loan to the Kuwaiti police, to identify the man so that the police could apprehend him.

I was badly shaken anyway and it was not a pleasant task, but such occurrences were seriously viewed in this largely Muslim country. As I led the way to the office, one of the plain clothes policemen nodded for me to open the door and go in. I shall never forget the look of horror on the man's face. He was standing in the middle of the room chatting to some typists and when he saw me and the police entourage, his jaw really did drop. He was arrested on the spot and later deported to Egypt, from whence he came. Apparently he was a cousin of the owner of the business who had given him a job out of kindness. But a pile of pornographic magazines were discovered in his office and he was clearly something of a menace to society. Grateful as I was to have escaped fairly lightly, I didn't relish the thought of him being roughed-up by the police, as I was told he certainly would have been before being deported back to his homeland.

The only other, but less threatening incident to befall me in Kuwait was when Mike and I fell out one Friday and our usual day at the seaside was put off. However, I wanted to go to the sea so drove off by myself in a fury. Driving through the desert, I calmed down and realised I had no water with me. Fortunately I remembered that there was a little shack selling 7-Up at a place called Ahmadi, where several oil pipelines met.

Having stocked up on this life-saver I continued on down to a beach we went to quite regularly. I then realised there was no bottle opener for the 7-Up and by this time the heat was intense and thirst was really biting. Searching around the car for a sharp piece of metal on which to wrench off the bottle tops, I found what I was looking for. My thirst sated, I changed into my bikini. There was no sign of life, just a smattering of small bushes, but while making my way towards the shore, I saw to my horror what seemed like a small legion of Arabs appearing from behind the bushes and coming towards me. Quick as a flash I made for the car and shot off in a cloud of dust. So there was no swim that day and I expect Mike and I had a good laugh about it once we had made our peace.

When Nizzar invited Mike to go fishing one afternoon, I and a colleague were able to go along too. The boat belonged to one of General Mubarak's bodyguards, a round and benign figure, whose quite small fishing boat was enhanced with an oriental rug for us to sit on. No sooner had our 'good soldier Zweig', as I had christened him, put down a cluster of bated hooks, than he hauled them out again full of wriggling red snapper. And so it continued until there was hardly room for us all in the boat. At one point I needed to relieve myself and hopped into the water. At this the 'good soldier' cried out: "Sharks", and of course this paralysed me and I climbed back into the boat in double quick time without having completed the object of the exercise.

When we returned to the shore again the tide was out, so poor Mike had to carry we two girls back to the shore. He and Nizzar had on shoes of some sort which was lucky because the shallow water was a mass of sea urchins. The 'good soldier Zweig' was not so lucky and by the time he had towed the boat in, the soles of his feet were full of their poisonous spines His friends on the shore lit a bonfire over which they held first one foot and then the other. This was to open the pores so that the spines could then be drawn out more easily. Poor chap! We left them engrossed in this foot-saving operation, but were kindly presented with a modest part of our haul, to be prepared by Ali and thoroughly enjoyed later.

Dame Violet Dickson

I was priviledged to know Mrs Violet Dickson, later Dame Violet Dickson, during my time in Kuwait. She was a matriachal figure, who held open house to people from all walks of life, including many of the Bedouin tribesmen and women, as well as visitors from England. By the time I knew her she was in her eighties. She lived in a grace-and-favour house near the shore which had been her home during her marriage to Colonel Harold Dickson.

As a young subaltern on leave from India, he had met his wife-to-be when calling in to his bank in London to collect his mail. She was working at the bank and handed him his mail. On his second visit he proposed to her. In her autobiography: 'Forty Years in Kuwait' she wrote, not surprisingly, that it was a difficult decision to make. However the two were married and after service elsewhere in the Middle East, Colonel Dickson eventually became the Political Agent in Kuwait and later Adviser to the Emir of Kuwait. He also became one of our foremost Arabists and wrote a definitive book on the Arabs. He was a well-liked and respected friend of the Ruling Families, not only of Kuwait, but also of Saudi Arabia and Iraq.

It was said that in 1937 he had a dream about a beautiful girl emerging alive from a tomb. A local soothsayer interpreted his dream, telling him that oil would be found near a conspicuous landmark, a lone 'sidr' tree, situated in the south of the town, rather than the north where drilling was taking place unsuccessfully. When a well was drilled in that area it struck oil and the site became Kuwait's most productive oilfield.

After her husband's death Mrs Dickson carried on his good work helping the Arabs in any way that she could. She used to be driven by her chauffeur, who, like the house, had been lent to her by the Ruling Family for her lifetime, to visit Bedouin families, who would confide in her their most intimate problems, knowing that any advice she gave them would be sound. The Dickson house, near the waterfront, was full of artefacts the couple had collected during their years in the Middle East, together with many watercolours painted by her husband. It was a veritable museum and such it was hoped to become on her death.

She became ill just as the Iraquis invaded Kuwait in August 1990 and although, initially, she was moved to a hospital in Baghdad for treatment, permission was later given for her to be flown back to the UK to a nursing home in Berkshire found for her by her son, where she died shortly afterwards. Tragically, the house in Kuwait was ransacked during the invasion and any hope of creating a museum there was lost.

I met her through Mike to begin with and although she was known to be less interested in women than the menfolk, we got on well and when I left Kuwait she gave me a present of a Maria-Theresa dollar on a chain and signed my copy of her autobiography with the words: 'With my love Angela Many Happy Years – Sorry you are leaving us. Violet. Kuwait 6.7.71'. For her services to Anglo-Kuwaiti relations she was awarded an MBE in 1942, a CBE in 1964 and a DBE in 1976. A fascinating woman and a legend in our time. The hope was that the effects of her series of strokes prevented her from realising what was happening to her beloved Kuwait.

There were so many interesting places to visit while in the Middle East and the nearer ones could be done from Kuwait, either for a day or on local leave. For some reason or other I had to drive up to Basra, at one point, probably to collect a spare part for my Peugeot 404. The Peugeot proved to be a popular make of car in the desert regions because it was tough and handled well in the prevailing terrain and mine was no exception. I had bought it very cheaply whilst staying with Rosemary and David Manger who were still serving in Berlin. The owner, a member of the British Military Government (BMG) in Berlin had used it only for holidays touring in Europe. It was pale blue and in immaculate condition until my trip to Basra. A fierce sandstorm was blowing and the road up from Kuwait was long and straight with desert on both sides and afforded no shelter from the all invasive sand. On arrival back in Kuwait the colour had been completely sandblasted off the front of the car.

Holidaying in Iran

Mike suggested we might spend a few days of local leave visiting Iran and I was keen to do this. We flew to the Gulf port of Abadan where we were met by car, complete with driver, a luxury organised by Mike. We drove first to Shiraz in blizzard conditions. The country was mountainous, bleak and uninhabited, except for the odd 'caravanserai' where camel trains would stop for refreshment and to stay overnight. At one point during the journey I had to make a 'comfort stop' and was very nearly blown away by the force of the icy wind. We had plans to visit Darius' Tomb, Persepolis and other well known historical sights in and around Shiraz, but I woke up the first night with a high temperature and a heavy cold. I managed to see Darius' Tomb but Mike had to do the rest on his own. An excellent doctor was called to wreak a miracle cure, which he did, and we were able to continue our trip to Isfahan some 48 hours later.

Isfahan was one of the most colourful and exciting places I have ever been to. The vast Maidan Square surrounded by so many magnificent mosques, their domes vying with each other in design, mosaics and sheer vibrancy and beauty, were sights never to be forgotten. We stayed at the Shah Abbas Hotel, named after the King, Shah Abbas the Great (1586-1628). It was sumptious in the extreme. Originally a 'caravanserai', it provided every possible luxury and was more like a palace than a hotel. There was so much of interest to see in the town and the enormous bazaar was teeming with vast amounts of tempting merchandise, most of it made locally and by hand. We bought some silver and lengths of colourfully designed materials and flew back to Kuwait utterly enchanted.

Sailing Round the Greek Islands

Another week of local leave was spent sailing round the Greek Islands in a yacht Mike had chartered at the port of Piraeus. He had gone back to UK to pick up a brand new Landrover, which he drove out to Greece, together with his younger son and girlfriend. The young then went off on their own and Mike came to meet me at Athens Airport.

We took ourselves off to see and wonder at the Acropolis and then drove on to Piraeus. We hadn't the time to see much more of Athens, but I wasn't altogether inspired to plan another visit, only partly perhaps because my bottom was soundly pinched by a passing Athenian. Mike had picked up the boat the previous day and spent hours cleaning her and making her sailworthy but even then we had to return for emergency repairs after half a day's sailing late on the first night. After that it was, as they say, plain sailing. The July sun was relentless, but with a canopy to protect us on deck we enjoyed it and got nicely sunburned.

We sailed from island to island, weighing anchor each evening, and early enough to do some sightseeing and have supper ashore. I loved Spetsai in particular, where no cars were allowed and transport was by horse and carriage and Hydros was immensely attractive and picturesque and home to a large colony of artists. It was all lovely, but sadly Mike kept having angry moods and half the time we weren't even speaking so it was a sad waste of what could have been a wonderfully romantic holiday. I never quite discovered what triggered these moods and whether shortcomings of mine were to blame or not. But it didn't bode well for any future we might have had together, although we persevered with the relationship, which in so many ways was a rewarding one.

Istanbul

After the week's sailing Mike's son and girlfriend joined us and we drove up to Istanbul. It was not the most comfortable of journeys in the Landrover but we enjoyed ourselves anyway and stopped off for a night at the age old city of Thessalonika on the way.

Istanbul, the only city in the world situated on two continents, pulsated with life, restrained only by the blue waters of the Bosphorus. Horses and carts vied with the motorised traffic and somehow survived. The manager of our hotel insisted that Mike was the spitting image of Kemal Atatürk, who led the Young Turk revolution in 1923, and he treated us with great respect. I had only one day in Istanbul, but managed to see The Blue Mosque and traipse round the enormous Bazaar. There was a cholera outbreak whilst we were in Istanbul and after having to visit a loo in the Bazaar I thought that if there was a chance of my catching cholera my visit there would have trebled my chances.

On arrival back in Kuwait, all travellers from Istanbul were immediately sent to an Immunisation Centre in the centre of the dockyard to have a cholera booster. It was heaving with people of all shapes and sizes bent on getting their injection before the next person. There seemed to be no order and when an old man used the melée to press himself against me, I'm afraid I gave him push which sent him flying. It was a desperate situation, but suddenly a voice of authority called down in English from a balcony above: "Come up here, please" and to my surprise and relief I was given an immediate booster injection and sent on my way.

XVII

Journeying Back to the UK

As my tour of Kuwait neared its end I made plans to fly home by a circuitous route calling at Beirut, Cyprus, The Holy Land and then to Rome to catch up with friend Dorothy Laing, who was currently the Ambassador's PA there. These plans were in danger of being severely disrupted, if not curtailed, when the day after I had secured a buyer for my beloved Peugeot, an Arab driver, no doubt feeling the effects of Ramadan, stopped suddenly in front of me. I managed to swerve, but caught the offside rear end of his car. The driver of the car behind me, a brand new Mercedes, crashed heavily into the back of my car and it was at that point that my dreams of using the cash from the sale of my car for the trip home receded with brute force. Oddly enough the dream was realised in the end. The buyer of my car, a British Army Major, decided to go through with the sale. The damage to the front was negligible, the engine intact and he knew that the bodywork at the back could be made good. The Egyptian Embassy, who owned the Mercedes, paid for most of the damage and my share of the damage to the car in front amounted to a mere 18 Dinars.

Serious Thoughts

It was clear that much thought had to go into what might well have become a long term relationship with Mike, once he had sorted out what he wanted to do vis-à-vis his marriage and his future in the Army. Those were decisions he had to make alone, but my feelings about the whole relationship were also important in helping him make up his mind. I was keen to marry and have a child, but didn't want my wishes to jeopardise whatever life his wife had to contend with, particularly when I wasn't one hundred percent sure that Mike and I were temperamentally suited to each other in the longer term. He knew of my earlier relationship with Allan and how much it had meant to me. My protracted holiday on the way home from Kuwait would, I hoped, give me some thinking time. And so we parted but planned to meet up again in Rome.

Beirut

Beirut was a city I had always wanted to visit and it proved to be no disappointment. Friends working for Shell in Kuwait introduced me to one of their colleagues in Beirut and Mike knew the Head of the British Council there. With these two wonderful introductions the visit couldn't have been better. The Shell man, an extremely urbane and kindly Lebanese, with a flat in London, indeed in Mayfair, took me on a sightseeing tour of the city ending up with a drink at the famous Hotel St Georges. As I said goodbye to him he was horrified to learn that I was going on to The Holy Land and looked nervously over his shoulder to see if anyone was within earshot as I dropped what to him was a small bombshell. It was an unfortunate gaffe on my part, and I realised at that moment that if a man of such urbanity and intelligence felt so strongly about the Arab-Israeli conflict, there seemed little hope of it ever being resolved.

On my second night in Beirut, Ella Fitzgerald was giving a concert at Baalbek within the magnificent ruins there and surrounded by some of the beautiful 'cedars of Lebanon'. The British Council man invited me to accompany him and a visiting friend to the concert. They planned to drive there in style in a chauffeur-driven car and have a champagne picnic on the way. It all sounded too good to be true, but the difficult bit was that somehow I had to acquire a ticket to the concert. Again fate stepped in, helped by the Diplomatic grapevine. One of the Second Secretaries at the Embassy in Beirut, who had a ticket, had gone down with mumps. He was David Spedding, who many years later became Head of MI6. So I went in his stead and what a memorable evening it was.

What seemed like several thousand people were milling about trying to find their seats when Ella appeared on stage. Within seconds you could have heard a pin drop. And so it continued throughout her performance. She looked and sounded magnificent, dressed in a stunning white evening gown, and I was not alone in shedding a few tears as she sang her way through so many well known and romantic songs: 'The man I love', 'You can't take that away from me', to name only two. The air was clear and warm and doves flew lazily over our heads between the ancient Doric columns around the arena. It was a magical evening but I must confess to being a mite disillusioned when, early the following morning as I was leaving Beirut, I saw Ella at the airport. She was just another rather heavily-built woman from the deep South chewing gum, accompanied by a diminutive Sammy Davis Junior-type musician dressed in loud checks. I couldn't resist thanking her for such a marvellous evening. "Thank you agin," she replied in tones from the deep South and I felt privileged to have met her, despite the lack of the glamour which had so entranced us the evening before. But then most of us might be said to look pretty drab at an airport, early in the morning with that slight feeling of uneasiness and the endless waiting, even without having entertained a large audience a few hours before.

Cyprus

On arrival at Nicosia Airport I had to get a taxi to my hotel and had been advised to make sure it was one which would take the shortest route through the Turkish sector to Kyrenia. Needless to say I got it wrong and ended up with a Greek-Cypriot driver who not only took me the more circuitous route, but made a pass at me on the way. A friend had recommended the hotel I was booked into, but it was a disappointment. I was tired and irritable and decided to go straight to bed without an evening meal. The dining room looked forlorn and as the sojourn in Cyprus was intended to be a 'rest and recuperation' stop I had serious thoughts about moving to the Catsellis Dome Hotel across the road the following morning.

My room had a balcony and the gap between the balcony and an adjoining roof was too close for comfort. I firmly locked the balcony door and the bathroom window. After downing a couple of modest brandy and gingers, I fell into bed exhausted. Something woke me and standing at the door of the bathroom was the figure of a man dressed in a black turban and black Arab dress. My immediate thought was how had he got in and how was I to get him out. His mien was grim and sent shivers down my spine. He somehow looked like a Turk. As these thoughts flew through my mind the figure just glided away through the wall. I switched on the bedside to light to find that it was exactly midnight. Had I seen another ghost? Totally unnerved I rang down to the concierge who came up to my room. He spoke only a smattering of English and certainly not enough to understand what I was trying to tell him. "No men here," he said, thinking I was completely deranged. "I go back to my telephone" he went on, preparing to leave, but when I somehow managed to explain to him that the figure was a Turk and that I wanted to move out immediately, he became more concerned and walked with me the short distance to the Dome Hotel.

Of course the receptionist there wondered what strange creature was arriving in such a state of alarm but gave me a room, where I felt happier. Nevertheless I slept with the light on, not only that night but for the remainder of my stay in Cyprus. There had been a feeling of evil and foreboding about the spectre, which proved difficult to banish. There were two possible explanations, if one gives credence to the spirit world. One was that a graveyard next to the hotel was being bulldozed and some poor soul might have felt displaced. The other was that it may have been some portent of what was to come, as the Turks invaded Kyrenia shortly thereafter. Who is to know.

Otherwise the few days I spent there fulfilled their role, with plenty of sunbathing and swimming from a private jetty belonging to the hotel and gentle trips to the surrounding countryside and Balapais Abbey.

Sitting at the next table to me in the hotel dining room was a slight, bearded and elderly Englishman. During most mealtimes his head was bent over a book, but we did have the odd conversation. I told him about my ghostly encounter and when I got to the bit where the receptionist thought I was slightly batty, my neighbour interrupted sharply to say: "Well you were, weren't you?" I recall that he was a former Governor of The Sudan, so felt I ought to take his comment seriously. Feeling rested and renewed, albeit rather glad to shake the dust of Cyprus off my feet, I headed for Jerusalem.

The Holy Land

This was a whole new world, a world in which The Bible came to life, as if in the twinkling of an eye the modern world had receded. It was fascinating to walk through the different quarters, Armenian, Muslim, Jewish and Christian and to see how each group lived, intermingling with each other whilst going about their daily business. The markets in Jerusalem were a bustling throng of Arabs of one sort or another and the vibrancy and sounds of the Middle East filled the air. I spent several weeks in the area totally enthralled, visiting the Dome of the Rock, the El Aqsa Mosque, The Church of the Holy Sepulchre, The Temple on the Mount, The Tomb of the Kings, The Mount of Olives, The Garden of Gethsemane and the Wailing Wall, where, like millions before me, I placed a little prayer in a crack in the Wall, while watching Greek Orthodox Priests banging their heads against it. I went to a Service at the Cathedral Church of St James and thanked God from the bottom of my heart for making it possible for me to do such a trip.

Hiring a car proved a rather time-consuming business. The garage had no small car and off I drove in one which was far too big for my needs. But as luck would have it, it stalled at the first set of traffic lights and refused to go any further. An Israeli policeman sauntered up and said I couldn't stop there. Once he became aware of the problem he agreed to stand guard by the car until I had alerted the garage. A further plus was that, not only did the garage then produce a smaller car, a Simca, but gave me it free for the rest of that first day.

I drove off posthaste to Bethlehem and was able to visit the Church of the Nativity before it closed for the night. Sadly the church and the whole area had become unattractively commercialised. But I climbed up the steps to the tower and marvelled at the view and the history it had been witness to. The sun began to set as I drove back to Jerusalem and the hills, the shepherds and the sheep were bathed in a red and golden aura. I'll never forget it.

During the next few days I drove to Nazareth, the Sea of Galilee and along the Jordan Valley. The man from whom I had rented the car had told me that it was quite safe to give a lift to any Israeli soldiers who might ask for one. Sure enough one fair and very good-looking soldier did so. He was armed to the teeth and as he got into the car he parked his pistol and automatic rifle on the car floor. I was making my way towards the Dead Sea and so was he. When asked whether he read English books, because if so I could recommend a very good one about the Dead Sea Scrolls called 'The Road To Shiloh', he replied sternly: "We have no time for reading in the Israeli Army".

I dropped him off shortly afterwards and parked the car near to the banks of the Dead Sea so that I could easily descend into the salt-ridden waters. Such a strange experience and I just couldn't get dry afterwards. On the road to Jericho I gave a lift to a young American couple, who must have wondered at the grubby little wodges of Kleenex scattered about the floor.

Driving down the Jordan Valley one could see camouflaged Israeli tanks lurking amid the trees on either side of the road. Suddenly a group of Israeli soldiers waved me down. Thinking that they wanted to check my bonefides, I drew to a halt. Without a word they began to pile into my car: "Stop," I said, "I don't want you in my car," at which they politely got out, apologising as they did so.

By this time I had begun to check my finances and suddenly realised that the car was costing me far more than I had guilelessly imagined it was. So I headed for Tel Aviv Airport where I had arranged to hand it back. On the way there I stayed the night in a small and primitive hostel in the town of Caesaria, where my room was like a little cell, with a stone floor. In the dining room there was a special table on which was an attractive array of what looked like a Scandinavian smörgåsbord, but as I made my way towards it I was firmly told that it was kosher food provided solely for their Jewish clientele. After this, not uncomfortable, but cheap night I decided to spend my last night in The Holy Land in the comfort of the the Sheraton Hotel. It was on the beach and I was able to have a swim in the sea before leaving for the airport the following morning.

Rome

I caught up with Dorothy Laing in Rome but stayed in a hotel for a couple of nights as the poor girl was exhausted after a long hot summer and a surfeit of visitors. When Mike arrived we moved to a charming hotel, which was part monastery, just outside the city. The following day we wore the soles off our shoes sightseeing and joined the throng of visitors making their way towards the Vatican to see, above all, the Sistine Chapel and we loved it all. Dorothy joined us for dinner and was happily in good form again.

The following day Mike decided to buy a smart-looking secondhand Fiat Spyder sports car he'd spotted in a showroom window. It was British racing green and he fell for it, so we continued on our way by car up to Moenchen Gladbach, where I was to be Godmother at the Christening of Andrew, Rosemary and David Mangers' first baby. This was an emotional occasion and we celebrated his safe arrival in style, while Mike continued on his way back to England in his little Fiat gem.

XVIII

Interlude in London

Back in England again, I reported in to the Office. Personnel Department were always interested in hearing about the Post one had just left and showed an interest in one's travels and adventures. It made coming back that much more personal. Apart from this, one was always eager to know what the future had in store. It was good news. A posting to Singapore was coming up in about six months time and I accepted it with alacrity. I found a tiny flatlet in Streatham in which to live for those six months in London and had Mike's Fiat Spyder to take me out of London and catch up with family and friends at weekends.

Christmas in Rhodes

Mike suggested we might meet up on the island of Rhodes for Christmas. He flew from Kuwait and I took a cheap night flight from London. Soon after reaching cruising height the Captain made his way up the aisle asking who was flying to Rhodes. There were three of us: an elderly and crippled French lady who walked with the aid of two sticks, an elderly Yorkshireman, turned Pommy, who had built up a flourishing bus company in Australia and me. The Captain, an Australian, told us that there was a 90 mile an hour gale blowing around Rhodes, so that he couldn't land the plane there. The two options he suggested to us were to land at Nicosia, where we would all be accommodated in a 4-star hotel and given dinner and breakfast the following morning when we would then continue on to Rhodes, weather permitting. The other option was for him to land at

Athens where we three would disembark and continue our journey immediately on a small twin-engined plane which could cope with the gale. Naturally we wanted to get there as soon as possible, so I said to the Captain: "My chap's panting in Rhodes!" The Captain drawled, with a twinkle in his eye: "Ayl bae thet in moind" and various passengers within earshot turned round to see what sort of a fortunate female I was. They were clearly amazed to see just an ordinary middle-aged woman and then we all dozed off to sleep wondering which option the Captain would decide upon. Perhaps in deference to 'the chap panting in Rhodes' he landed in Athens. The three of us hopped off – well those of us who could hop – and were treated to a magnificent breakfast while the British Airways staff moved heaven and earth to get us onto a fully-booked plane bound for Rhodes.

Somehow they succeeded and replete but very weary we climbed into the tiny plane. We seemed to spend ages just sitting on the tarmac. The elderly Yorkshireman-cum-Pommy suddenly jumped to his feet shouting: "Can't they get this bloody crate off the ground". I managed to calm him and eventually we were on our way. On arrival I suggested to the French lady that we stay put until the others had disembarked and I would try to arrange a wheelchair for her. I wasn't sure whether Mike would have made it from Kuwait because of the weather, which was a bit of a worry. However he was there waiting and when we all appeared some time after the rest of the passengers, he cut a very disconsolate figure. On seeing us he raced across the tarmac and enveloped me in a strong embrace, from which I emerged to say in a shaky voice: "Could you get me a wheelchair please?" His disconsolate mien returned until I introduced him to my two elderly friends and there were smiles all round. In fact we saw quite a lot of the indomitable French lady and weren't a bit surprised when she opted to go up into the hills sightseeing on a donkey one day.

It was strange being out on a limb in Rhodes over Christmas, but interesting to see how the islanders celebrated it. Certainly on Christmas Eve they scurried round like the rest of us buying last-minute presents and the all-important goose. Our hotel produced a delicious Christmas Dinner and it was lovely to wake up each morning with the sea lapping onto the beach below. The sun shone and we sat on a jetty eating the mince pies Mike had brought and trying to picture the lost city of Atlantis rising out of the sea before us. We did the sights and talked about a possible future together. Mike presented me with the gift of a plain gold ring and although he wasn't in a position to marry me at that point, it was clear that his intentions were serious. But I never did wear the gold ring; it was one size too small.

Marriage Prospects

Immediately I got back to London I decided to try and see Allan to find out what effect that would have on my muddled emotions. He was just off on a trip abroad and said he would pop in en route. His timing was uncertain and two friends were in having a drink with me when he arrived. It was clear to them that this was something special and the wife of the couple whispered: "Would you like us to go"? "No, don't," I nervously replied. But when, after the introductions, Allan helped himself to a handful of pistachio nuts thinking they were peanuts and had to dispose of them in the bathroom before he choked on their shells, I said to them "Perhaps it would be a good idea if you went," and they did.

We had an unforgettably happy time together and Allan left the following morning. I had explained to him about Mike, whom he knew as they were both from the same regiment. He asked if I was in love with Mike and in a small and uncertain voice, I answered that I thought I was. Had I said, more honestly, that I had thought I was until now, I doubt that it would have made the slightest difference. A letter from him came to me in Singapore some time later which was a poor appreciation of the happy time we had had together.

<h1 style="text-align: center">XIX</h1>

More Foreign Postings

British High Commission, Singapore

The time came for me to go off to Singapore and as there seemed to be nothing to keep me in England as far as my love life was concerned, off I went. One of the First Secretaries and the secretary I was to replace met me off the plane and asked what I'd like to do first. "Take my vest off," I replied. It was hot and humid in Singapore, something I never got used to. Safely installed in a comfortable little hotel a stone's throw from the High Commission and very near the lovely Botanical Gardens, it was agreed that I would find my way to the office myself the following morning. Easier said than done as the hotel lift broke down with me trapped inside it. Alarmingly, it took an extremely long time before I was released, so my arrival at the office was seriously delayed. No harm was done, except perhaps to my nervous system, and everyone was kind and sympathetic. Leaving aside the lift incident, I was completely bowled over by the greenery everywhere and the intoxicating smell of the tropics. It was different from Venezuela, much more humid and consequently rather more enervating.

About a week after my arrival we had a Royal Visit. The Queen, accompanied by Prince Philip, came to lay the foundation stone of the new British High Commission. It was a splendid occasion and we all got seats in the stands to watch the arrival of the Royal Yacht 'Britannia' and the Royal Party. We watched as the red carpet was put in place and as Lee Kuan Yew and the other local dignitaries gathered to greet the Royal Couple. The husband of one of the locally-engaged staff, who clearly had a Colonial past but who should have known better, looked with horror as two Chinese Hakka women, complete with their red headdresses, tried to clamber up the scaffolding behind us to get a view too. "Get down, you buggers," he shouted. They did, but it was a misplaced request, badly expressed, and it cast a bit of a cloud over our enjoyment of the occasion.

Oddly enough, the official opening of the new High Commission building took place just as I was about to finish my posting there. Special bullet-proof windows had been sent out, some of which arrived broken, so in order that the official opening could take place on the due date, ordinary glass windows were put in as a temporary measure, held in place by some temporary means. A team of British Army soldiers were detailed to stand guard and they and an armed guard in the foyer proved a successful deterrent to any would-be marauders. I believe the troops included some who had been confined to barracks for various misdemeanors, so in truth we were probably more at risk from them than any other assailants. Sam Falle our High Commissioner became Sir Sam Falle during this Royal Visit and a number of other worthy souls were awarded well-deserved medals.

Malacca

I drove up to Malacca one weekend with one of my secretarial colleagues, Susanna. We found miles of beautiful and empty beaches and settled down in the middle of one with our books and plenty of lovely sunshine. Suddenly two teenage boys appeared on bicycles and, thinking we were mother and daughter, began with lurid gestures to ask my permission to have their wicked way with Susanna. The only weapon in sight with which to chase them off was one of those waxed Chinese umbrellas, but it did the trick and off they rode chortling. They were soon followed by a group of young Malay women, who settled down beside us and proceeded to try and relieve us of anything they could lay their hands on. There was nothing for us to do, sadly, but to remove ourselves.

We later hired a boat to take us to one of the many small islands in the South China Sea and there we were undisturbed for the rest of the day until the boat arrived to take us back to Malacca. We then had a wonderful time mooching round the antique shops and both bought one or two worthwhile pieces of china and I also bought a couple of very old spoons.

Susanna first met her husband, David, a Naval Officer, when he visited Singapore on a Naval Visit during her tour there. They had a lovely wedding some years later and were married at the Chapel of King's College, London. Susanna's father was Chancellor of King's College at that time and it was a supremely happy occasion. Years later they lived quite close to me with their two super teenage children, Thomas and Eleanor; at the time I was living in Dorset and so we were able to meet fairly regularly over a number of years. They also came to my part of Spain twice on holiday so we were able to catch up with each other once again. Needless to say we never failed to reminisce over those funny times in Singapore.

Discovering Golf

I learnt to play golf at The Keppel Club in Singapore and later became a member of the Royal Tasek Utara Golf Club in Johore Bahru also. Weekends were invariably spent driving over the Causeway to Johore very early in the morning, so as to miss the queues of cars doing likewise, playing as many holes as my energies allowed once the sun began to shine with a vengeance.

After relaxing with an ice cold drink, I usually drove to one of the various local restaurants serving chilli crab, and finally on to the Keppel Club to swim and sleep by the pool. I got to know one or two of the members and was once invited to join a group of beer-quaffing men. One of them was a Singapore-Chinese airline pilot and with a certain amount of bravado, probably intensified by his beer drinking, he launched into a commentary on how he would save his aircraft if it got into difficulties. I privately hoped I'd never be one of his passengers. However, some time later the plane he was piloting did get into severe difficulties and what is more he did do all the right things and saved it from crashing, thereby becoming a local hero. So much for my character-assessment.

Another day I had a rather hesitant phonecall from a man professing to have met me at the golf club in Johore. Would I play golf with him? I agreed and we duly met. He was a Malay civil servant and when asked what his handicap was, he replied: "A wife and two children". A bit of a wag, but a nice enough fellow. After our game he invited me to the rather splendid Civil Service Club for a drink. Although doing his best to drink me under the table, he didn't quite succeed and I arrived back safely in Singapore feeling weary and just a bit the worse for wear.

Another young Malay asked if I would play a round with him and mark his card for his handicap. I agreed and we chatted as we played. He was anxious to know where I lived. I explained that it was just off the Bukit Timah. This was safe enough as this road runs the length of Singapore Island. However, he kept narrowing it down until he was satisfied he knew where it was I lived. He then asked if I had a dog. "Why?" I asked him. "Because I'm afraid of dogs," he replied. I believe I said I had a dog at that point, but he didn't pursue matters and again he was a pleasant young man.

A friend from the Australian Foreign Service, Pye Cormack, with whom I sometimes played golf, surprised me one day by saying she had just bought a little island in the South China Sea and would I like to come with her to see it. Small and mostly overgrown, the only signs of habitation on the island were two tiny little huts. But the beaches were lovely and as we sat by the sea a kitten came and joined us. Pye played with it and needless to say it scratched her. Imagine our horror when we went to look at the second of the two huts and saw the word RABIES scrawled across the door. Worse still, when we returned to the beach the dead body of the kitten was lying on the shore. This put Pye in a dreadful dilemma. Should she have an anti-rabies shot or not? Needless to say I was all for her doing so, however unpleasant it may have been. Pye, though, decided not to and in the event she didn't get rabies. Relief all round.

Frasers Hill and The Cameron Highlands

There were two popular hill stations in Malaysia where one could shake off the heat and humidity of Singapore. I went to the nearest one, Frasers Hill, with friend Dorothy Laing who was at that time PA to the High Commissioner in Kuala Lumpur. We stayed at a very comfortable rest-house belonging to the Malay Railway Company. Everything was spotlessly clean and highly polished, rather like a Pullman train, with lots of shiny brass. During the night I had an awful nightmare about bloody joints of meat. I discovered in the course of conversation the next day that the house had been a hospital during the Insurgency.

Playing golf on the little 9-hole golf course was a happy antidote to this rather macabre experience and it was good to escape the heat of Singapore. Dorothy as almost always was good company and we had a lot of laughs. She met her husband-to-be in Kuala Lumpur and until her sad death a few years ago I saw them both fairly frequently when we had all retired to the UK.

I was lent an air-conditioned car for a trip to the other popular hill station, the Cameron Highlands. On the journey north two bottles of Dubonnet which were on the back seat broke when I suddenly had to break rather sharply. No harm was done to the interior of the car as the trim was the same colour as the wine, but the alcoholic fumes threatened to engulf me for the rest of the journey.

I had booked myself into Fosters, a chintzy English-style country house hotel overlooking the golf course, some 400 kms north of Singapore. Having specifically asked for a room overlooking the golf course, I was horrified when shown into a tiny single room overlooking the well of the hotel. After a few words with the Manager I was given the bridal suite, complete with four-poster bed and wonderful vases of flowers all over the room. Such a waste on my own but needless to say I thoroughly enjoyed my stay. There had been a faint chance that Allan might have joined me there as he had to pay an official visit to Australia around that time, but in the end it just wasn't feasible.

Stan Foster, the owner, had chanced upon the house years ago as a soldier serving in Malaya and vowed to come back and make it into a country house hotel. He realised this dream and also had a very popular restaurant, Foster's Smoke House, in Singapore and later another beautiful hotel in the Cameron Highlands.

Another unexpected blow struck when I discovered that the golf course was closed as the entire Malaysian Royal Family had taken it over for all of five days; the area was littered with Rolls Royces. The disappointment and anger I felt were soon dissipated when one of the hotel staff offered to take me on a tour of the nearby tea plantations and the rose gardens. The area was so beautiful and the tour turned out to be well worthwhile and really something of a bonus. Also, I got to know Stan Foster and his lady well enough to be invited to a private dinner with them one evening, which happily relieved the monotony of dining alone.

When I arrived at the Golf Club on the sixth day the The Tunku was about to leave in a helicopter, watched by the local populace, who couldn't have failed to see me driving off the first tee. It was with some surprise and relief therefore that I watched my ball land a reasonable distance away. Halfway round the course I noticed two men bearing down on me and as I started to wave them through, the elder of the two men came over and introduced himself: "Samed Noor, Deputy Minister of Defence." "Angela Barry, British High Commission," I countered. At this he told me that one of his children was engaged to be married to one of our High Commissioner's children. I can't now recall who had the son and who had the daughter, but the ice was well and truly broken and this charming man invited me to join the two of them for the remainder of the round. Although I explained how much of a beginner I was he insisted and of course I ended up losing all my golf balls and then his. But it was all great fun and at the end he introduced me to his equally charming Malay wife. They kindly invited me to visit them on my way back to Singapore, and although I couldn't manage to do this, it was a welcome invitation despite my poor showing on the golf course.

It may look as if I spent most of my spare time in Singapore playing golf, but no, there was a good social life as well and eating out was a particular pleasure as I was fairly addicted to Chinese food. Rather indelicately, I liken a Chinese meal to a multiple orgasm, in that one could feel totally sated but then keen to start again in no time at all.

The car park at the 'Cold Storage' supermarket turned at night into an open air restaurant. As dusk fell the little carts started to arrive, pushed by the usually quite small cooks in spotlessly clean white vests. In no time their woks were bristling with very hot and tempting mixtures of Chinese food. In fact my taste buds are beginning to quiver at the thought.

One ate at rather rusty little iron tables on wobbly iron chairs and it was always packed. I never ever heard of anyone being ill after eating there. In fact I was taken there while still suffering from the effects of a tummy bug caught elsewhere and was able to eat some mussel soup. It looked rather grey and unappetising, but I persevered and felt completely recovered afterwards. It was probably the result of the copious amounts of garlic they had used.

Sightseeing in Singapore
On the whole I found Singapore overly hot and humid but it had a lot to offer in sightseeing terms. 'The streets of the dead' were fascinating, because people did actually go to the death houses there to wait for their demise. Funerals took place all the time with decorated floats and little saucers of tasty morsels so that the dead would not go to their graves hungry; loud music accompanied them on their way.

Bugie Street on the other hand, which was a great tourist attraction, came alive at nightime when the local transvestites paraded among the cafe tables dressed in sumptious dresses which barely restrained their well-endowed figures. If one didn't know that they were men one would be hard put to believe that they were. In fact a British merchant seaman sitting at our table had set his cap at one of them and our dire warnings that he might well be clobbered in a nearby alleyway and lose his wallet had no effect whatsoever and off he went.

There was a table nearby full of more raucous British merchant seamen, one of whom stripped and danced naked on top of their table. Of course this attracted the attention of everyone and until he was apprehended stole all interest away from the transvestites, much to their ill-concealed anger. As my escort and I were leaving, one of them decided to get into the taxi with us, but luckily he was dissuaded.

One day I took the car down into Chinatown, parked it and went off shopping. When I returned a group of Chinese were standing where my car had been. They were looking upwards. I followed their gazes and there in the air was my car in the process of being removed. "Hi" I shouted, "that's my car." After a moment's hesitation, the machine that held it in its claws gradually lowered it down to the ground and the perpetrators just fell about laughing, which is what the Chinese tend to do when they are embarrassed. I decided not to remonstrate in case I might have been parked illegally, rather than being the victim of a robbery and drove off feeling lucky to have got there just in time.

Social Life

Apart from friends within the High Commission, there were four couples who made life interesting and stimulating and with whom I had a lot of fun. They were Iain and Ruth McAllum, whom I had known in Berlin. Iain ran the British Council in Singapore during the time I was there and I remember particularly spending a lovely Christmas with them and their two children Frances and Justin. We renewed our friendship years later when we lived near to each other in the West Country.

Frank and Pam Hickley were another couple with whom I spent some wonderful times. Frank had lived in Singapore most of his life and had been a prisoner in Changi Prison during the Japanese occupation of Singapore. Pam had also lived there for many years and the couple were married soon after Frank's release. He was a shadow of his former self, but survived to tell the tale and was always full of fun. They were a most civilised and hospitable couple whose paramount interest was the collection of blanc de chine porcelain. They travelled far and wide in quest of rare and beautiful pieces and had one of the finest collections in the world. Some year's after Frank's death, Pam gave the whole collection to the Singapore Government and it is now part of the National Collection. Pam was a cousin of Group Captain Leonard Cheshire and worked unstintingly for the Leonard Cheshire Home she had helped set up in Singapore, for which she was awarded an MBE.

Then there were Ruth and David Porter and sometimes their three lively daughters. David worked originally for the BBC and came out to Singapore to help the Singaporeans establish their own network. They loved the country and spent many years of their retirement there before returning eventually to the UK.

Robert and Katherine Du Cane came to live in Singapore towards the end of my tour. I had originally met Robert when he came out to Caracas to sell warships to the Venezuelans on behalf of Brook Marine, so it was lovely to have the family in Singapore. By this time Robert was working for Vosper Thornycroft, in which there was a family connection. They were immensely hospitable and great party-givers. Again, we kept up with each other after moving to Dorset and Cornwall respectively.

Diplomatic Bag Run to Bangkok

A stroke of luck came my way when I was chosen to do a Diplomatic Bag run to Bangkok. I say chosen, because there were several others, particularly among the High Commission Registry staff, who would normally have done this, but as I was about to leave Singapore and was very keen to visit Bangkok, they all stepped back and the Head of Chancery let me do the run. It happened to be on my birthday so it was a fairly unique way of celebrating. Free champagne was served as an aperitif on the return flight and if I remember rightly the dinner was pretty delicious too.

As the timing of the flight back allowed for a night in Bangkok, I was able to cram in quite a bit of sightseeing the following day. I did a whirlwind tour of the town by taxi, although whirlwind is a bit of a misnomer because even in those days the traffic was diabolical and carbon monoxide fumes pervaded most of the city centre. But it was just possible for me to see some of the more important sights and even look inside the main temples. I then caught a boat and did a relaxing trip through the canals. It was absolutely fascinating to see the canal life both on the canal itself and along the banks; to see the little punt-like boats full of fruit and vegetables and other necessities of life being sold to the canal dwellers. Then there were boats on which the Thai women cooked delicious morsels and sold them, piping hot, to their boat-bound customers. We passed the famous Oriental Hotel, which, sadly, had just suffered a fire, so that parts of it were just a mass of smoke-stained wreckage. It was restored to its former glory, but not until some time later.

There was time too to look at some of the shops selling beautiful sapphire jewellry and Thai silk. My pennies didn't run to such things, but I did buy a lovely bowl made of some gold-coloured metal. It was attractively designed and still affords me great pleasure in the centre of my mantlepiece full of potpourri.

Touring in Malaysia

As my time in Singapore was drawing to a close, Mike came out to stay. Sam Falle, the High Commissioner, who had known Mike in Kuwait, kindly let him stay in the house of one of the staff who was on home leave. This simplified things a lot and a modicum of propriety was observed. Mike had by that time left the Army and was casting around for something to do and somewhere to live. He had managed to find a comfortable home for his wife, run by nuns, who charged as much as their patients could afford. This had put his mind to rest on that very difficult problem. But he was unrelaxed and although we did a marvellous trip round Malaysia, which should have had a calming effect, the holiday nearly ended in serious tears.

We were staying somewhere near Kota Baharu in the north of the country in a delightful hotel with little chalets, run by a most interesting man, who we had a chance of talking to as a result of high drama. Mike and I had a furious row one evening, after which he took an overdose of sleeping pills. I was only alerted to this when he began to mutter to himself as if delirious and I had no idea how many pills he had taken. To be on the safe side, I rang the local hospital, who told me that the police would have to be informed if it proved necessary to admit him into the hospital. Naturally this would have caused serious repercussions and the hospital authorities then suggested sending an ambulance to see just what sort of condition Mike was in. Fortunately, the medicos said that, provided I kept plying him with strong coffee and didn't allow him to lapse into sleep again, he would be all right in a few hours. By this time the hotel manager had been told and came over to see how things were. He was extremely kind and courteous and saw that his staff kept up a continuous supply of hot, strong coffee. By the afternoon Mike's condition had stabilized, thank goodness and we were able to leave for Singapore with me doing the driving. It was a long haul, but luckily we made it eventually.

When this incident had blown over, we talked at length about the future and I suggested that he might go off to the Channel Islands to see if there was anything there which would be of interest to him. He came back elated, having bought a house on the island of Alderney. The owner wanted to get rid of it quickly as his wife had died there recently. He sold the house fully furnished, together with a car and a boat for a ludicrously low figure and it was a stroke of very good luck for Mike.

He had had ideas earlier about buying a house on the Balearic Island of Formentera south of Ibiza. He thought we could use it as our home but also as a sort of hotel for our friends in the holiday seasons. At that time the island was without water and electricity and too primitive by half for me to consider living there. In the event, he got a job in Saigon, working for the Save the Children Fund and lent his house on Alderney to a mutual friend who had just left her husband. I later heard that he had had some sort of liaison with her, which helped my wavering emotions vis-à-vis a possible future together.

It was the last straw and enabled me to pluck up the courage to end our relationship. We had had many happy times together and he had done so much to make me happy, particularly in the early days, but in retrospect the good times didn't outweigh the difficult times. By this time I was nearing 40 years and any hopes I had of having a child had to be discounted. This was a great sadness, as was the break-up of the relationship.

Back to the UK by Sea

In those days it was not unusual to return home by ship and this I did on the small cargo ship, the 'Ben Lyon'. It carried eight passengers including the wife of the Captain. Our first stop was at Kuala Lumpur and we stayed there long enough for me to have a round of golf at the rather splendid golf club there. However the run of farewell parties in Singapore had left me exhausted so it was with relief that I settled down to the relaxing routine of life on board. The Indian Ocean was as calm as a mill pond, so calm in fact that I was allowed to take the helm for a time. In contrast, the last Ben Line ship to make this trip had been hit by a massive rogue wave, which damaged the ship to the extent that the passengers had to be winched off by helicopter. But our turn was to come later.

We stopped next at Port Elizabeth and three of us took a taxi round the town to get the feel of it. I couldn't believe it when seeing notices on park benches saying 'Whites only'. Our next port of call was the Ivory Coast where scavenging vultures hovered overhead. We were offered local wares, including to my horror pornographic photographs, by a rather sinister-looking group of assorted touts. After some haggling I bought a fine carved mahogany mask made, they told me, by the local pygmies.

When we approached the Bay of Biscay a storm blew up and we watched with increasing anxiety as the waves came crashing over the deckhouse. Enough is enough I thought and retired to my cabin for the night. And what a night it was. The ship rolled precariously from side to side, pausing with a shudder at each turn as if deciding whether to turn right over or to roll back. Luckily it rolled back, but this uncertainty carried on hour after hour throughout the night. I was terrified. In making my way to the bathroom I was flung against the cabin wall and nothing would have induced me to make that effort again. There was a great crash outside at one point and I waited for shouts of distress to follow. It emerged that the chap in the next cabin had attempted to cross to the cabin opposite to check on his two small boys. He was thrown towards the stairway, was saved by the banisters, but hit a fire extinguisher which went off, surrounding him with foam. He believed for a moment that he was already in the sea. When he eventually struggled back to his cabin he ended up sprawled across a table which had been turned upside down for safety's sake. The two little boys slept peacefully through it all.

A pale and bedraggled group of passengers appeared at breakfast the next morning, all thankful to be alive. As I thanked the First Officer for getting us through it safely, he muttered: "just say getting us through it". It appeared that our captain was anxious to get to Hamburg on time and instead of heaving-to as most of the other ships were doing he attempted to beat the storm and continue. The car belonging to two of the passengers had broken loose in the hold and was badly damaged, but the ship was reasonably intact and after a day in Hamburg we made the last lap across the North Sea to London.

Mother and Dick were waiting at the quayside and looked pleased to see me. I should say here that Mother wrote to me regularly whilst I was overseas and kept me au fait with what various members of the family were doing; and I always enjoyed visiting them all in between postings and seeing how the younger members were growing up in leaps and bounds.

London

Although the Personnel Department had decided that it was time for me to acquire a cat and a canary and settle down in London again, this decision was almost immediately thrown to the winds and I was offered a posting to Geneva. I accepted this posting; it was another challenge, but little did I realise just how much of a challenge it would prove to be. By this time I had grown accustomed to living in the sun and wondered how easy it would be to adjust to the climate of northern Europe. Both the Herlenius and the Köhncke parents were by that time living most of the year in Corseaux, a small village near Vevey on the shores of Lake Leman, which was an added incentive to go to Geneva. They later moved, respectively, to Vevey and Lausanne, both attractive places to visit.

Whether it was due to the knocking about I had received during the storm at sea, or the result of touching my toes in an effort to cast off some of the added weight engendered by five meals a day on board ship, I had somehow injured my back. The Office doctor prescribed bed rest for six weeks, but in view of my imminent departure for Geneva I said that this was not possible. He then referred me to a top London osteopath who did some noisy manipulations, during which I was sure that my neck and back would be broken, but was assured that in no time I would be back to normal. I have to say that, if the pain was excrutiating before I saw the osteopath, it was, if that were possible, even worse afterwards. My friends had to help me to dress and any movement at all caused me to turn a sickly green. However, it was just possible to get ready to go to Geneva and off I flew, desperately hoping that the words of the eminent osteopath weren't just 'pie in the sky'. Of course he was absolutely right and I was soon back to normal, but not soon enough and I more or less limped into my new posting.

British Consulate, Geneva

My first impression of Geneva itself was relief that it was such an elegant city; and when the sun shone and the lake glistened in the sunlight, and when the mountains were alight with colour or covered in snow, it was also very beautiful. After some difficulty finding the time to hunt for a flat, I eventually found the perfect haven. It was the upper and quite separate half of a lovely timbered villa overlooking Mont Blanc and the lake and only a stone's throw from the French border at Divonne, where there was a very fine golf club.

The British diplomatic presence in Geneva was divided between various United Nations Missions, headed by either an Ambassador or other senior diplomat and the Consulate General. I worked in the Consulate. A Second Secretary attached to one of the Missions lived with his wife and small children in the bottom half of my house so one wasn't completely out on a limb.

Paddy Ashdown, who was attached to one of the Missions, lived quite nearby too. The Ashdowns were a super family and it was difficult to relate the 'Paddy Pants-down' figure created by the media during his tenure as Leader of the Liberal Democratic Party, to the same man I knew in Geneva. He used to tell a very funny 'shaggy-dog' story about 'raping and pillaging' – I can't remember quite whether they were Vikings or who they were doing the raping and pillaging or what the punchline was, if there was one, but when I heard him speaking in Parliament I was always reminded of this story, because he always spoke so quickly.

The thing that struck me most about the area of Geneva where we worked and where the cluster of United Nations buildings were sited, and to whose restaurants we often went for lunch, was the lack of any animated expression on the faces of the hoards of people of all nationalities who worked there, presumably debating and thrashing out problems of great pith and moment. But for the most part there was no hint from their demeanor that they were being successful or that they were enjoying their jobs. I never got to know any of them or to find out 'what made them tick'. One's social life mostly revolved around our own little diplomatic circles, apart from that generated by my Swedish 'families'.

Working Conditions

In the office, one thing after another conspired to make life difficult. Days after I arrived, the secretary with whom I worked most closely went down with pneumonia. Once recovered she fell in love and soon left to marry and accompany her new husband to New Delhi. She was replaced by a stunningly energetic young secretary, Amanda, who was renowned for rushing round London on a motorbike. She was good news, and in no time at all she too fell in love and married but, happily, came back with her husband who was also serving in Geneva. About two weeks after their return, however, she was struck down by a serious viral illness, which apart from being extremely debilitating caused a paralysis down the whole of one side. She was hospitalized and then returned to the UK for treatment. During her absence we were sent a temporary replacement who wasn't altogether ideal. Added to that another colleague was just completing her tour and was replaced by a girl who was slightly disabled and who was terrified of driving her car, so had to be given lifts everywhere. She very soon met and married one of the security guards and left Geneva.

Another good secretary arrived and her only quirk seemed to be that she thought she was a mouse. She left little messages everywhere signing them 'Mouse' with a picture of a mouse for good measure. But she was a fit and a happy person who spent some of her weekends skiing up in the mountains with David Cornwell (alias John le Carré), the author and his family. Her presence in the office was a great relief, but the earlier dramas, whilst being 'all part of life's rich pattern', had not been conducive to a smooth-running modus operandi. The work had to be done and it was done, but it was tough going and after eighteen months of my posting, I fell by the wayside so-to-speak and arrived back in the UK in a wheelchair.

The Specialist I saw in London explained that I had overtaxed the automatic nervous system, the physical part of the nervous system, and he judged that it would take some six more weeks of rest and recuperation for this to renew itself. The Office decided I should stay in the UK to recover and not finish my tour in Geneva and although this was a disappointment, bringing with it a feeling of failure, in my heart of hearts I think it was something of a relief.

Social Life in Geneva

That was the downside of my final posting abroad. But at the start of the posting, I discovered many diversions outside the office, energies and time permitting. Soon after settling in I walked up to the first tee at the Divonne golf course to see the sort of people who were playing there. They all seemed rather intimidating and I wondered how best to start playing and eventually elicited the help of the locally-engaged Vice-Consul, Jack Berner. Jack was a dear, as was his wife, Joan. They had spent many years in Geneva and knew a great many people. Jack's pride and joy was his Rolls Royce and it was said that many local people thought he was an Ambassador and he certainly looked the part in the car and with his clipped moustache and a rather austere mien; and I rather think he liked to give this impression. Anyway he kindly introduced me to a retired British merchant banker who had been a member of the golf club for years. This elderly golfer used to go round the course, accompanied by a caddy, in a golf buggy. I would go round with them, but on foot. He would shout instructions to me now and again on how I should play a particular shot and I well remember him saying one day: "You move your body about too much when you are driving. Imagine you are standing between two pillars as you address the ball." I drove off rather unsuccessfully and he asked: "What happened there?" "The bloody pillars got in the way," I replied. I didn't get to know many other people there but at least I got a game of golf most weekends.

One weekend our Consul and his wife with their youngsters took me up to Les Diablerets, a very sophisticated and popular resort for expert downhill skiers. On the way we stopped for supper at a little tavern where a jolly party was going on and some country dancing to the music of a concertina. We had no sooner sat down than one rather buxom, red-cheeked wife invited the Consul to dance and round they whirled like the best of them to cheers and laughter from the assembled company. The poor man was actually recovering from a bout of flu, but true to form he rose to the occasion.

The following day the family went off to do some downhill skiing and we arranged to meet for lunch at the open-air restaurant at the top of the mountain. I had taken the precaution of bringing a pair of cross country skis to get from the cable car to the restaurant; not out of deference to the only flat piece of land, but because I had no others. As we sailed up in the cable car my fellow travellers just stared with disbelief at my skis, and with Germanic inquisitiveness a voice finally said "You not go down on this skis, yes?" "Oh yes," I couldn't help saying, but finished by telling them the truth and with some hearty laughter the ice was broken as they signified their relief.

Having the Herlenius and Köhncke parents nearby was an enormous fillip and provided some lovely family weekends and some interesting social occasions. There was a very large Swedish community around Vevey and Lausanne consisting mostly of wealthy people who had been driven to spend half the year away from their home country because of the heavy taxes there. I gradually met a number of them, particularly at the annual Swedish Christmas Fair, run by the local Swedish church, with which they all helped in one way or another. Apart from the social side of the Fair it was also full of attractive Swedish handicrafts which made splendid Christmas gifts. Without exception, the Swedish expatriates had beautiful homes, some of them containing priceless works of art. They entertained well and I was sometimes included, along with my Swedish 'families', in their lunch and dinner parties.

Jonas Herlenius was still a keen walker, despite his great age and he and I did some gentle Sunday walks round about Lake Geneva. Afterwards we repaired to one or other of the lakeside cafes serving delicious pastries and were joined by Elsa for a typically Swiss Sunday afternoon treat.

On other occasions we drove to a nearby health spa, Lavez-les-Bains in France, where Elsa and I swam in the health-giving pool and Jonas spent the time enjoying a leisurely lunch in the hotel. The pool water was actually quite heavy with various natural minerals and notices around the pool warned of the dangers of exercising too energetically. In fact anyone with heart problems was advised to seek the in-house doctor's advice before entering the pool. An hour's rest in the salon overlooking the pool was mandatory afterwards. I always loved this hour and spent it watching the bathers, especially the French, chatting nineteen to the dozen to each other in the water, whilst enjoying the jacuzzi jets round the sides of the pool.

Chasing Romance to Lake Como

During my time in Geneva, Allan wrote that he was going down to Lake Como for a golfing holiday with friends. We hadn't seen each other for over two years and I decided, rashly, I knew, to drive down at the weekend to see if they had arrived. It is quite a long drive from Geneva to Lake Como, across the Alps, but it was all so beautiful and well worth the journey for the drive alone, I kept assuring myself. With something like relief, however, I heard at their hotel that they would not be arriving for another couple of weeks. Well, I had had no idea how I would explain my sudden arrival, so that was that, I was spared and could now enjoy myself.

The golf club was above a little town called Lanzo, where I'd booked myself into an old-fashioned but comfortable hotel and I spent the weekend playing golf and doing some local sightseeing. Lanzo is in a magnificent position between Lakes Como and Lugano and the views were stunning. It was all thoroughly enjoyable and I arrived back in Geneva tired yet contented, but for a tiny mishap. Backing the car outside my garage I drove over a bag containing a precious bottle of Scotch I'd bought on my travels and of course it shattered, releasing a wonderful whiff of the hard stuff into the ether; such a waste and I certainly needed a stiff drink at that moment.

As the next two weeks passed, I began to think I might just make the journey to Como again, despite my serious apprehensions. Once more, caution was thrown to the winds and I drove off through the Alps to Lanzo. It was the Whitsun weekend and traffic was heavy so the journey took longer than expected. As I was on my way to book into the same hotel as before, I noticed a grey Mercedes about four cars ahead. Could this be Allan and friends, I wondered, as this was, I knew, the make and colour of their car? To my horror as I got closer it seemed that there were two men and two women in the car. This was not the scenario I had envisaged – another woman – and my heart missed a beat or two. But happily it wasn't them.

A room secured, I drove straight to the golf club to see if there would be any problem getting a game during this busy weekend. On returning to my car, the hairs on the back of my neck suddenly stood up and with an immense frisson I saw a Mercedes driving in with Allan at the wheel. When he saw me, he appeared completely unfazed; he introduced me to his friends, John and his wife, Tessa, and asked how my golf was. "Not good enough to play with you at this moment in time," was my reply. "Oh come along, we'll see you on the tee in a minute," he said and marched off. Needless to say, I was in a frightful state and as they disappeared round the corner, I dived into my car, took out a handy bottle of Dubonnet and took a good long swig to supply the Dutch courage needed for what lay ahead.

As we set off Allan said: "You'll probably beat us hollow as we've been drinking a fair amount of gin over lunch." I laughed to myself, thinking of the Dubonnet and followed them down the fairway. Fortunately, I didn't do too badly considering that the drive from Geneva had taken hours and I'd had no lunch. At the end of the game I thanked them all and took myself back to my hotel, completely shattered.

After a long hot bath and a good rest, I went down to supper, my mind in a turmoil ('the things we do for love' as the song goes). The manager introduced me to an Italian sitting in the hall, who, he said, was a golfer. It emerged that the man owned a large hotel at Bellaggio and had an English wife. He invited me to join him for dinner, which was nice and took my mind off the day's events. After dinner he suggested we take a drive up the hill to see the magnificent view and all the lights. At first I demurred, but he eventually persuaded me. He said he couldn't understand why I wasn't married. Little did he know the little drama that was being enacted that weekend. He then told me that there were two English Generals playing at the club. "Yes," I told him, "I've been playing with them today." He looked suitably impressed and asked: "Will you be playing with them tomorrow"? "No, I'm not really a very good golfer," was my rather feeble answer, but better than "I haven't been invited."

127

"Then could you play with me instead, I'm not very good either?" Why not, I thought and we met up early the next morning.

As we pottered rather slowly down the fairways, I kept looking back towards the first tee, wondering why the others hadn't yet appeared. They soon did appear and very soon caught up with us. Allan's face was a picture, but as we waved them through and waited for them to putt out, he sank an extremely long putt. As I congratulated him, he said with a big smile, "It must have been the calibre of the onlookers that did it," and forged ahead to the next tee. But my day had been made and after our game the nice Italian took me off to lunch with some charming Milanese families. What a day it was. The remainder of the weekend was spent sightseeing in the area and I even managed to see the sublime Von Thyssen Art Collection at Lake Lugano before heading back to Geneva, mission accomplished. But for the timely appearance of the Italian hotelier, my ignominy would have been far greater, although it had been, after all, an important adventure.

As far as local leave was concerned, I sometimes visited the Köhncke family at their house in the mountains at Villars and on one occasion Elsa and Jonas invited me on a wine-tasting trip to Beaune for a few days with a group of fellow Swedes. One of the vineyards we visited was Bouchard, Pierre et Fils and the tasting took place in the cellars of their ancient chateau. We were given a menu of six wines and as we tasted them, I gave them my own starring system, because my French wasn't good enough to understand what the guide was telling us. Strangely enough I seemed to have given the right stars to the right wines; a Gevrey Chambertin was by far my favourite. In those days a decent bottle cost about £15, but would probably be about double that now. We went on to the prestigious Chateau Clos de Cougeot nearby, where members of the Chevalier du Tastevin meet some 17 times a year to promote Burgundian wines and bestow awards on those they consider to be the best.

We also paid a visit to the famous Beaune Hospice and then wended our way to Vezelay to see the splendid cathedral there. It was from there that one of the original routes started for the pilgrims heading for Santiago de Compostela in Northern Spain.

Yet another of our secretaries, Sue, had recently returned to the UK to get married and I went over for the wedding. Her father was at that time Sheriff of London, and it was a rather grand affair. The wedding took place at one of the old City of London churches and the Reception was held at the Barber Surgeon's Hall, home of one of the City's ancient Livery Companies. Sue's parents gave a pre-wedding lunch for close friends and family at the Tower Hotel at London Bridge, where they were all staying and I was lucky enough to be invited. So too was poor Amanda who was still on sick leave in England and could only manage either the lunch or the wedding and opted for the former. It was good to see her, but she was at that time a shadow of her former ebullient self.

After lunch we guests made our way to the Church and took our seats, but no bride arrived. She had been all but ready to leave the hotel when we did, so where was she? People began to look uneasy, especially the waiting bridegroom and there were urgent whispered exchanges amongst the family (the mobile phone had not yet been invented). But she eventually arrived, some twenty minutes late, looking none the worse for wear, but slightly pinker about the cheeks. We heard later that, just as they were about to leave, fire broke out in the hotel and no lifts were functioning. They made their way safely down several flights of stairs to the front door only to find that their wedding car was trapped between the fire engines. When the fire was extinguished they finally got away much to everyone's relief and the wedding could hardly have been a happier one.

About three quarters of a way through my Geneva posting, at the end of a particularly hectic week, culminating in the arrival of my Australian friend from Singapore days, Pye Cormack who was doing a French Course at one of the French universities, I more or less collapsed, as I mentioned earlier. It was a great pity because, apart from anything else, I had had great plans to show her around the area. But it was not to be and she set to and did the shopping and the cooking and was wholly supportive. After consulting my local doctor, who advised a period of total rest, arrangements were made for me to fly back to London with the aid of a wheelchair at Geneva and London airports. This, I discovered, is quite the most comfortable way of dealing with pre and after flight procedures. Once the Specialist in London had given his prognosis and his estimated recovery timetable the Office, not surprisingly, made the decision to curtail my tour in Geneva.

Where to stay when coming back so unexpectedly? Marvellously, the newly-married Sue took me into their home on the Cator Estate in Blackheath for a day or two, which was particularly kind as the couple had barely settled in after returning from their honeymoon. As luck would have it, another Office friend, Doreen, who had stayed with me in Singapore, gave me a bed in the flat she was renting, also on the Cator Estate. It all fell amazingly into place and my love affair with Blackheath was off to a good start. The flat was just far enough away from the village to provide a physical challenge and if it proved too much, which on some days it did, there was always somewhere to rest. I did the shopping and cooked the supper and looked forward to Doreen's return and some gentle chatting. It was a cosy routine and coincided with one of the hottest summers for many a year. Blackheath, with its village atmosphere and the vast swathes of green of the Heath itself was a far cry from the hustle and bustle of Central London and Tranquil Vale, the name of one of the main roads through the village, said it all.

Once recovered and before starting work again I had to return to Geneva to pack up the flat and drive my car back to the UK. Everyone was kind and helpful, particularly Patricia Hutchinson, the fairly newly-arrived Consul-General, whom I had known earlier in Stockholm. She kindly invited me to stay, which I did happily for part of the time. The rest of the time was spent packing up my own flat.

The drive back to the UK went well until I reached the Customs at Dover. The Customs officer told me to pull in and park the car. He then carried out an aggressive interrogation chiefly about my car, adding disparaging remarks about the Foreign Office whenever he could. It all seemed totally unnecessary and having travelled all over the world with no such trouble it was an unprecedented hitch. In the end, I told the officer that I would not be treated like a Third World immigrant and later filed a strongly-worded complaint to HM Customs Service. The reply was long and extremely apologetic and advised always to ask for the senior Customs Officer if this sort of treatment should ever happen again. It was certainly an unpleasant eye-opener.

XX

Returning to Work in London

One of the unexpected advantages of coming home early from the Geneva posting was that I became eligible to transfer from the Secretarial Branch of the Foreign Office to the Executive Branch. This meant that promotion prospects were greater and one was no longer at the beck and call of demanding bosses, well not quite in the same way, that is. I managed to get through the usual hoops of this transfer and enjoyed most of the jobs I did in this Branch. They were all based in London.

Home Owner in Blackheath

During all my years overseas, I had never once wished to be back living in the UK. Life abroad had been rich in the extreme: a satisfactory career, a varied and stimulating social life, including some memorable concerts, often followed by an Embassy Reception when one had the chance to meet musicians such as Sir John Barbirolli and his delightful wife, also a musician in her own right; politicians like Lord Carrington and Lord Butler to name only a couple; not to mention meeting many different nationalities in their own surroundings and absorbing different cultures, while at the same time being cushioned by the inherently British family atmosphere of the Embassy. But it never crossed my mind to lament the end of all this when suddenly there I was back in England. At last I was ready to settle down and make my own proper home; very much a first in my life. I'd enjoyed making temporary homes in the rented flats I'd lived in abroad, but to actually own a property had been one of my dreams. I knew instinctively that this would have to be in Blackheath. Here was history, elegance and style, with Greenwich, the Park and the Thames but a stone's throw away It was also only a short train journey into London, not a tube train, but a real one from a distinctive Victorian station.

Doreen Foster had just bought and moved into her own flat so that I was able to arrange a six month lease in the haven which had contributed so much to the recovery of my health. Now the hunt was on. Of course the attractions of Blackheath hadn't escaped the notice of several thousand other people and therefore property prices were high and higher than I could then afford. Eventually I settled for a little maisonette in what I thought of as 'a thin house'; that is to say in a rather charmless 1960s block of four flats in Shrewsbury Lane right at the top of Shooters Hill about half a mile out of Blackheath village and also Woolwich and Plumstead, rather more modest areas, but not without their own charm and histories. The flat had a tiny garden with rose bushes and a postage stamp size lawn. It also had a magnificent view and on a clear day, with the aid of a telescope, one could see into the centre of London. I think the flat cost some £16,000 and the mortgage payments, even then, were a bit daunting. But it was well worth it.

Furniture was for the most part discovered in antique or bric-à-brac shops in and around Greenwich for a fraction of the cost of buying new. The greatest bargain was a Georgian drop-leaf dining table marked at £27. The manager's wife had put this price tag on by mistake and her husband very honourably let me buy it at that inordinately cheap price. Another good buy was a large single bed with beautiful American mahogany carved head and tailboards and a virtually new mattress. I spent a lot on having curtains made by Sandersons and Peter Jones and they were well worth splashing out on. That being said, however, Sandersons' first effort had to be returned because there were biro marks all down one side and, to quote from my letter of complaint: "they were so crumpled that it looked as if the entire staff of Sandersons had slept between them". Their second effort, for which they had to comb the country for what remained of the particular print I had ordered, was, in the end, perfect.

There was a slight drama with the pair from Peter Jones. I rarely drew these curtains as the sitting room had a large picture window which was not overlooked. It was only when, months later, during a game of bridge, we were discussing curtains – as one tends to do at ladies' bridge fours – that I drew these curtains, only to discover that carpet beetles had made meals of large sections along the pleats at the top. Luckily this bean feast was discovered before the curtains cascaded to the floor. A hunt was then started to find out where these greedy little insects were coming from. It emerged that they came from an adjoining flat, the owner of which had died and the flat had been left empty long enough for these wreckers to invade it and by extension encroach upon the adjoining flats. They were successfully annihilated before more damage was done.

Being a 'thin' house and high above London itself, it was very cold in winter and there was no central heating. Each morning I shot out of bed to light the oven to warm up the little kitchen, so at least it was warm enough for breakfast. In the evenings a single gas fire had to suffice in the sitting room. Later on I had double-glazing installed on the 'never never', which did a lot to keep out some of the chill. But London was a good deal warmer than many of the houses I visited in other parts of the country at weekends. It was lovely to catch up with old friends, but very often at the price of being cold. I still ran the blue Peugeot I had bought in Paris whilst en poste in Geneva, and although this made quite a hole in the flimsy budget, it was a worthwhile expense. I had been putting £4 a month into a life insurance policy for years and when it eventually matured I spent most of it on having the rust removed from the car. Needless to say, this was a complete waste of money as the rust soon came back; I had had to learn the hard way.

The oldest golf club in the world, The Royal Blackheath GC, was close by and I soon became a member. Golf dates pepper my diaries from the mid-seventies and the eighties. Being such a venerable and I have to say, rather pompous club, it had a beautiful Georgian clubhouse and any number of splendid traditions. One of the less splendid traditions was that Ladies were not full members when I first joined, were not taken very seriously and on some occasions hardly tolerated by some of the male members. Happily this changed after concerted efforts by successive Lady Captains. Needless to say it was a far cry from the more relaxed clubs at which I played while on holiday in Scotland. That being said, however, I remember being smuggled by a former Committee Member into The Royal and Ancient Golf Club at St Andrews to enjoy, as a lady, a furtive look round and to have the honour of being shown the Muniments Room with all the trophies. It was great fun to have been inside and later to play a round on one of the less popular courses, but sad that the visit into the hallowed clubhouse had to be done so furtively.

Golfing in Scotland

Mary, my old flatmate in London in 1950, had married a charming and attractive American, Jimmy Freeborn, who was also a successful business man. After years of living in exotic places abroad they eventually retired to St Andrews in Scotland, Mary's home territory. In June 1992 they invited me to join them on a motoring trip to Loch Lomond where we stayed at the very special Creggans Inn. We played a little golf at Elie on the way back and altogether had a wonderfully relaxing holiday, driving through some of the most beautiful Scottish countryside and properly catching up with each other, after years of brief and spasmodic get-togethers.

Once back in St Andrews, Mary gave a lunch party at her golf club, St Rules, the St Andrew's Ladies Golf Club; her two brothers Ian and Sandy, as men, were of course long-time members of The Royal and Ancient Golf Club. The lunch was fun and, small world as it is, one of the guests turned out to be the mother of one of my ex-colleagues from The Consulate in Geneva in the 1970s. Another was the little girl L.S Lowry painted and befriended many years ago and who when he died inherited many of his extremely valuable paintings.

Having been lent a house at Pitlochry by the ex-colleague mentioned above and her husband, I had two golfing holidays there in the summers of 1978 and 1979. The first happened to coincide with the Annual Ladies' Open at the Pitlochry Golf Club and James Wilson, the Pro there, insisted that I should take part. This I did, mainly because my holiday would otherwise have been wasted. Most of the other competitors were 'tigers' with very low handicaps and formidable swings. The whole thing was something of an experience, including the parties before and after, and at the end I was announced the winner of the 'Booby Prize' just as I was sneaking off to the bar to get a reviving brandy. Actually the first five holes were seriously uphill and to survive these was in itself no mean feat. The house I was lent was a bit too creaky and spooky on my own and at night a funny white light was to be seen hovering around the skirting boards in my bedroom. I never did work out what it might have been. But sightseeing in the area and playing various courses, including the famous Rosemount Course, made up for the slightly nervous nights.

Chasing Romance Again

Driving back from Scotland in August 1979 after one of these golfing holidays, I had a sudden rush of blood to the head and decided to call on

Allan. We had not seen each other since I gatecrashed his holiday at Lake Como some two years previously. Mike, I had bumped into one day coming out of the Army & Navy Stores. We had had a cup of tea together, caught up on each other's news and as we parted Mike asked for my phone number. I gave it to him but he never did phone, for which I was grateful. That was the second time we had met by chance, but why, I wondered could I never seem to bump into Allan?

I suddenly decided to take matters into my own hands and turned the car towards Henley-on-Thames where he lived. Butterflies began to flutter in my tummy, but this failed to deter me. When he opened the door, his first words were: "What are you doing here?" "Oh I was just on my way home from Scotland and thought I'd pop in on you," I replied. "There must be more direct routes home, but come in," was his rejoinder. After a rather tense conversation he suddenly said: "Would you like a chop?" I laughed and said, "Yes please," and he busied himself in the kitchen, producing an impromptu supper in no time. I left soon afterwards, thrilled to feel that the magic was still there and drove to London on 'cloud nine'.

As it had all gone so well, I called on him again a month or two later. His eldest daughter Jackie was there and quite clearly it was a bad moment. He remarked that they were very busy. After a short chat with Jackie, I left vowing never to do this again; nor did I and it was some 15 years before we met again.

Another unexpected reunion with friends from the past also happened around that time. My step-sister's children were being confirmed at a church near Guildford and as I looked round during the service, there among the crowded congregation were Andy and Sheena Skiöldebrand, friends from Stockholm days, now 18 years ago. They had adopted a girl and a boy, Louise and Robert, in the intervening years, having despaired of ever having children of their own, and it was Robert who was being confirmed. They couldn't have chosen a better time or place. We exchanged telephone numbers and continued a very rewarding friendship, although now without Andy who, sadly, died in 2003. What a charmer he was. He could turn his hand to anything and after he retired took up furniture restoration and then watch and clock-mending. He loved reminiscing about the past and when he and Rutger von Seth got together their conversation always turned to their days in the Swedish cavalry and how uncomfortable they had been on exercises in the snow and the cold in the mountains during the winter.

Soon after our fortuitous meeting, the Sköldebrands invited me to a lunch party, where I saw among the many guests a senior member of the Foreign Office, whose farewell party I had recently attended. I asked him what he had bought with his farewell cheque. "A new set of golf clubs," he told me. As I asked him which golf club he belonged to, I somehow knew before he said so that it was Huntercombe, the club to which Allan belonged. He told me that Allan was currently their Captain. We chatted further and as we said goodbye I charged him with letting me know should anything untoward happen to Allan as we were no longer in touch. He promised to do so.

He and his wife Paddy invited me to their home for a weekend soon after this and during dinner my host said: "I'm sorry I couldn't get Allan Taylor along but he is golfing in Cornwall". I heaved a sigh and thought that it just wasn't meant. In the event, it was Allan who told me some years later that our friend, Desmond, was seriously ill and of his death quite soon afterwards.

Quite soon after returning to England I met Tita and John Shakeshaft, both of whom worked in the Foreign Office. Tita was just recovering from a divorce and was being seriously wooed by John. She was adamant, however, that she was never going to marry again and was concentrating on making a career for herself. I spent a lot of time trying to convince her that, if she married John, she would have a splendid husband – and children – and could still have her career. It looked for a long time as if she was going to follow her own agenda, but she didn't. She married John and had two sons, James, my godson, and Hugo. I have always thought of Tita and John as my surrogate children and their friendship has meant and still means a lot to me.

For about twenty years it has been a tradition to spend New Year's Eve with them along with a group of about ten other friends; nearly always the same group. It is usually a splendid occasion to which we always look forward as the Christmas season approaches. John and Tita between them produce a gourmet dinner with very very fine wines. At midnight, following what I have always thought of as a Swedish custom, I usually climb onto a chair or a sofa, sometimes with another intrepid soul and as the bells ring out heralding the New Year we leap down to the floor and into the New Year. Photographs have been taken of this spectacle each year and Tita compiled an album of the annual 'leap' which shows just how few new dinner dresses I had over the years, as well as giving an up-to-date picture of my increasing age.

The following rather emotionally sterile years in London did have their brighter moments. Old friends were always coming to the metropolis and these visits were happy occasions on which to show off the delights of the area: The Cutty Sark, Gypsy Moth, the Trafalgar Tavern, with its famous plates of fresh whitebait, Greenwich Park and the stunning views of London from the top of the hill, the contours of which were always changing and slowly dwarfing the magnificent dome of St Paul's Cathedral. The antique and bric-à-brac shops, the market and finally the Painted Hall and the Naval College, now a University. The list was endless and I never tired of visiting each and everyone of them. By travelling further afield it was easy to get to Sir Winston Churchill's home, Chartwell, Sissinghurst Castle and its wonderful garden designed and tended by Vita Sackville West and her husband Harold Nicolson, and Knowle, the home of the Sackville family, to name but three wonderful homes.

I remember taking Elsa Herlenius to Sissinghurst when she came over to stay shortly after Jonas died. At one point I came upon her sitting under a tree listening to a blackbird singing its glorious song as if in sympathy at her loss. It was magical. When I took her to Knowle she insisted on knowing who was depicted in most of the portraits. As portraits filled every wall of room after room, I was hard put to it to do better than say: "Oh another of the Sackvilles." As she was a stickler for historical facts, which I knew from our Grand Tour in Italy, this didn't quite fill the bill. But she knew my shortcomings only too well; history had never been one of my strong points.

Christmas in Switzerland

A couple of months before Jonas died, I spent Christmas with them both at their home on the shores of Lake Leman (aka the Geneva Lake) just outside Vevey. Before retiring on the night of my arrival, Jonas explained, rather apologetically, that there was a slight change of routine in the mornings: "As I take so long to dress these days we now have breakfast in our dressing gowns. I hope you don't mind. And would you like bacon and egg for breakfast?" Bacon and eggs had always been a feature of breakfast at their home in Sweden, but in those days Jonas never set foot into the kitchen except to select and open the wine before a lunch or a dinner party. The next morning there he was at the kitchen stove cooking breakfast for us. He was, I think, 92 years at that time.

It was during that Christmas that we were invited to a lunch party on Boxing Day by a charming Swedish couple, Margit and Jan Wingårdh. It was a large party but Margit had cooked and prepared everything herself. Her table epitomized the attractiveness for which the Swedes are famous and her Christmas fare was all totally delicious. We were still eating at 5 p.m.

When we arrived home, I announced that I would like to have a little lie-down. But Elsa cried: "No and waste good talking time; come and sit down here!" Feeling totally replete and not a little sleepy, I did as I was told. Jonas, lucky man went to have a rest. He reappeared about an hour later clutching a bottle of the Gevrey Chambertin he had bought on our trip to Beaune a year or two earlier. "Come along now, we are going to have gravad lax (marinated salmon) and some Stilton with this good wine." I couldn't believe that anyone could have contemplated another meal after the feast we had enjoyed at lunchtime. But Elsa was game too and my protestations brought forth her suggestion that I should take one of her pills which, she assured me, guaranteed instant digestion. "They are on my bedside table," she said. As I found them and took one, she exclaimed "No, those are my heart pills!" But it was too late and I daren't think what effect they might have on me or my heart. However, it turned out that they were the right pills after all and within minutes my appetite had returned as if by magic.

When the day came for me to fly back to London, I asked Jonas, rather tentatively, if I might have a tiny drop of brandy to prepare me for the flight home. He poured one out for me, smiling gently and then we were off to Geneva Airport. That was, very sadly, the last time I saw him. He died very shortly afterwards, a nobleman to the end and a friend.

Celebrating Christmas and Easter

Christmas and Easter are both times for contemplation and celebration and I have never been able to face either on my own, nor have I yet had to. In a long life this is something for which I'm very grateful. On these important occasions I prefer to be with family or friends and, wherever possible, go to church and experience the whole spiritual panoply, be it in Canterbury Cathedral or in the tiniest village church in Suffolk. However much we may bewail the inevitable pressures that are involved, there is no doubt that the spirit of Christmas does on the whole prevail. It may not be for long, but it is there and with it there is hope, however faint; something we all need in these treacherous times. Easter is something different and to believers, of even more infinite importance.

I spent several very happy Christmases with Rosemary and David Manger and their two children, both in Germany, where David had been posted and in Melton Mowbray once they returned to the UK. The German Christmas usually involved a lot of snow and freezing temperatures, but the warmth of their welcomes made up for this in a big way and it was great fun to be in a military ambience again, with plenty of socializing of the sort I had enjoyed in Berlin. It was fun to watch their children grow up over the years and visits on other high days and holidays made for really close friendships to be cemented with them all.

Other very happy Christmases have been spent with Andy and Sheena Skiöldebrand in their lovely old cottage in Dennington, Suffolk to which they had moved from West Byfleet. It was always a wonderful family Christmas with Louise, their daughter and Robert, their son and later her husband Tony and their small son Fred. Later on Louise and Tony began to host Christmas at their 15th Century farmhouse at Boxted near Bury St Edmunds, which also lends itself to wonderfully happy family Christmases with a roaring log fire and a visit by Father Christmas delivering Christmas stockings filled with goodies. The family has grown to include Flora and Anna, two delightful little girls. I once gave Flora a pair of colourful, striped tights which turned out to be a size too big for her. She thanked me with great enthusiasm and said about the size: "Don't worry, they'll soon grow in to me"

Because Andy was Swedish and he and Sheena had lived most of their married life in Sweden, the family always celebrated a Swedish Christmas Eve. Andy was a dab hand at mixing various delicious kinds of marinated herring and Janssons Frästelse (Johnson's Temptation). Then on Christmas Day there was Turkey and Christmas Pudding, English-style, before which we went to a nearby Suffolk country church to attend Matins. Sometimes we played a chilly round of golf at Aldburgh Golf Club, once we had prepared the vegetables and brandy butter.

One year when attending Matins, all the children had been asked by the vicar to bring one of their Christmas presents up to the altar to be blessed. As Fred made his sturdy way up the aisle carrying as his present a small ball, I whispered to his Uncle Robert, whom I have known since he was a small boy: "Have you ever had your balls blessed," to which he replied with suitable reverence: "Yes, but not in church!" A bit of a naughty exchange, but it was added to the family's Christmas memories, to be recounted year after year with a smile.

For many years after returning to the UK, I was invited to go along with Mummy and Dick to either Chris, my brother's family or to Janet, my step-sister's family, but as both families got bigger and bigger, there wasn't really room for me as well and that is how I started going elsewhere and mostly to the Mangers and the Skiöldebrands.

Apart from the joy of being with family or friends, my total belief in the Almighty has always been strengthened at such times. I have never thought to pose academic or scientific questions on the meanings within the Christian or any other religion, although I have read a modest number of books about things spiritual: 'The Spiritual Crisis of Man' by Dr Paul Bruton, and several others by him, 'Evil and the God of Love' by John Hick, 'Love's Endeavour Love's Expense' by W.H Vanstone, 'The Meaning of Paul for Today' by Professor C.H. Dodd to mention just a few, as well as a number of books on spiritual healing and on Angels, who I believe to be around us guiding and helping us. One book which I came across in a secondhand bookshop was a small much-handled leatherbound gem called: 'The Pursuit of Holiness' written in 1871 by the then Dean of Norwich, E.M Goulburn, formerly a Chaplain in Ordinary to Queen Victoria. It was dedicated as follows: 'To The Earl of Derby, K.G., The Accomplished Scholar, The Brilliant Orator, The Eminent Statesman; who has thought it a task not unworthy of his Genius to instruct children in the parables of the Divine Wisdom; and to Whom therefore a Plain Work of Practical "Instruction to Righteousness" may be not inappropriately dedicated; These Pages are, by his Kind Permission, Inscribed with the Utmost Respect and Gratitude'. Written in the flyleaf and at the back of the book in minute and beautiful copperplate script are personal quotations from the Bible dated 1st January 1875.

This book in particular reinforced the strong faith I have in the goodness of God. I don't expect to understand the whys and wherefores of His ways, but I think He is present in us all and it is up to us to accept this and to seek to recognise Him in everyone we meet. Answers to our prayers and questions come to us in many ways and often from people we meet, both known and unknown. He does indeed work in mysterious ways. I think 'awareness' is everything and I count myself very lucky to be blessed with such a faith.

Weekends in Blackheath

Also sacrosanct, but on a different level, were my Sunday games of golf at The Royal Blackheath GC. We sometimes played matches with neighbouring Ladies' teams, and Mixed Foursomes with male members of the Club. But mainly I played with one or other of the Lady Members. My favourite was Irene Yate, a lady of advanced years with the heart and animation of a young girl. We became great friends. Irene had led a charmed life, with a happy marriage, a lovely house and garden in Eltham and opportunities for worldwide travel. Her husband owned a business in London selling sports equipment. When he died, which was before I met her, she decided to carry on with the business, the everyday running of which she entrusted to a senior member of her staff. The business fell prey to several serious burglaries as well as financial problems, as a result of which she and the firm were declared bankrupt At this time she was approaching her 90th Birthday and the shock would certainly have killed a lesser person. But she was a true Londoner who had spent the whole of the war in London and was made of stern stuff. Her last years were difficult, although we managed to have many good chats and laughs despite her worries and seriously diminished lifestyle. She became something of an icon at the Golf Club and I'm happy to say was made Lifetime President of the Ladies Section, where she was loved, respected and admired by all.

Visiting Morocco

One of my first holidays abroad after returning to live in England was to Morocco, where I stayed with an Office colleague attached to our Embassy in Rabat. After a fascinating few days exploring Rabat I took the train down to Fez. This in itself was an experience. As lunchtime approached I wandered down to the food bar, but decided not to indulge in some bread rolls filled with a delicious-looking salad for fear of catching a tummy bug. A beer wasn't quite enough to quell the hunger pangs, and as I sat wondering what to do, the Moroccans in my carriage started to take down their picnics from the luggage rack. I watched with envy and then realised that everyone was inviting everyone else to share their food. My fellow travellers included me in this generous exchange despite the fact that I had nothing to offer in return and I ended up eating with relish a sandwich similar to the one I had disdained at the bar. Needless to say, I did succumb to a tummy bug but whether it was from this or not I will never know, but I have seldom enjoyed a sandwich more.

Just before the train arrived at Fez I paid a visit to the loo. There was no time to turn to lock the door before a young Moroccan shot in after me and was about to close the door on us both. Quick as a flash I pushed him out with a force which sent him staggering down the corridor, This little episode seriously unnerved me and I wasn't quite out of the wood even then. The train drew into Fez Station and as I looked around for a taxi to take me to my hotel, which was some distance away, a couple of Moroccans with whom I had shared a carriage came and asked if they could be of help. As I explained my need for a taxi, a little man who had been listening, apparently idly, to our conversation, suddenly said: "I am a taxi." Actually he was, but as I climbed in in the pitch dark of Fez Station I felt far from sanguine. But it was all right and he did take me to the hotel.

There, a dark and goodlooking young man came up and said: "I am your guide for tomorrow". I took the precaution of asking at Reception if he was indeed a registered guide. He was, so all boded well for the morrow. He told me his name was Rashid and he turned out to be a most personable young man. He managed to produce a car the next morning so that we could take in more of the sights, such as The University, once we had seen round the town. The one thing he refused to do was to allow me to take a photograph of him sitting on a donkey. He explained that the donkey was the lowest of the low and it would be insulting for him to be photographed on the back of one. Luckily he was fairly good-humoured about it so nothing was lost. But I don't know how the donkey felt. Rashid took me to various carpet shops in the street market to buy a Moroccan rug. This was no sinecure and involved imbibing a lot of strong coffee or mint tea but was very entertaining. I ended up buying a strong saffron and blue-coloured rug, which, despite its rather loud colours still remains a favourite. It graces the floor behind my desk and the years have toned down the colours a bit but it still produces a surge of happiness as I look at it.

Back in Rabat my chum had one or two memorable social occasions lined up as well as a game of golf with one of the Embassy chaps at the Royal Rabat Golf Club.

The first social occasion was a rather grand Cocktail Party hosted by the Defence Attaché and his wife at their large attractive home, where the Band of the 1st Battalion the Light Infantry, from nearby Gibraltar, were playing in the garden. It was magical and a scenario well-suited to being the background for a Somerset Maugham short story. One of the tunes which I found particularly haunting was called: 'High on The Hill' in which two buglers echoed each other from their respective hilltops. I was able to ask them to play it again the following evening at The Queen's Birthday Party held at the Ambassador's Residence. They did this with great pleasure and it made an already evocative occasion even more special.

My visit contrasted strongly with the one experienced by an attractive blonde with whom I chatted on the plane out and also on the return journey. She explained that she always had one holiday a year without her husband and she had booked to fly to Morocco on the spur of the moment. She flew initially, as I did, to Tangier and, having nowhere booked to stay she took a room in my hotel..

We went off to the Bazaar together, where she attracted quite a following, partly, I think, because she was a blond and partly because she appeared to court attention. I was glad to be able to continue my journey to Rabat the following day without her. But on the plane home her account of her week in Tangier was fascinating. She had got in with a crowd of people who seemed to be taking drugs during a meal she had with them. She was then courted by a man who turned out to be a policemen, who was later arrested by another policemen as the couple walked along the beach together. It didn't seem to add up, but, reading between the lines, I imagine she had attracted police interest because of the people she was spending time with. A background which, say, Raymond Chandler might have used in one of his thrillers.

All in all I loved Morocco: the sun, the vibrancy and colour of the landscape and the friendliness of the ordinary people. Actually, the touts who roamed the Bazaar were also reasonable if one made it clear firmly, but kindly, that one would prefer to be left alone. I loved the glaring whiteness and beauty of the State buildings in Rabat and the shops full of handmade shoes and clothes. And I arrived home in one piece, which was something of a surprise given my initial forebodings.

Celebrating a Birthday in Sweden.

I went back to Sweden on a number of occasions and particularly to Irma and Christer Borlind's house near the sea at Haverdalstrand for one or two Christmases and the odd summer holiday. One such visit that stands out was to celebrate Irma's 50th Birthday. The Herlenius family and friends turned out in full force, all splendidly attired in evening dress. A huge marquee went up in the garden between their villa and that of Christer's parents, Bethan and Ove Borlind.

Those of us who arrived early were put to work straight away cleaning chairs and tables, setting the tables and decorating the marquee with birch tree branches. Then several of us were despatched to gather armfulls of wild flowers from the surrounding countryside and put them into huge containers to add to the decoration. Meanwhile large quantities of gravlax (marinated salmon) had to be recovered from a cold room in the kitchen of a hunting and fishing friend and landowner, Thord Hansson, and then sliced and laid up onto silver salvers taken out of a silver store in Bethan's kitchen cupboards.

Excitement grew as party time approached and more and more guests started to arrive. The weather was sublime, but Irma had a slight problem. Christer had taken us all out in his motor boat to a nearby island for a picnic the day before. Somehow Irma had toppled backwards into the heart of a prickly bush and the whole of her back was a mass of tiny thorns and scratches. Her party dress was backless so her lovely smooth, suntanned back which she had been working on for days before looked rather as if she had been soundly whipped. But in the event I think only she was conscious of it until the party got going and her attention was distracted towards the fun and the warmth with which she was being fêted.

It was a real Swedish summer party. Conversation and laughter flowed along with the schnapps, the skåls, the live music and the food and wine, which was interspersed with moving and amusing speeches from her husband and children, her brothers and her friends. And then we danced. She couldn't have wished for a happier celebration, which continued the following day with a smaller, but nonetheless well attended family lunch party

London and Politics

Having always been a Conservative, I began to feel increasingly restless about the Labour Government which was then in power and as the General Election approached in 1979 I felt it was time that they were ousted. A day or two before the election I happened to be invited to a lunchtime drinks party in the Office, at which a number of Personnel Officers were present. At one point the conversation turned to the forthcoming Election and primed of course by a couple of gins-and-tonics, I said to one of them "Well, if the Labour Government is re-elected you can have my job because I shall be leaving the country". Needless to say in the wee small hours of the next morning, I thought: "Whatever have I done – or, rather said?" To my utmost relief Labour were ousted and Mrs Thatcher became Prime Minister.

To my mind she halted the rot and brought back a feeling of pride in the country, in what it had achieved in the past and could go on achieving in the future. She encouraged a feeling of respect for oneself and for one's fellow men. We were all heartily sick of seeing piles and piles of rubbish and detritus all over the streets of London to name only one of endless failings of the Labour Government. She managed to break through the general apathy once she had broken the power of the Trades Unions led by Arthur Scargill and his miners and won the Falklands War. Things could only get better, I felt, and they did for a good number of years so I was again happy to be in England.

As mentioned earlier, Jim Spicer, husband of my old flatmate, Winfy, went into politics some years after he had left the Army in protest over the Suez action in 1956. He was the Conservative Member of Parliament for West Dorset when I caught up with them both again after returning to live in the UK. They used to host a large reception in London for political colleagues, old Army friends and assorted friends on a fairly regular basis. I was lucky enough to be invited on a couple of occasions.

The first time the party was held at the King Henry VIII Wine Bar in the cellars of the Ministry of Defence. It was all a bit awe-inspiring and as I could see neither Winfy nor Jim nor indeed anyone I knew on arrival I went up to a kindly-looking man and said: "You don't need to talk to me, but could I just stand here?" He roared with laughter and took me under his wing. I asked him which category of guest he was and, like me, he was an old friend. However, he had also been Lord Mayor of London in the Queen's Jubilee Year and was at the time we met a Trustee of the Royal Maritime Museum. Needless to say, I told him briefly about my Capt Cook project and he repeated Lord Lewin's reservations about funding such a project (More of Captain Cook later). He than regaled us with some of the amusing incidents during his tenure as Lord Mayor. He said that there were two sets of official robes, one for fat mayors and another for thin ones.

It was a happy beginning to the party and later Winfy, as was her accomplished wont, introduced me to a host of other interesting guests, including Lord Mayhew, Secretary of State for Northern Ireland and Lord Chalfont, a former Minister of State at the Foreign Office. When Winfy introduced me to him as a member of the Foreign Office, I was conscious that he stiffened very slightly. However, as soon as I told him that our hostess and I were very old friends, he visibly relaxed and we had a short but easy conversation. I asked one of the MPs I met during the course of the evening whether his mind ever went blank as he stood up to address The House. "Oh yes," he said, "and it usually happens when my wife is in the Chamber!"

The second of these Receptions I found less daunting and met a charming couple, General Sir Geoffrey Howlett and his wife Elizabeth, who were to become good friends some years later when I went to live in Dorset. At the time of the Reception Geoffrey was C-in-C Nato Northern Command in Norway and I was suitably awed, although both he and his wife were completely unstuffy.

The Royal Family

As the Wedding of Prince Charles to Lady Diana Spencer approached in 1981, I like most people awaited it with growing excitement. I even bought a commemorative mahogany mantle clock bearing on its face the respective coats-of-arms of the Royal Couple and the date of their marriage. The evening before the great day Michael Parker had organised what was to be a firework display to beat all firework displays in Hyde Park, which almost ended in tears for a lot of us, as I have described earlier, when paying tribute to Michael Parker's prowess at arranging spectacular Royal Events.

I have to say that, beauty apart, I was never a fan of Princess Diana, but have always had a lot of time for Prince Charles. In this respect I have found myself at loggerheads with some of my greatest friends and have not always practised the art of diplomacy on the subject. The Queen, on the other hand is for me, as for millions of other people, beyond reproach and her stoicism and self-restraint over decades of difficulties have been quite remarkable. When Windsor Castle was burning down and the Press was baying for her to foot the cost of restoring it, I felt driven to writing a letter of encouragement to her. I was prompted to do this after seeing a photograph in the paper showing her standing in the rain watching the fire and suffering, it transpired, from a streaming cold, the picture of sadness and dejection. I had never written such a letter before and was pleasantly surprised to receive a letter of thanks from her Lady-in-Waiting. In addition to the fairly stereotyped typed reply she had added a handwritten paragraph saying how much the Queen had appreciated my letter and my loyalty, so perhaps the Queen had actually seen it.

I also wrote to The Daily Telegraph to complain of a scurriless article about the Royal Family written by none other than Alistair Campbell who was at that time Editor of The Daily Mirror before becoming the Prime Minister, Tony Blair's Press Officer. No reply was forthcoming. Optimistically I hoped that perhaps the paper had had so many complaints that they couldn't cope with replying to them all, but I rather doubt it.

XXI

Captain Cook Researches

As mentioned earlier, I had grown up with the belief, handed down from my family, that we were direct descendants of Captain James Cook, the great Navigator and Explorer who, as is well-known, was famous for having discovered Australia and many other parts of the World. He also charted the Transit of Venus at the behest of The First Lord of the Admiralty. James Cook was born in 1728 and died at the hands of natives, who were also cannibals, in Hawaii in 1790.

I spent many of my Saturdays doing research into his life at The National Maritime Museum and in and around Deptford, from whence his famous journeys began and in East London where he was married and where he lived with his wife when ashore. During my holidays I also did a lot of research in Great Ayton in North Yorkshire, where he lived and went to school as a boy, and in churches, churchyards and local records in and around the area. The Cook Museum at Great Ayton and those at Whitby and Middlesborough were mines of information and interest. I visited the house in which he spent his first years, Aireyholme Farm and the nearby hill, Roseberry Topping, where he played with the other local children, the peak of which became badly distorted due to the quarrying of ore over many years. The owners of the house were eager to help and to talk about the great man, of whom as a fellow Yorkshireman they were of course justly proud.

It was also great fun exploring North Yorkshire as prior to that I had only been familiar with East Yorkshire, my birthplace. My cousin John Lineham and his wife, Jean who had lived in North Ferriby for most of their married life, were a welcoming port-of-call on these trips.

One day John took me to the studio of an artist called Tom Harland who had been having increasing success in marketing his watercolours, particularly through Harrods in London. Tom was the grandson of my Grandfather's chauffeur, who, when asked to report for duty used to say of his uniform: "Well I'll just get me 'at and jacket". I commissioned a painting of Roseberry Topping from Tom Harland, but it took him three years to produce and by then he was asking three times the price we had agreed on for it. I didn't much like the painting as it turned out so John bought it instead.

XXII

The Cook Project

As a result of learning more and more about my illustrious forebear, I felt that it was about time there was a 'living/working' memorial to him. Statues of him abound across the world but I felt something else was needed to act as an incentive to youngsters who had no academic bent or weren't born 'with a silver spoon in their mouths'. After all Cook got where he did by sheer diligence and hard work, teaching himself about navigation by candlelight in the cold attic of a house in Whitby, which, incidentally, was fairly recently bought by The Cook Society and now houses the splendid Cook Memorial Museum.

My idea was to set up a variety of craft workshops in memory of Captain Cook, which could be rented by craftsmen and women and where youngsters could be taught to make useful and beautiful things. I knew that such a scheme was flourishing in The Rocks area of Sydney, Australia, the Jam Factory in Melbourne and the Meat Market in Adelaide. At that time, the London Docklands were about to be developed and I had pinpointed a likely site where the old Surrey Docks farm used to be.

I needed to put this idea to someone of authority who was also a Cook lover. By chance I happened to switch on the television one evening as it was showing a programme about The Cook Memorial Museum at Whitby. It was a programme to celebrate the great man's birthday. The figure presenting the programme, whoever he was, was exactly the person I needed to get in touch with. The next morning I telephoned the TV station to ask who this man was. He was, I was told, Admiral Sir Terence Lewin, the current Admiral of the Fleet and also the Chairman of Trustees of the Maritime Museum. I had chosen well, but how could I approach this august figure?

As luck would have it, he was shortly to be the guest of honour at a supper party at The Maritime Museum, where he was to give a talk on Cook's travels. Such an amazing stroke of luck! Lord Lewin's presentation was fascinating and it was clear that James Cook was one of his heroes. During the interval I vied with a good number of people all eager to have a word or two with him. There was one lady in a very red dress who was determined to have more than her fair share of his attention and my impatience grew. However my chance came and in double quick time I managed to tell him of my purported connection with Cook and my plan concerning the craft workshops. He appeared unphased by the fact that I believed the connection to be from 'the other side of the blanket'. "Write to me about it all," he said.

I did this and enclosed an outline of my business plan. In reply he wrote a two-page manuscript letter, saying that the Maritime Museum had been offered a site near the area I had proposed for a boat Museum, which, he believed, provided a "window of opportunity" for my idea as well. He said that one would have to be prepared for the many problems inherent in such a project, not least of which would be the funding of it. He referred me to Stephen Reilly at The Maritime Museum whom, he said, was dealing with the Boat Museum project. Stephen Reilly, in turn, wrote me a long and interested letter in which he drew my attention to the fact that Deptford Creek was also going to be developed. As it was from Deptford that Cook's ships set sail on their voyages, he thought it would be a good idea for me to explore that avenue as well. He introduced me to someone in the Greenwich Society who, when we met seemed far more interested in putting forward a plan of his own, which had nothing to do with Cook.

Disappointed but undeterred, I continued my search for other interested parties. Jim Spicer put me on to Lord Mellish, who had recently been Deputy Chairman of the London Docklands Development Corporation and he in turn put me on to Peter Turlik, Business Director of the LDDC. Everyone I met showed an interest in the idea of The Endeavour Workshops. It was clear that producing a proper Business Plan would be one of my first considerations. I had enrolled in a short Business Enterprise Course held over three weeks at The Greenwich Polytechnic in the evenings and at weekends to learn the rudiments of this subject. I have to say that 'it wasn't a giggle a minute', but turned out to be very useful in a way I hadn't expected.

Robert Fletcher, who ran this course, and with whom I had discussed my plans, very kindly agreed to set his fulltime students the task of producing a Business Plan for the Captain Cook Endeavour Workshops as part of their training. When they had completed it, they invited me along to The Polytechnic where they gave a Presentation of their Plan. This was all great fun and clearly they had much enjoyed doing it and handed me a copy which they had all signed. I would like to have been able to say that the whole scheme got off the ground, but it was not to be.

Australia

During the period from 1985-1989 I had been dogged by various infections and after one particularly virulent attack of flu, my boss decided that I needed to get away for a week or two, perhaps to a more temperate climate. The 'powers that be' endorsed this suggestion so I began to make a swift plan. This was an ideal chance to visit Australia, something I had always wanted to do and which, with the help of various loans, I did. Elsa and Jonas Herlenius had introduced me to an Australian couple, Joy and Bob Hutchinson, whom they had originally met through their son Göran during a tour of the Carlsberg Brewery in Copenhagen, since when they had become firm friends.

The Hutchinsons lived in Sydney and I had met them when they were on holiday in London and where they had a small pièd-á-terre in Duke Street, St James's. (They always enjoyed being able to say that their local grocer's shop was Fortnum and Mason!) They had repeatedly given me an open invitation to visit them in Sydney and here was my chance to do so. My cousin, John Lineham gave me a list of our Australian cousins, several of whom I had met over the years when they came over to 'do' Europe and, quite incredibly, one family of cousins lived 5 minutes away from the Hutchinsons. Given the size of Australia, this must surely rank as more than just coincidence.

All I can say about the flight out to Sydney was that it was far too long. Once there the Hutchinson's virtually took me over. They had two apartments in a very tall block called Blue Point Towers situated at McMahon's Point on the other side of Sydney Harbour from the town. The views from their windows had to be seen to be believed. I could lie in bed in the mornings watching from my window huge vessels sailing in and out of the harbour. There was a ferry stop just below the block of flats from where one took a small boat over to town and which took only a few minutes. On the day of my arrival Bob and Joy were insistent that I could have only a short siesta to recover from jetlag, as a long one, they insisted, would confuse the body clock. I bowed to their greater knowledge and joined Bob for a stroll along the waters edge at McMahon's Point to get my bearings.

They had put together a marvellous programme of sightseeing, visiting and dining with their friends and on my first night Bob took me to a performance of the opera 'Fidelio' at the magnificent Sydney Opera House. I had of course seen countless pictures of this building, but the reality of it was even more impressive. The inside was less so. But I enjoyed the performance of 'Fidelio'.

The couple had a weekend home on the coast near Newcastle, a few miles north of Sydney, at a place called Worra Worra, where we spent a few days. There was a risk of sharks off the beaches and crocodiles in the waters around the houses there. I was able to cycle round the area but wasn't allowed to go off by myself for a swim in the sea; Bob always accompanied me to the beach. They introduced me to Sydney Bay oysters, the largest I had ever seen and took me to small Korean restaurants which served delicious and inexpensive dishes and like Chinese food they went down well. I was surprised when at one point Bob, a most equable man, suddenly turned to the people sitting at the next table and berated them for smoking. Equally surprising, they stubbed out their cigarettes without a murmur. Bob had built up a Health Shop empire throughout Australia, but had recently been the victim of a takeover and was at that time buying and selling paintings. It was more of a hobby than anything and there were some interesting examples hanging in their two apartments.

I have to say that my chest infection disappeared like magic in the Australian sunshine and I enjoyed every minute of my stay. Sydney buzzed with life and I loved being there, using this opportunity to visit craft workshops in The Rocks area. They were functioning more or less as I had envisaged my 'Endeavour Workshops' project might function and I foresaw the possibility of exchanges between Australian and British craftspeople. In fact there were a number of British craftsmen and women working in many of the Rocks' workshops. The Australians were busy preparing for their Bicentenary, scheduled to take place in 1988 and I met a number of the people involved with the planning, as well as the Director of the Crafts Council of Australia, with a view to interesting them in my project. Without exception they did show great interest and came up with various helpful suggestions. Needless to say, when the question of funding came up, their interest waned a little, not surprisingly, as the funding of the forthcoming Bicentenary celebrations was at the forefront of their minds.

I had tentatively earmarked in my own mind two people whom I thought might help with the funding of my project. One was Robert Holmes à Court and the other was Alan Bond, both very wealthy philanthropists in their different ways. The former was an Australian who at that time owned, among many other things, a number of London theatres. Sadly, he died quite a short time after I had seen him at the opening of an art exhibition in Canberra. Alan Bond was a well known character, an Englishman who lived in Australia. He was convicted of fraud some time later. But he did build a copy of Cook's barque 'Endeavour' which sailed across the world and which I visited when it was moored at Greenwich. I even have a photograph taken at the helm as a momento. He might well have agreed to fund or help fund my project as he was obviously a Cook man. But in the light of his conviction, perhaps it was as well that I didn't get round to asking him.

From Sydney I went on to Melbourne and found it a much staider city than Sydney, but nonetheless very attractive with some stunning modern buildings as well as very imposing older ones and many picturesque houses by the sea. It had a much more English feel about it than did Sydney. I visited the Jam Factory where the craftsmen and women were busy at their workshops and was again fired with enthusiasm for my project.

Towards the end of my stay the Hutchinsons were motoring down to Canberra to attend the preview of an Art Exhibition. They took me with them so that I could see a bit more of the country, but the landscape we passed through was rather boring and very dry, almost desert like. The Art Exhibition was a spectacular affair opened by the Labour Prime Minister, Bob Hawke. Apart from some stunning French Impressionist paintings, there was also a room full of works by Australian 19th Century painters like Sidney Nolan, Frederick McCubbin and Tom Roberts to name only a few. Bob Hutchinson, who had recently taken to buying and selling works of art, took me round and gave an expert commentary on each painting.

Pye Cormack, a friend from the Australian High Commission in Singapore, was back at the Australian Ministry of Foreign Affairs in Canberra and had invited me to stay with her. After paying a fond farewell to Bob and Joy Hutchinson, who had been such wonderful hosts, I joined Pye in her attractive little house in a new area of the city. At that time Canberra was very much under development as a capital city with great potential. We played golf at the Royal Canberra Golf Club and I treated myself to some kangaroo skin golf shoes – which I still have and which are to my mind infinitely more desirable than the dreaded 'trainers', which seem now to have become something of a status symbol the world over. Pye and her friend Judith took me up into the mountains to get some idea of the area and the skiing possibilities in the winter. Again, it was the sunshine which was part of the great attraction.

One morning as Pye left for the office, she said: "I've put some muesli out for you in that jar; I don't eat it any more because it makes me fart on the golf course." As I sat musing over my plate of muesli, I saw to my horror that it was moving. It was full of maggots, which unknowingly I had been eating. Ugh! Only a doctor would be able to say what, if anything, they might do to me, but I didn't want to embarrass Pye over the incident. Luckily, a tiny little lump had suddenly appeared on my forearm, thus providing a reasonable excuse to visit a doctor. Pye made an appointment for me to see her own very agreeable Hongkong-Chinese doctor. He was reassuring about the maggots and told me that a patient of his who had been a Japanese prisoner-of-war, had survived because of the protein in the maggots in his meagre food. The doctor prescribed some pills to rid me of the creepy crawlies, but when I saw on the box that alcohol should not be taken at the same time, I decided to wait until the end of the holiday before taking them. The lump on the arm was the result of carrying a very heavy handbag and hardly life-threatening, but it had fulfilled a useful purpose. History doesn't relate how and when Pye found out what was in the muesli jar. But I quite understood why she had been afflicted with flatulence on the golf course.

Hong Kong

I flew to Hong Kong from Australia. It was a lengthy flight of some 10 hours and there was free champagne to be had at the touch of a bell. As we landed in Hong Kong the steward presented me with a magnum. "For the champagne lady," he said with a wide smile. Oh good, I thought, it would be a nice addition to the bottle of Scotch I had brought for Pat Gibson, with whom I would be staying for four days before flying home. I had always wanted to visit the island from where my father had sailed with the Shipping Company, Möllers, in the 1950s.

On arriving at the Customs Hall an unsmiling female Customs officer in military style jacket confronted me and said in an accusing voice: "You have too much," meaning the alcohol, "you will have to pay." Now I didn't want to have to pay duty on the present from the steward, so I said, "Well, I don't want to pay, so please keep the champagne." But I had only got as far as "I don't want to pay," when a posse of senior policemen emerged, seemingly from nowhere and demanded to see my passport. I have to say that the thought of being arrested on the spot wasn't something I had envisaged. The senior policeman looked at the passport and said "HM Diplomatic Service, what you do here?" I replied that I was on holiday and what was more I was going to stay with a member of Special Branch. As I explained this last fact to the police officer, he visibly blenched and said as he handed me back my passport: "Is ok, don't do it again". So Pat got her champagne after all and she certainly deserved it.

Pat and I had served in Berlin together and she had later left the FCO to work for the Hong Kong Police. She was well ensconced in a nice flat and ran a racy little MG sports car. She whirled me round the town in it and out to the New Territories to peer over the border into mainland China. We shopped at the famous Stanley market and I bought a number of very cheap cotton shirts, which with great regret I had to deem too old and faded to wear in 2004, almost 20 years later. The last, a once strong pink one, was consigned to the ragbag only a couple of weeks ago – i.e. Spring 2006. They had collars, unlike the T-shirts of today. Raw silk dresses could be had for a pittance and, slightly more expensive, was a small blue and white ginger jar, which added to my modest collection of blue and white Chinese porcelain.

I have to say that, apart from being on the island, seeing the sights and being royally entertained by Pat and meeting her many friends, Hong Kong didn't really appeal to me. I have never seen so many people scurrying like mice about their business, faces taut with intent, or felt an atmosphere so heavy with carbon monoxide from the traffic which more or less throttled the thoroughfares, except perhaps in Bangkok on the brief visit there on the 'bag run'.

The flight back to Heathrow with British Airways was a nightmare as my seat was next to the Stewards' and Stewardesses' hidey-hole. When they weren't clattering china and dispensing drinks they were talking loudly and incessantly with no regard for their sleepy passengers. We touched down briefly in Calcutta at some unearthly hour of the morning and a team of Indians came on board to clean round us. It was at this point that I insisted on moving to a more peaceful seat and thankfully things improved.

XXIII

London Again

Back at the Office, the good news was that I had passed the Civil Service Swedish exam. I don't think at that point there was any financial benefit as there would have been had I been serving in Sweden, but, nevertheless, I felt a slight modicum of achievement.

Commuting into the Office had gradually become a lengthier and more disagreeable experience. The trains were dirty and full of graffiti and became more and more crowded; there were frequent cancellations and not a few strikes. During the strikes, those of us from the Office who lived in and around Blackheath would take it in turns to drive the others into town, starting at something like 6.30 am in order to miss the rush hour traffic. We all had our favourite 'rat runs' which saved us quite a lot of time. The advantage of these early starts was that we got a great deal more work done as the phones didn't start ringing until much later and we were able to knock off halfway through the afteroon. I used this opportunity to put my flat on the market and search for a bigger one in Blackheath itself.

My maxim that something good very often emerges from something bad was borne out when I succeeded in finding the most splendid flat at the Blackheath end of the Shooters Hill Road. It was the top floor of a most attractive Edwardian villa, complete with quite a big secluded garden and a garage. The

156

rooms were large and the ceilings high. I couldn't have wished for a more attractive abode and lived there extremely happily until my retirement in 1989.

The ground floor flat was owned by a kindly couple with a young daughter and the basement flat by a charming young man and his girlfried. They were friendly but unobtrusive and until he became seriously ill with Parkinson's Disease, Michael from the ground floor flat took it upon himself to keep the garden in order. When he did become rather too frail to cope, it was with great reluctance that he allowed two gardeners from Greenwich Park, whose help I had secured, to take over the maintenance of the garden.

The move into this new home was fairly inexpensive and painless as it was no distance from the other flat. The only panic I can recall was when doing a final run between the two flats. I had my jewel case in the hand so-to-speak, for safety's sake. Imagine my horror when I couldn't find it on arrival. As I emerged from the car, it was where I had put it as an interim measure of course, on the roof of the car How it hadn't rolled off into the road, I simply don't know. Perhaps it was the weight of the gold inside that kept it on the roof. But over the years I had to sell off several of those pieces of jewellry to pay my heating bills. It was worth it though to go on living in such a lovely flat.

During the famously bad storm which hit the South East of the country one night in October 1987, the house shuddered alarmingly. Although it had stood its ground safely since 1860, despite a bomb in the front garden during the war, I wasn't too certain that it would survive this massive onslaught and got out of bed to make a calming cup of tea, but this wasn't enough. The branches of a large willow tree in the garden were being blown towards the house and it looked as if the tree might topple over onto the house at any moment. A large whisky was needed at this point, after which I fell into a deep sleep and was woken by the ringing of the telephone. It was a good friend calling to see if all was well after such a violent night. It was, although the willow had come crashing down, fortunately just missing the house. There was no chance of getting into London and the scene as one walked down towards Greenwich Park the next day was almost unbelievable: so many trees uprooted from the pavements along the sides of the road, but this was nothing to the devastation of centuries old trees in the Park itself. The scene there really likened the proverbial 'elephants' graveyard'.

Riffling through my diaries for those years in London, I see and had almost forgotten how many friends and relations from all over the place came to visit.

157

I have always found cooking and entertaining a bit of a chore, although friends tell me I'm good at both. But I do love seeing old friends so do tend to make great efforts when they come to call or to stay. The family came up on a fairly regular basis for Sunday lunch and I think they enjoyed this and our wanderings round the Park afterwards.

There was nothing I liked better, however, than solitary weekend walks in Greenwich Park. Apart from being a beautiful and beautifully kept park, every inch of it exuded so much of the nation's history and the view from the top of Point Hill to the Thames and St Pauls never ceased to capture my heart and imagination.

There is a lovely garden within the park just inside the Blackheath Gate and in the summer I used to take a folding chair, lie in the sun and watch the world go by. One Saturday afternoon as I was lazing there I must have dropped off to sleep, but woke suddenly to see a black youth a couple of yards away with his back to me, checking it seemed to be sure we were alone, and drawing a knife out of his belt. 'Goodness', I thought, 'it's like being in the jungle.' I must have made a slight movement, but as he turned some people came along and he ran off. A lucky escape.

This was another feature of living in London; one needed to be on one's guard the whole time for just such incidents. I remember leaving my car, locked, outside a car hire firm one evening. I can only have been gone a couple of minutes, but nevertheless a window had been broken and a lovely suede holdall taken. It had been a Christmas present from Elsa from Switzerland and was particularly elegant and I was sad to lose it. But I laughed at the disappointment the thieves must have felt when they saw that it contained a sort of spinster's survival kit: a pair of high-heeled shoes, a spare tampax, a packet of hormone replacement pills and a loaf of bread.

The colleague whose flat I rented to begin with in Blackheath during her absence overseas had returned home. She was a keen concert goer and I had almost forgotten the number of wonderful concerts we went to together during those years, particularly in Greenwich at the splendid baroque church at the Naval College and at The Ranger's House, one of the beautiful and historic mansions in Blackheath, where Lord Chesterfield lived and close to Montague House where Queen Caroline of Brunswick lived when King George IV abandoned her. It was magical to wander into the garden with a glass of wine during the interval and gaze over the Heath, with the memory of the music still gently holding sway.

On another occasion I went with Nick Siddle, my cousin and his wife Jo to see The Northern Ballet Company's depiction of the life of the artist S.L Lowry. The dancers managed so well to mirror the figures from his paintings, who though in groups leaving their work in the mills, playing on the beach or just talking to each other, had nevertheless that solitary, emotionally isolated look about them, which expressed a fairly common feature of the British character.

Then there were wonderful exhibitions to be visited. I saw a number of these with Philip Haslett and sometimes his good friend, Peter Dryland, friends from Berlin days, who had by then retired from the Army. They were members of the Army and Navy Club in St James's Square and after doing the exhibitions we would wind our weary way there for a gin-and-tonic or two followed by lunch and a relaxing chat in the splendid drawing room overlooking Pall Mall, the one room, apart from the restaurant, in which members were able to entertain their wives and other lady guests.

In 1999 Andy and Sheena Skiöldebrand celebrated their Ruby Wedding with a party in London. Always good party givers, this one was no exception and it was a joy to meet up with old friends again on such a happy occasion. One such was Rutger von Seth, a Swedish Count, who had been one of the regulars who sailed with Andy and Sheena on 'Foresight' in the old days in Stockholm. I hadn't seen him for twelve or thirteen years and as we chatted about those days he suddenly said, "You and I never had sexual relations did we?" As is often the case when one would least like it to happen there was something of a lull in the general conversation around us as I replied, "No, we didn't," adding jokingly, "and if you speak a little louder everyone will hear." Rutger became a good friend (and we never did have sexual relations!) He had been married three times and at Andy and Sheena's party he met up with a girlfriend from student days, Jane Gross, a lifelong friend of the Skiöldebrands, as was Rutger who had been Best Man at their wedding.

When Jane's husband, David, died very sadly of cancer some time later, she and Rutger got together and I saw a lot of them in the ensuing years. Rutger had inherited an estate in the south of Sweden, which he sold with a view to investing in forest land in Scotland. Instead he rented Barscobe Castle near Dumfries, belonging to a former Lord Mayor of London, Sir Hugh Wontner, who had restored it and for which he won a Scottish Heritage award. It was a fitting place for Rutger to live, enhanced by his lovely old and gracious Swedish furniture and family porcelain, not to mention the odd case or two of vintage malt whisky.

Rutger was an unusual man with an odd, but wholly benign temperament prone to suddenly coming out with strange turns of phrase in perfect English. I remember when he, Andy and Sheena and I were having dinner at the Spyway Inn at Eggardon Hill in Dorset the night before my 60th Birthday Party; he suddenly left the table, wandered over to the bar where he ordered a double whisky and engaged the owner of the pub in earnest conversation. The poor man looked totally uncomprehending and he must have had plenty of odd conversations in his time, so poor Rütger wandered back to join us, probably totally unaware that his words had been too obscure to be understood by the barman.

France

The five of us had a splendid holiday on a narrow boat on the Canal du Midi in 1992. It was Rutger's birthday treat for Sheena's 65th Birthday. In fact he treated us all, such was his generosity. Andy was at the helm and we 'girls' did our stuff manning the ropes as he steered the boat through the interminable locks. We ate very well, mostly at the small restaurants close to the banks of the canal. On one occasion we went by foot or on bikes slightly further afield to a chateau which appeared to be closed when we reached it. But once we had beaten on the door and told them how hungry we all were, they opened up the kitchen and provided us with a delicious lunch and some of their own wines. Rutger bought a couple of cases and we left them late in the afternoon, vowing to return soon again. Would we have been so hospitably treated out-of-hours in England we asked ourselves.

We reached the ancient town of Carcassonne on a pouring wet day, but braved the elements to do some exploring there. We sheltered in and thoroughly enjoyed going round the basilica of St Nazaire and wandering round the walls of this medieval town, a World Heritage Site, and when the rain was at its worst found a good restaurant to lunch and dry out in. Rutger was having a bad day because he had fallen and badly grazed a knee the day before whilst helping with the ropes as we went through a lock. It had been some 30-odd years since we had been sailing together on 'Foresight' and none of us was as nimble as we would have liked to have been. But all-in-all it went very well, although we were quite glad by the end to motor to the luxury of Jane's second home at Monseigne near Bordeaux for the weekend, where we relaxed in hot sunshine and were thoroughly spoilt by our hostess before flying back to London.

XXIV

Health Problems and Early Retirement

In 1985 my stepfather Dick's health was failing and he had two serious operations to clear an artery to enable the blood to get through to his brain more easily. His condition affected his temperament so that he easily became angry and even violent. This naturally put a great strain on my mother and in turn affected her equilibrium. After his death in October 1985 she eventually rallied and began to take on a new lease of life, which was a great relief to us all.

As to my own health problems, I still seemed to get infections of one sort or another on a fairly regular basis, despite the healing holiday in Australia, and it was after a bout of 'flu in 1987 that things began to become more serious. I had booked to go on holiday to Irma and Christer in Sweden and my doctor advised me to go as planned but prescribed another course of penicillin to take with me. I decided to go but just didn't seem to get any better as the days went by. Sten Jacobsen, a friend and a surgeon, examined me and pronounced that it was a virus, about which nothing could be done and that it would go in time.

He was right. In fact it was what has now become a recognised medical condition, that of post-viral fatigue syndrome or ME (Myalgia Encephalomyelitis), originally known as 'Yuppy Flu' because so many ambitious and upwardly mobile young people were going down with it. No-one seemed to know how to cure it at that time. It was Claire Francis, the well known round-the-world yachtswoman, who campaigned for it to be recognised by the medical profession as an illness, after she had suffered from it for many years. Well, to cut a long story short I suffered with it on and off for some 12 years. At the beginning I was so debilitated it was difficult to find the strength to turn over in bed. The doctor's advice was to do as much as I could manage and to go for short walks, which I did.

I used to take the car into Greenwich Park, sit on a bench until strength enough returned to walk to the next bench and so on and back again in the same way, resting on each bench. One day as I made my slow way towards a bench, I saw that there was a man sitting there with what looked like a golf club in his hand. In fact it was a white stick; the man was blind. We didn't speak and he soon got up and continued on his way. I was still sitting there on his way back and we chatted. He told me that he lived alone, but often went on what he called sighted walks, i.e. with a group of people who weren't blind. He said that he would get up early on a Sunday morning, make himself sandwiches and then take a train into London, all on his own, where he met up with the sighted walkers and off they would go into the country. He became quite animated as he described these walks. He said, "At one time I was walking with a grave-digger, so was well ahead of the others." This struck me as being very forward thinking and very funny. I left this brave and permanently disabled man feeling humbled but cheered and ready for the next challenge.

These totally debilitating attacks came and went and in between them I was able to carry on with my job. I particularly enjoyed the job I was doing at that time and felt desperately frustrated with each bout of sick leave. The Office was extremely good about it, but eventually I came to the conclusion that soldiering on was fair neither to myself nor to the Office and the colleagues who were shouldering the burden of my work during my absences. My local doctor set in motion the necessary steps in support of my decision to retire early on medical grounds. She considered it to be a wise one, and later, after interviewing me, the Treasury Medical Adviser sanctioned this.

It was a sad time. The Office and the people in it had been such an important part of my life for so many years that leaving it all felt prettywell like a bereavement. A fair number of people turned up for my farewell party, for which I had prepared some heartfelt, but I hoped, amusing words. The nervousness beforehand had been assuaged with one or two drops of 'the hard stuff' kindly supplied by my boss's secretary, but soon after embarking on this little speech, rather like that MP addressing The House, my mind went completely blank, although the spiel had been endlessly rehearsed, in the bath, in the bus and in bed. Ignominy! However, I heard myself saying very calmly: "Now the words seem to have left me, but let's all take a sip of our drinks and hopefully they will return." Well, quite amazingly they did and were well received, so honour was satisfied. It had been so important for me to do this and at last I could begin to enjoy the party and my retirement.

Visiting Italy

In October 1988, a year before retiring, I took a Page & Moy package tour to Italy to the area of Lake Trasimeno, more or less in the centre of the country and quite near to Perugia and Assisi. A coach met us at Rome Airport and took us on our way to our base, a charming little town called Passignano on the lakeside, from where we toured round the area, including the ancient hill town of Castiglione. My fellow travellers were cheerful and pleasant and there were no problematic souls, which sometimes tend to cause varying degrees of unease within such a party. On the way back to Rome Airport we spent a couple of days in Florence and I was able to revisit my favourite sights with no time wasted wondering how to find them. The trip had the effect of rekindling my keen interest in this fascinating country. So much so that during a serious bout of ME the following year I went again, but this time for health reasons.

I headed for the spa town, Abano Terme, in Northern Italy, which I'd visited a couple of times with Elsa and Jonas Herlenius in the 1950s, but by this time the prices had risen at the Hotel Orologio causing me to find a similar but somewhat cheaper hotel in the spa town of Montegrotto Terme, quite near to Abano. It was perfect and later in the week I took a bus to Abano to look again at The Grand Hotel Orologio. Sadly, it had been modernised and extended and was just like any other five-star hotel in any part of the world. Most of the old world charm had gone, so I was better off at the unspoilt Miramonte Hotel in Montegrotto.

The doctor there recommended six mud (fango) treatments, but bearing in mind the cost, I settled for three. He found my blood pressure to be rather high, but I didn't let on that it was probably because of the price of six treatments and that it would be sure to sink once we had agreed on just the three. Very early the next morning the telephone rang to say that the first treatment was now due. A couple of Englishmen I had met at the swimming pool described the mud treatment: "It's a bit claustrophobic," they said, "and don't let them cover your hands and arms with mud because it makes it even more so." Of course that is what happened, but this didn't appear to worry me as it had done them. The mud was very hot and I was encased in it for about fifteen minutes and then shown down into a Roman bath where the mud was hosed off, rather like a jet car wash.

Soon after returning limply to my room there was a sharp knock on the door and a burly Italian masseur came in and proceeded to pummel the life out of me. But so sure was I that it was bound to be doing me a great deal of good, that after a short rest I went for a walk. However, the treatment had so devitalized me that it seemed to be touch and go whether I could make it back to the hotel at all, but after resting at the roadside for nearly an hour, strength enough did return. Things improved and after a day or two I was able to take a bus into Padua to see some of the the sights I had so loved during my first visit there with the Herlenius family. The church of St Anthony of Padua was the most important, closely followed by the University. And then the next day to Abano for old times sake, before returning home and back to the office the following morning feeling a lot better.

During the bout of illness which prompted me to set in train early retirement in 1989, thoughts naturally turned to where I might live when this became a reality. London was out of the question and the thought of settling down in the country in England as a 'single girl' somehow filled me with apprehension. Italy was fresh in my mind and somehow, somewhere I had picked up a brochure advertising a month's Course of Italian lessons at the University for Foreign Students in Perugia. Accommodation would be found by the University and the price was reasonable. Why not, I thought, go and do that Course, health permitting, and look round the area, which included Passignano, with a view to finding somewhere peaceful to retire to. This idea, oddly enough, seemed much less daunting than the thought of retiring to somewhere in the UK. It would be something entirely new, it would present an interesting challenge and, importantly, the climate would be better than in England.

Over the years I had toyed with the idea of retiring to Lincoln, because of the Cathedral and because it was close to my roots in Yorkshire; Pitlochry, because of the golf and in a heavenly part of Scotland and then Sidmouth in Devon for the sea and the Devon countryside. But none of these places beckoned when the time for retirement approached.

In the event I wrote off to the University and booked a place starting at the end of October 1989. Just as I was preparing to leave for Italy, Irma rang to give me the very sad news that Elsa had died the day after driving down with two old friends to her home in Vevey in Switzerland for the winter. This was not unexpected as she had been failing gently for some time and had been searching round for somewhere to end her days in comfort. This problem resolved itself with her death, but her passing left a very big hole. I had so much to be grateful to her for. The very direction my life had taken was in no small part due to her continuing interest, help and guidance. I joined the family for her funeral at the little Swedish church at Vevey and from there took off for Perugia, a move which, I'm certain, would have had her approval.

The University for Foreign Students, Perugia

On arrival I could hardly wait to go into the centre of this ancient town, founded by the Etruscans and taken by the Romans in 295 BC. It is situated on the top of a hill overlooking the Tiber valley and is the capital of the Province of Perugia in Umbria. It has a massive Etruscan town gate, the Arco d'Augusto and its University proper dates from 1276. Rather than go into the wealth of detail which such an historic town deserves, I will just say that lovers of Italy and its art who haven't already done so, should pay a visit there and see for themselves. I spent a month at the University for Foreign Students and grew to love the town and all it had to offer aesthetically. But it wasn't all plain sailing by any means.

To begin with I was told by the Admissions Clerk at the University that there was a shortage of accommodation at that moment. My heart sank; there was no way I could afford to stay in an hotel for a month. After what seemed like an endless wait, she gave me the name and address of someone she thought might be able to put me up. Finding the house was a nightmare. It was a hot day and although a policeman on traffic duty pointed me in what he thought was the right direction it wasn't and I eventually waved down a car-load of policemen on the outskirts of the town. They couldn't have been more helpful. One eager beaver went off and found the house but they weren't able, they said, to give me a lift to the house in their official car, but got a taxi and waved me off with many encouraging smiles.

It was a large house down a tiny lane on the opposite side of which a huge car park was being built. The door was opened by a sharp-featured little woman, who spoke only Italian and German. She showed me into what was nothing more than a broom cupbard with a bed, a chair and a wardrobe. My heart sank again, but she then showed me a bigger room with a wonderful view over the valley below the town and said that, once the present occupant moved out in a few days time I could have that room, but it would cost more. I accepted the offer and returned to my hotel feeling fairly shattered, but more hopeful, although I didn't take to my landlady-to-be.

On the Monday morning I got the hotel porter to ring her to arrange a time when it would be convenient for me to arrive. This arranged I duly set off in a taxi. Miraculously the driver found the house and off he went. I rang the bell but all was silent. I could have wept and because of the suitcases couldn't go anywhere to get help. The builders on the car-park site looked down with curiosity, but with no incentive to help. Gloomily, I wandered up to the shuttered window of the little room she had offered me and pulled open the shutters to find the window wide open. The one chair was just inside the window so I lifted it out and climbed in. The builders had by this time increased in numbers, their curiosity further aroused. No sooner had I brought in the suitcases through the front door than the Madame returned. I whispered a rather triumphant apology, which she could only accept. However, she had her revenge the next morning when I wandered into the kitchen to put the kettle on. Watching me she said: "Oh, you can't use my kitchen." After I had protested that breakfast was a must, she produced a little camping stove and a cup and saucer, a plate and a knife and fork and spoon, at extra cost of course.

There were ten other students staying in this house, mostly younger than I was and we all took great exception to her manner. Add to that the fact that she kept the heating down so low that we had to sit in our overcoats to do our homework in the evenings, it was no surprise when the younger students revolted one weekend when she was away attending a family wedding. All the lights in the house were left on overnight and the heating was turned up as high as it would go. Revenge was certainly very sweet that night.

There were some 2000 foreign students of every conceivable nationality at this University The atmosphere was one of unforced bonhomie, especially at mealtimes as we all queued up for our generously subsidised lunches in the enormous dining hall. I palled-up with an older American couple, a young coloured girl, a lawyer, also American, and a charming German who, it finally emerged, was a publisher. He and I had the odd meal out in the evenings and went to some excellent concerts given in an ancient and beautiful theatre and in the equally old and beautiful Town Hall. Although the concerts started late and finished around midnight, it was quite safe to walk home, even on my own, and there were still many people just strolling around the town at that late hour.

The lessons during the day were fairly intense and only Italian was spoken. Our Professor was a dynamic lady who was said to be an ardent Communist, but sensibly she did not attempt to bring politics into the classroom. The only time politics was the subject of our conversations was when the Berlin Wall came down and the German publisher's wife, a Berliner, had gone back to her home town to join in the celebrations. We had a first hand account of the joyousness of the occasion from her husband after she had telephoned him about it.

At one point a group of unruly Palestinians joined our class, sat in the back row and had clearly little interest in learning Italian. They disrupted the class with their chunterings and finally the good Professor firmly upbraided them and they didn't appear again. A young Kuwaiti student confided in me during lunch one day, that rumour had it they might be terrorists using the lessons as a cover whilst planning some nefarious activities. But we lost track of them once they had left our class and the status quo returned.

House-hunting in Italy

I spent what spare time there was visiting and loving Assisi and saw some of the nearby hill towns as well as looking at various properties in the vicinity of Passignano on the shores of Lake Trasimeno. There was an estate agency in Passignano run by a Dutch man who spoke excellent English; just what was needed. He showed me round a number of properties in the area, some of them virtual ruins with great potential had I been able to contemplate such renovations. He told me that Peter Hobday had a house nearby. I had no idea who Peter Hobday was and the agent enlightened me, showing some surprise that I'd never heard of him. He told me he was a well known radio personality with his morning programme, 'Today'. Some years later, whilst living in Dorset, I met Peter Hobday and his wife at a drinks party and was fascinated to hear all about their house near Lake Trasimeno.

Eventually I viewed what seemed to me a dream property. It was the bottom half of a two-bedroomed villa in the hills above Lake Trasimeno and as well as a sitting-cum-dining room it had a long salon, stretching the length of the house, with picture windows along the whole of one side and a spectacular view overlooking the Lake. There was an open fireplace at the far end of the room. It also had a small garden with access to a proper asphalted road running down into the town. It was within my price range and after little consideration over the madness of living on my own in such a location and with only a smattering of the Italian language, I put in my offer and it was accepted. The estate agent explained the various hoops to go through in buying a property in Italy and I left him to arrange a 'notario' on my behalf. I met the couple who were selling the house, who seemed nice enough. Once back in Perugia I had great fun telling my new-found friends in the language class all about it. They were all keen to come and stay and made sure they had my address before the course broke up at the end of the month.

XXV

Moving to Dorset

After spending a weekend with Irene Kohncke and her husband Marino in Rome on the way back, I returned home to Blackheath with a song in my heart; mission accomplished, or so I thought. My elegant flat on Shooters Hill Road had been on the market for only a short time and was snapped up fairly quickly, although there were the usual last minute hitches. By Christmas the sale was agreed and I left, rather sadly I have to say and headed towards Dorset to spend Christmas with Winfy and Jim Spicer, the car laden with luggage to keep me going until I left for Italy. I recall that it was a particularly wild night with high winds and heavy storms, which brought back memories of the great storm of 1987.

My brother-in-law, John Morley, who owns a holiday home at Mudeford, near Christchurch in Dorset let me stay there prior to my intended move to Italy, so as soon as Christmas was over I took off for Mudeford. Rather surprisingly I found that winter was a good time to be at the seaside. It was mild and there were very few people about apart from the local inhabitants. A daily walk along the beach became a regular habit and my heart sang with the sea air and the sense of freedom from the responsibilities of doing a job and owning a house. It really was a carefree time. Things didn't seem to be moving as quickly as I had hoped with the house in Italy and I began to get slightly cold feet and decided to elicit the help of an Italian lawyer in the City of London to take over the conveyancing on my behalf.

During the following few days I drove over to Christchurch to have a look round its famous priory church; famous because of a legend and for having the longest nave in the country. It was said that one night, as building was about to begin, the building materials were mysteriously moved to another site. As it was generally believed that The Almighty preferred the new site, building was started there. Two strange things then happened. The first was that an extra builder whom nobody knew arrived to take part in the construction work and the second was that one of the main beams had been cut too short. Again, mysteriously, the builders arrived one morning to find the beam in place and the right size and the unknown builder had disappeared. I was enthralled by this story and went to view the beam, around which there is a spotlight and a plaque describing this apparent miracle.

I took the opportunity of saying a little prayer asking for advice on my Italian venture. The following morning a letter arrived from the Dutch estate agent, explaining with abject apologies that the vendors had decided to withdraw their property from the market. So that was pretty much that. As this decision had been taken as soon as my Italian lawyer had taken over the conveyancing, there may have been something not quite straightforward about the sale, but I shall never know. All I know is that, with hindsight, it would probably have been complete madness to have gone through with this project at that point in time. Was it Divine Intervention? I've always believed that it probably was, although it was deeply disappointing at the time.

Back to the drawing board, as they say, and I began to look at properties in the Christchurch area. But it just wasn't my scene and the prices were high. Winfy Spicer invited me over to Beaminster for a weekend and suggested I look for something in that area. Mindful of Jim's high profile as the longstanding Conservative MP for West Dorset, I was chary of living too near them in case they felt in some way responsible for my welfare, so I started looking at houses over the border in Somerset. Also, the prices there were marginally lower as was the Council Tax.

In the end I bought a small cottage in the village of Hooke, a few miles from Beaminster in Dorset. Winfy who had been house-hunting with me seemed to have no qualms about my living close by; in fact she seemed to welcome it as Jim was up in London most of the week at the House of Commons and busy with various directorships, while she was extremely committed to representational and other tasks within the Constituency. She worked tirelessly

Left: My brother Chris
Right: With Winfy Spicer before my 60th birthday at the Spicer's home in
Beaminster

With my mother after a pub lunch

Elsa Herlenius at home in Råda, Sweden

The Herlenius family enjoying their annual cousins' party given by Hans-August and Birgit Herlenius at their home in Falun, Sweden

Malcolm Herlenius and me at a cousins' party in Falun, Sweden

Göran and Leena Herlenius at the Sandborn Museum

Andy and Sheena Skiöldebrand and Rutger von Seth at Jane Gross's house in France after our week on the Canal du Midi

A crayfish party at my cottage in Hooke, Dorset

Poised to jump off the sofa at Tita and John Shakeshaft's
annual New Year Party

Allan Taylor visiting Mapperton Gardens, Beaminster

Lunching with Kerstin at their home in Mexico City

Winfy, Mary and me, flatmates in London 56 years ago, with Owen Scholte at my 70th birthday party

With Rosemary Manger and Tita Shakeshaft at my 70th birthday party

With Jane Gross at Heulyn's home in Periana

My car outside my house in Antequera

The Alcazaba just behind my house in Antequera

in fulfilling her role as an MP's wife, but such a life can be slightly isolating in some ways, and having an old friend of some 40 years standing living nearby to relax with could prove to be no bad thing. Jim's energy was boundless and their joint commitment to so many good causes as well as to the Conservative Party was prodigious.

For my own part it couldn't have been better. It had been so long since I had had the time and energy to enjoy a proper social life and with such little initial effort on my part, it was all too good to be true. Within a very short time the Spicers had introduced me to many of their friends in the area and although earlier I had reservations about settling in the UK as a 'single girl' I had no cause to worry on that score in Dorset. I soon felt very much a part of Dorset life, although the 'hunting, shooting and fishing' scene was quite new to me. Everyone was immensely welcoming, although I have no doubt that being introduced to them by Winfy and Jim provided a head start.

Winfy insisted that I brush up on my very rusty bridge and even found a congenial bridge class for me to attend. I have never been a good bridge player, but have been able to hold my own in so-called 'kitchen bridge', with supper and a lot of chat and laughter.

On one occasion I was invited to a bridge supper with three very good players and although I forewarned them all that I was something of a novice, our host, my partner, assured me that as long as I did my best there was no cause to worry. The effects of ME still plagued me and I tended to tire easily so towards the end of the evening I made a silly mistake. My host rounded on me angrily and it was all I could do to stop my lips quivering as a prelude to bursting into tears. Our hostess, who was not a bridge player, but who had been sitting nearby sewing, got up and left the room. She later returned and when the time came to go home and I thanked her for a lovely evening, she cried: "It was not a lovely evening; they were perfectly beastly to you and now you know why I don't play bridge!" Her husband rang to apologise for his impatience the following morning and we were able to refer to it after a time, when we met, with some amusement.

Trying to find someone to cure me once and for all from the effects of the ME became a top priority. Apart from the tiredness and debility, the disease also seemed to affect my emotional stability, or emotional lability, as the books on the disease describe it. This added to the usual uncertainties of retirement and moving to a completely different life, albeit such a promising one. Winfy proved to be a wonderfully kind friend and took me along to many and varied events at which she was often the guest of honour, including some splendid concerts. She was an encouraging and tireless listener as I regaled her with endless memories stretching back to childhood and the ongoing problems with my mother.

A year after my arrival she arranged a stunning lunch party for my 60th Birthday at their home in Beaminster, to which I was able to invite lots of old friends, many of whom she knew, together with the new friends I had made in Dorset. The summer had been a wet, cold and windy one, but on that day the sun shone and about 40 of us sat down to a delicious feast in the garden. Jim gave a kind speech and with trembling voice I replied. I felt that my cup was full and the thought that anyone could make such a kind gesture involving so much work quite overwhelmed me.

But what I failed to realise some time later was that the one thing I had sought to avoid, which was that neither Winfy nor Jim should feel any responsibility for my welfare, appeared to have happened. After all, I had been, until then, fairly adept at managing my own life, so where had I gone wrong now? It was a crushing blow to think that I had somehow breeched a code of which I had always been mindful. It was up to me to prove that this was not in fact the case.

Cured of ME (Myalgia Encephephalomyelitis)

To work on becoming emotionally and physically strong again and to rid myself of the effects of ME became more essential than ever. My local GP could only advise that I take short walks and gradually increase the distance. I went to a man who practised Polarity Therapy, which is rather like Acupuncture but the pressure points are manipulated by hand. This helped in a general sort of way, but the effects soon wore off. Acupuncture helped too but didn't cure me.

Eventually I heard from two separate sources of a Homeopathist called Dr Robert Jacobs in Verwood who had treated them for various chronic conditions with great success. I was by this time rather sick of trying new treatments, which although helpful didn't do the trick, but the fact that two people had recommended him gave me some hope. Amazingly, he cured me completely over a period of nine months.

He had various electronic diagnostic machines which showed there to be two viruses in my system which, he thought, could be causing the problem. He made up a potion of minute amounts of the viruses, diluted to such an extent that only the energies of the viruses were left and eventually this did the trick. I was cured. Needless to say it was marvellous to feel well again after some twelve years of spasmodic chronic debility and I spread the word locally, so that a number of ME sufferers who were brought to my attention were able to reap the benefits of his treatment.

I had been asked by General Geoffrey Howlett, who had by then retired from the Army and lived close by, whether I would like to consider joining the local Leonard Cheshire Homes Committee. He was Chairman of the Charity at the time. I had long wanted to do something useful and although Jim Spicer put my name forward as a possible non-executive director of one of the local National Health Trusts and although the man who interviewed me, yet another General, was optimistic that a positive outcome was fairly certain, I was turned down. Whether it was on health grounds, or whether, as some said, my candidacy might have had political repercussions, because Jim Spicer had put me up for the job, I don't know. Whatever the reason, I must confess to having been rather relieved and settled instead for joining the Leonard Cheshire Committee, eventually becoming a Deputy Chairman.

I think Winfy had probably hoped that I might join one or other of her many Committees, but I didn't want to expose our long friendship to possible disagreements in the course of committee meetings, so instead helped wherever I could in more menial capacities. Selling raffle tickets at Conservative Party and the Joseph Weld Hospice events seemed to be my metier and I enjoyed doing it. Apart from meeting masses of people, it also enabled me to either meet or observe at first hand two Prime Ministers, Lady Thatcher and her husband Denis, and John Major and his wife Norma, as well as other MPs who came to address the local Conservative Association.

When John Major came down I decided to form up to shake his hand as he made his way round the guests at a Reception being held in his honour. I joined the mélée of others anxious to do the same. As my turn came, he was just in the process of taking my hand when his PPS claimed his attention. Instead of leaving me in the lurch, as I had expected, he held onto my hand and said "Don't go away," so I stood firm, but the sudden rush of blood to the head which had enabled me to make what for me was a bold move, fell away and I was left, a quivering mass, wishing I'd been a million miles away. A slight exaggeration, and of course when he did turn his attention back to me I was able to thank him for all the good he was doing. There are many who would disagree with me on this, given, for example, 'Black Wednesday' and the fall-out from that, but I admired the innate honesty with which he tried to lead the Country.

Life in Hooke Village

I enjoyed living in the village of Hooke, where everyone was consistently friendly. Allen and Sheila Hill made me especially welcome. They enjoyed entertaining and more often than not included me in their parties and this contributed very positively to my new life in the depths of the Dorset countryside. They lived at the other end of the village in 'The Mill House', which had originally been a working mill, beside a gushing spring and their own little lake. It was more or less derelict when they bought it but they restored it into a beautiful home from which Allen ran a flourishing trout farm. As with the house, they started and built it up together over some 30 years to become one of the major suppliers of trout in the country.

We became great friends and had a good deal of fun together throughout my years in Dorset and beyond. Sheila has been one of my staunchest friends in good times and in bad and remains so to this day. In the early years she and I collected together a group of like-minded friends and formed a painting class in Beaminster, under the guidance of one Ray Gray, whose life seemed to be one long drama, episodes of which he regaled us with each week. Not many of us succeeded in the art bit but it was always a congenial gathering with much gossip and laughter.

Through Allen and his fish farm connections I was able to buy sweet water crayfish at a very reasonable price; in fact buying the dill to cook them in cost more than did the crayfish. It was great fun giving crayfish parties and introducing my Dorset friends to this traditional Swedish form of feasting. Not all of them appreciated tearing the crayfish apart with their fingers and sucking the juices, most of which tended to run down one's arms. Others made hay with the accompanying schnappes, once with fairly disastrous results.

Another spell of feasting, but in the English style was when Malcolm and Kerstin were over from Mexico and made a stopover in England to come to Hooke for the weekend to meet my other Swedish friends, the Skiöldebrands and Rutger von Seth. Malcolm and Rutger had been at school together and even shared a room at Lundsberg, the Swedish public school fashioned on the lines of, I believe, our own Rugby School. They hadn't met since then but got on well together and I was in my element providing for and sightseeing with such very dear and close friends from different phases of my life.

As far as village life was concerned, I'm afraid I did not get too involved, but did fairly modest things like cleaning the little church of St Giles once a month, helping to sew kneelers and in 2000 contributing to the Millenium Gate leading into the churchyard.

During my time in the village, there was a school, St Francis School, for young unstable and emotionally disturbed children who came mostly from London, Kent and the South West to be rehabilitated and educated. It was run at the manor house, Hooke Court, by the Anglican Friars from nearby Hillfield Priory. Hooke Court had been the home of among others The Earl of Sandwich in the late 19th Century and in 1919 Sir Thomas Salt, a Liberal politician and Banker. The school was started in 1947 and closed down in 1992, when many of the old boys came to lament its closing down and to say farewell. Holy Communion was celebrated and the current Earl of Sandwich gave a speech. He had made a strong case in The House of Lords for it to remain open. Sadly his efforts were to no avail due to the colossal government grant needed to keep it going. It was rumoured at the time that it cost more per boy to run than was the case at Eton College. It is now a very successful school of quite a different sort.

When I moved to Hooke in 1990 the village was described to me as "just a damp little place". This did no justice to the quite considerable and interesting history it has had dating back to 1086, when it was called La Hoc. Professor Duncan Harris, who built a house at the bottom of Green Lane, near to my cottage, researched and wrote a fascinating history of Hooke Village called 'Paupers, Dukes and a Prince' in 2005.

Many friends and relations came to visit me during the 10 years I lived in Hooke and once each year I collected Mummy and her friend Phil Milner from Mudeford where they were holidaying. I usually took them sightseeing to nearby places of interest in Dorset like Thomas Hardy's Cottage and Lawrence of Arabia's house and brought them back to my cottage for a night, returning them to Mudeford the following day. This always proved to be a great strain and I dreaded it. But they clearly enjoyed themselves so it was worth the effort.

175

On one such visit we went down to the beach at Burton Bradstock. It was a hot and sunny day and they were both intent on having a paddle in the sea. I warned them not to go too far into the sea as the waves were unpredictable. They were standing right at the edge when suddenly a wave did bowl them over and although Mummy kept her balance, blood began to pour down her paper thin shin, whilst Phil struggled out of the water, her clothes wet through. It wasn't the end of the world, but needed some sorting out before we could continue our journey back to Mudeford.

XXVI

New York and Washington

Quite out of the blue one day a letter came from a very dear American friend, Nickie Benjamen, inviting me to stay with her at her home in New York and then to take the train to Washington for a couple of days. Nickie and some student friends had visited London and our flat at De Vere Gardens in 1950. We had given them a whirlwind tour of London and they thanked us by sending over a huge food parcel when they got back home. What excitement when it arrived after the wartime years of food rationing!

Nickie and I became friends right from the start and kept in touch by letter over many years. She married a successful young lawyer and they had two sons, Bobby and Bruce and she was clearly blissfully happy. I then lost contact with her until a sad letter came telling me that her husband had been killed in an air crash just after she had given birth to their second son, Bruce. It was a cruel blow from which I don't think she ever really recovered. She subsequently paid a surprise visit to me in Copenhagen in 1963 and I spent a couple of days with her and the boys in New York on my way back from Caracas in 1969. Her invitation so many years later was too good to let pass. As she so rightly said: "We aren't getting any younger Ange...." So off I went and had a wonderful time.

Her apartment was in an imposing block on Park Avenue, complete with a uniformed doorman and an elegant, mirrored and tastefully furnished hallway, so it wasn't altogether surprising that I should fall completely in love with New York from the very start. I had an overwhelming desire to run down the streets of Manhattan singing: "NEW YORK, NEW YORK........", but didn't.

Although still beset by bouts of weariness caused by ME during that visit, before Dr Jacobs cured me of it, they were not serious enough to stop me making the most of visits to the Metropolitan, The Modern Art and the Guggenheim Museums, the Frick Collection and the Morgan Library, or from taking a boat to The Cloisters Museum with its wonderful collection of medieval art, mostly from Europe.

On the boat going there I settled myself on a chair near the rail with a perfect view, but suddenly two men came and stood right in front of me. Without looking up, I said indignantly: "Would you mind moving please?" A very sinister voice replied: "You move!" I looked up into the face of an Al Capone look-alike and nearly died of fright. Oddly enough, though, they did then take themselves off and I enjoyed an unobstructed view all the way to the tip of Long Island.

In Washington Nickie had arranged tickets for a tour of The White House, with which I was duly impressed and found it all a great thrill. From there she was proud to take me round the Smithsonian Museum and then to a concert at the newly opened John F Kennedy Concert Hall. But she insisted that we went even the smallest journeys by taxi because of the ever-present fear of street crime. And in New York she gave me strict instructions to watch my back and not to get into conversation with anyone. Needless to say I did so when leaving The Cloisters in search of somewhere to have lunch. I enquired of a perfectly normal couple out walking their dog in which direction I should head to find a reasonable restaurant. They told me and I set off on foot only to be stopped by the same couple offering me a lift in their car. Nickie's warning clicked in and I thanked them warmly and said I needed the exercise and off they went. Had I escaped some dire threat, I wondered, but happily I would never know.

On another occasion some two years later I was fortunate enough to be in New York when Malcolm Herlenius married Kerstin in the Swedish Church there. Elenita, Malcolm's first wife, had been killed in a tragic car accident in Sweden shortly after Elsa's death some years previously. Strangely enough Kerstin's husband had also met his death in a car accident, in Mexico, so the two of them well understood the anguish they had both suffered at the time.

But this was a joyous occasion and it was lovely meeting up again with Malcolm's now adult children and, of course, Kerstin herself and her two daughters. After the church service they had arranged a dinner party at The Waldorf Hotel for the children of their first marriages and a few friends, mostly from Mexico. I don't know when I have enjoyed a wedding more. Gustav, Malcolm's son remarked: "You are representing our family and Swedish friends, Angela". This observation 'warmed the cockles of my heart', so much so that I managed to join several of the others, in true Swedish style, to say a few heartfelt words to the happy couple during dinner. One thing which stuck in my mind was that Kerstin's mother, who was then in her mid-eighties, had flown over from Sweden the previous day for the occasion and she and Kerstin spent the wedding morning visiting the Matisse Exhibition at the Museum of Modern Art, a not inconsiderable feat for either of them on such a day.

XXVII

Romance

In 1993 the one thing I had always hoped might happen, did at last happen. Sitting next to a retired former Tank Regiment Brigadier at a dinner party one evening I asked him if he knew Allan Taylor. "Very well," he replied. "We play golf together quite frequently. A group of us from the regiment take it in turns to host a day's golf at each of our clubs." He promised that the next time he hosted the golf match he would give a dinner party to which he would invite me, so that I could meet up with Allan again. And there it was; fate had moved in after years of waiting. I couldn't believe my good luck.

The dinner was planned to take place in October 1993, but was postponed at the eleventh hour as a member of the regiment died and the funeral took place on just that day. So I had some months to wait before it did take place. When the day dawned I was in a state, not quite knowing how it would all turn out. Allan had been told that I was coming and initially suggested that perhaps it wasn't a good idea to invite me. To this Mike ventured: "Well actually I've already done so" to which Allan had apparently replied "Oh good".

When I arrived at our host's house and heard Allan's gravelly voice echoing along the corridor I knew that all would be well. He burst into the drawing room, gave me an appraising look and with a great twinkle in his eye announced "All ticketyboo!" We had a lot to catch up on and I'm afraid the other guests didn't have the benefit of his usual ebullience that evening.

Needless to say it was I who made the next move and invited him to a dinner party a month or two later. After some initial uncertainty he accepted and the evening was a success. We then began to meet very happily indeed on a regular basis for about six years.

Initially, when we got together again, I was able to agree with Allan's wish that, as before, there should be 'no commitment' and was quite sure then that I could handle this. The very mention of the word love caused him to become seriously agitated. But the physical attraction was still there 'in spades' and we had a close relationship, which I certainly could not have sought to rekindle or continue with had there not been a deep rapport between us. However, I vowed within myself that if the going got rough again, love or no love, I would call it a day.

He went through a very rough patch a year or two later when he was diagnosed as having throat cancer. Very fortunately this was treated successfully, helped probably by his very positive attitude to it all, but it took time and caused him a lot of pain and discomfort, which he always made light of. He made a trip down to Dorset and agreed to come to a lunch party given by the Howletts when he could hardly eat or speak, but he made great efforts on both counts. Geoffrey Howlett had served with him in the past and Elizabeth had acted as his hostess on a number of social occasions.

To aid his recovery I found a splendid cookery book full of recipes to help various illnesses and took him bowls and dishes of tempting morsels that would slip easily down his sore throat and help keep up his strength. The cancer certainly didn't stop him living life to the full as was his wont. But it did stop him hogging the conversation with his friends at the golf club each day for a while, which he was the first to admit.

Those years with Allan back in my life made an enormous difference to my life in general and were almost the answer to the many years of wishing and hoping. I say almost, because of course being happily married to him would have seemed the obvious zenith. But it wouldn't have been, as he had known from the start and as I with the years had come to realise and accept. I was more than grateful for what we had.

XXVII

Difficulties of life in Hooke

When I first came to live in Hooke, on retirement, the fears and forebodings I had had earlier about settling in the country as a 'single girl' had become a reality. Although I had made some very good friends and socially my feet hardly touched the ground, there were difficulties. On the whole I learnt to manage them, but there were occasions when I couldn't and in 1993 I decided to put my house on the market and start afresh. I looked at houses over a fairly wide area but saw nothing I liked and in any event the house market was at a low ebb and I couldn't get the price I wanted for my cottage so took it off the market.

Things settled down a bit but in 1997 'neighbours from hell' moved into the cottage next door to mine. Up until then I had been very lucky with neighbours, but everything changed almost from the day they arrived. As I knocked at their open door to introduce myself and to offer any help they might need, there was a great rushing noise and a big brown bull terrier threw itself at my back and nipped my collar. Apologies all round, but the die was cast. They were a young couple and both were social workers. They had five cars between them, a couple of these bearing rude and provocative stickers on the windows. The cars took up all the available parking space and very often prevented me from getting in and out of my garage. I tried reasoning with them but to no avail and as relations became impossible there was nothing for it but to put my house on the market once again. My one hope was that they would be out of sight when any potential buyers came to view the house.

XXIX

Mexico

Things had got seriously on top of me at this point so when Malcolm and Kerstin invited me to stay with them in Mexico City, I leapt at the chance and spent a glorious three weeks there. The flight out was not without its dramas as my luggage, along with that of sixteen other passengers was not transferred to the onward flight to Mexico when we changed planes at Houston. When they met me off the flight and heard this news, they were completely unphased and Malcolm calmly said that we should await the arrival of the next flight from Houston "otherwise we may never see the luggage again". We sat drinking whisky in an airport restaurant for what seemed a lifetime and exchanging years' of news until the flight arrived and, miraculously, I was reunited with my luggage. By the time we reached their home I had been travelling for the best part of 24 hours and was more than ready to 'hit the hay', as were they.

I have seldom enjoyed a holiday more. Malcolm and Kerstin were the most wonderful hosts and the three weeks sped past in an atmosphere of total enjoyment and a great deal of fun and laughter.

Their house, in an attractive neighbourhood high above the city, was light and modern and one of about eight similar houses within a compound surrounded by high walls. Entrance to the compound was through a massive, electronically-operated metal gate attended by two guards. Some 200 yards down the road was a police checkpoint and everyone and every car was scrutinised before being allowed to proceed further. As armed robbery was fairly rampant in Mexico City all this lent a comforting sense of security.

The only outing attempted on my first day, suffused as I was by jetlag, was to a huge shopping centre full of modern shops and restaurants. I think the shop selling music in all its forms was the largest and most impressive. At one point we sat on a marble bench savouring delicious yoghourt icecreams. As part of mine melted and fell to the spotless marble floor a cleaner appeared from nowhere to mop it up. I apologised to her and she answered with a smile: "That's what I'm here for."

Not all the Mexicans in the busy streets of this massive, straggling city looked so well-disposed and I was glad to be escorted everywhere by Malcolm. We drove by car through dense and endless traffic and the air smelt strongly of diesel fumes. We did a tour of Mexico City and then out of town to the Teotihuacan Pyramids. I climbed a bit of the way up the narrow steps of the Pyramid of the Sun but was glad to be back on terra firma again after the steep and precarious descent with nothing to hold on to and was ready for a cooling drink. As we sat outside a restaurant overlooking this vast and ancient landscape, I noticed an English couple sitting nearby. The man seemed to be a familiar figure and at first I wondered if he was one of our ambassadors, but then the penny dropped; it was John Mortimer, the playwright, and his wife.

On another day we visited the museum which was the home of the artist Freda Kahlo. The walls of the courtyard outside were painted a rich blue and rather gloomy trees and potted plants prepared one for the interior of the house. The memory of her anguished mind and tortured body seemed all-pervading; the result of her marriage to the famous Mexican painter, Diego Riviera, and the accident she had as a young woman, which crippled her. The walls of the house were hung with her strange self portraits, mirroring her painful existence. I went to an exhibition of her works in London some years later and found myself buying the Exhibition book. I don't think I have opened it since, but I did buy at her home a print of one of Diego Riviera's still life paintings and never tire of looking at it.

Kerstin was still working at The Swedish Trade Council in Mexico City so couldn't join us during the days, but one evening all three of us went to a wonderful concert commemorating the 90th anniversary of the Swedish telephone company, L M Ericsson's presence in Mexico, the company for which

Kerstin's first husband had worked. A champagne reception got the evening off to a good start and may well have contributed to the lively performance which followed. The piece which really gave me the greatest pleasure was called 'Huapango' by José Pablo Moncayo and the skill, energy and downright enjoyment shown by the Conductor was wonderfully reflected in the animated and happy faces of the members of the orchestra. What a success. I made sure to take a recording of that special Mexican piece home with me to lighten the darkness of the winter evenings.

These were just some of the highlights of that Mexican visit in 1994, but there were more to follow in 2000 and 2003. In the meantime there was my move to Sherborne to contend with.

XXX

Moving to Sherborne

I decided to move to the Abbey town of Sherborne because it seemed to be civilised and attractive, with a singularly beautiful Abbey Church to which I had been going on occasions ever since moving to Dorset. Hooke was without a doubt a bit isolated, looking towards a time when driving a car would no longer be feasible. Selling my cottage did prove a real problem. It took time and the sale was fraught with difficulties which seemed to drag on and on and on. Nevertheless, there is a time for everything and the protracted sale allowed me to find a gem of a house right in the centre and two minutes from the Abbey, in South Street. South Street had been called Duck Lane in earlier days when the water from the old Conduit, which was where the monks did their ablutions, flowed down the street, to the delight of the ducks. Allen Hill always referred to it as 'Dirty Water Street'!

The house was in a pitiful state of repair as a lady of 92 years, who had recently died, had lived there for some 30 years without doing a great deal to it. Sheila Hill and Elizabeth Howlett came over to view it, and then, leaving me in discussion with an electrician, they returned later clutching details of several other, "more suitable" houses. When Winfy saw it she exclaimed: "You can't possibly live here and with only a downstairs bathroom." However, my mind was made up; the price was very reasonable and I applied for a mortgage to renovate it.

It never occurred to me to employ a builder to oversee the work and thank goodness I didn't; it would almost certainly have taken very much longer than the five weeks it eventually took to replace some floorboards, damp proof and spray the house against woodworm, insulate the loft, install gas and put in central heating, fit a new kitchen and new windows. At one stage it was all rather overwhelming and I suddenly realised that the new carpets were to be fitted the following day and there were piles of rubbish both upstairs and downstairs. How to get rid of it quickly? Eventually I rang the man in charge of the town rubbish tip who went by the splendid name of Mr Murgatroyd. We discussed his name and my mother's maiden name, Farthing, for a bit and then I put my plea to him. "I'll just get on to my Guv'nor and ring you back," he said. True to his word he called back within minutes and asked when I wanted the stuff removed: "Midday tomorrow, please," I replied. "It'll cost you £50," he said and at midday the following day a huge dust cart turned up and cleared the house of rubbish. It was probably the best £50 I had ever spent, thanks to Mr Murgatroyd.

I reckoned that some 40 people were in some way involved in getting the house together, including the estate agents, lawyers, workmen and inspectors. Only the electrician proved unreliable, but he 'came good' finally after some sharp words.

Whilst the work was underway Fiona and Andrew Boggis very kindly offered me the use of their holiday cottage at the bottom of Green Lane in Hooke village and I drove to Sherborne each day to oversee the work which was being done on the house. There was a slight worry about timing as the Boggis family were coming down for Easter so it was important that my house be ready to move into before that deadline. Thankfully it was and the garden, an important feature of the property, was a mass of daffodils and looking lovely. I moved in during the last week in May 1999.

Death of my Mother

Early on the morning of 7 June I had a telephone call from Sheila, my sister-in-law, to say that Mummy had died in the night. In her final years she had become totally blind and although comfortably housed in a little flatlet in a congenial nursing home, the quality of her life was quite naturally badly diminished and she had had enough and wanted to die. She suddenly became ill late one evening and Chris, my brother, was summoned. He drove her to The Royal Berks Hospital, where the medical staff, after examining her, said they could find nothing wrong. They ordered an ambulance to take her home and after an interminable wait, with Mummy becoming more and more distressed,

Chris decided to drive her home himself. However, as he tried to get her out of the car and into the house she barely had the strength to stand. By that time it was midnight and none of the staff were about to help at first. Someone did eventually come and Mummy was put to bed. Chris kissed her goodnight and left. During the night she became extremely restless and agitated and cried for water. The night nurse, who was sitting with her did what she could and was with her when she died a short time later. Her pulmonary artery had burst. So much for the views of the medical staff at the hospital. Chris and I arranged her funeral and fortunately a vicar she had known in the past at Christchurch in Reading, where she and Dick had worshipped for so many years, was available to take her funeral. He asked me to write a short summary of her life on which he could draw for his eulogy. In the end he decided to read what I had written as it stood and I felt that she too would have been happy with it.

Although our relationship was a disappointing one for both of us for most of my adult life, we seemed to get on better towards the end, when probably we had both mellowed. Her death filled me with a great sadness, not entirely because she had gone, as it had to happen and she was at last at peace, but because we had failed to be to each other what each of us had wanted. It is an extraordinary thing that, since her death, not a day goes by when I don't think of her or hear her giving me advice, usually sound advice on the minutae of every day living. It is almost as if, in failing me in life, as I always felt she had, she is now making up for this and I welcome the advice which I frequently spurned in my youth. Furthermore, I see her every time I look into the mirror, which isn't quite so comforting. But as Oscar Wilde once said: "All women become like their mothers".

Not long after she died, I had a dream in which she appeared looking very glum. It's not a bit like I thought it would be, she seemed to be telling me, at which I thought that, as in life, she was never really satisfied. Some time later she appeared in another dream and this time she looked happy and radiant and was waving goodbye to me. This was the happiest of conclusions for someone who had fought in a single-minded, uncompromising way throughout her life for what she believed to be right. The nurses who cared for her latterly described her with great affection and respect as 'a feisty lady' and most of them came to her funeral.

Immediately after the funeral I drove down to Cornwall to join the Askerswell Painting Group, which I had been invited to join some years previously. They were enjoying a week's painting holiday near Padstow. It was a lively group of like-minded people and we always had a good deal of fun together. Many of them were very accomplished painters of a standard to which I never aspired. But I enjoyed our weekly sessions in the Village Hall at Askerswell, deep in the heart of Dorset, a short distance from Eggardon Hill, or as Thomas Hardy called it in his book 'The Trumpet-Major': 'Haggardon Hill' and the 'hill fortress of Eggar' in 'My Cicely'. It has an Iron Age hill-fort at its summit where, on most days, a continuous stream of dog-owners can be seen walking round it's perimeter come rain or come shine. A herd of wild deer can sometimes be seen grazing below, among which there used to be one white one. It is said that a ghostly band of Romans on horseback gallop up the hill at the dead of night. We very often used this road when returning home from parties, avoiding the main roads for obvious reasons, and I never once did so without wondering if the ghostly Romans would overtake me, but they never did.

It is an unbelievably beautiful area, just within sight of the sea. From my home in Hooke I could motor down to the beach at either Burton Bradstock or West Bay and be in the water in about 25 minutes flat. This I did almost daily each summer when the weather was reasonably good and the sea not too rough. There was a small cafe on the beach at Burton Bradstock, which produced the most delicious fresh crab sandwiches, so even if swimming wasn't possible the crab sandwiches were a great draw. Two of my Askerswell painting friends, Mary Gibson and Phyllida Horniman, relished daily swims pretty much whatever the weather or the temperature of the sea and seemed to suffer no ill effects. More power to them.

Dowsing

Towards the end of the painting week in Cornwall I came down with a tummy bug. To begin with the doctor thought it was a reaction to Mummy's death, but when I failed to recover tests were done and I awaited the results with some anxiety. The Consultant, a cancer specialist, had to consult a gastro-enterologist to help interpret the results whilst I waited with bated breath. Finally he said "When the body has been abused for a long time it suddenly says: 'Sod it, I've had enough.' Be careful what you eat and don't watch the television when you are eating." A really confidence-inspiring diagnosis which left me relieved but speechless with rage.

I wondered if the water in my new abode could have been the cause, and had it tested. Nothing dangerously untoward was discovered and eventually I got a dowser to bring her crystal to bear in various parts of the house. In the sitting room the crystal began to spin ferociously as it also did just outside in the garden. She deduced that there were strong negative energies in these two areas, which could well have a detrimental effect on my health. Then her assistant, whose crystal had also been spinning violently, went out to their car and returned with a metal stake which he drove into the ground at the top of the garden. We waited about ten minutes for the negative vibes to give way to positive ones, as they explained, and then they left assuring me that I would feel a lot better very soon. They thought that there might be water running beneath the house which, they said, would exacerbate any ill effects I had been experiencing. To cut a long story short, it was discovered a couple of years later that I was suffering from ceoliac disease, and after going onto a wheat- and gluten-free diet I felt a great deal better – and not before time.

Keeping up with the family

Although I had visited Mummy regularly after returning to live in England, I had rarely seen the rest of my immediate family on my own. After she died I began to see Chris and Sheila, my brother and sister-in-law and very often their family too in my own right so-to-speak. I still do to this day and these are always relaxed and happy occasions. They live a completely different life from mine and I envy them being so happily married and surrounded by children and grand-children. Their eldest daughter, Julie, is one of my Godchildren

I also keep up with Janet and John Morley, my step-sister and brother-in-law. They have a happily married family and six grandchildren and their youngest son, Chris, is one of my Godsons. John and Chris are the keen owners of an AUSTER J1 Autocrat 1947 plane which they both enjoy piloting. Chris became a civilian pilot when he left the Army but John gained his pilot's licence much later in life. Janet, one might say, 'sews for England' and produces mountains of hats, teacosies and the like as a hobby and sells them at local shows and fêtes with great success.

In the same way, I have kept up with Mummy's half-sister, Penny and Geoffrey her husband and their families. When motoring up to Perthshire to play golf, I usually spent a night or two with them in Poulton-le-Fylde in Lancashire when they arranged a lovely programme of sightseeing and very often a Halle Orchestra concert in Manchester. They eventually retired to Chichester to be near to their daughter Hilary, her husband Nigel and their two children. My visits there have been much more frequent and always very enjoyable. I must say that at one point when I felt like moving away from Hooke to be in a town, I toyed with the idea of looking for a house in Chichester, which in a way is a bit like Sherborne, although bigger, but with a lovely Cathedral and a particularly good climate. And of course the sea has always been a great draw. However, I settled instead for Sherborne.

One of the advantages of living in Sherborne was that it was a mere 20 or so kilometres from my old home and my old friends, all of whom I was able to keep up with, including my long-suffering old friend Winfy when her busy and altruistic schedule allowed. Helen and Tony Nunn, with whom I had played a lot of bridge over the years, lived at Longburton, a 10 minute drive from my house in Sherborne and they continued to be staunch friends in every way until Helen died a few years ago; no-one could have been more sadly missed. I made several more friends fairly quickly in and around Sherborne because one or two ex-FCO colleagues lived in the area and introduced me around. South Street itself was full of particularly friendly souls.

One of the most important of these was Pauline Willis who arrived in Sherborne shortly after I did. She had been working for the Editor of 'The Guardian' newspaper for many years but had had to retire early when she developed Parkinson's Disease. We got on well right from the very start, although our views on many things were poles apart. We begged to differ, usually quite amicably but most of the time avoided talking about the things on which we disagreed, which needless to say included politics. She was gentle, amusing and stimulating in the most relaxing way. She and two nice men, John Allan and Tony Sparshott, who were also retired, lived next to her in Bainton House, which had been split into large and attractive flats, although Pauline's was more of a little house, with a gravelled courtyard at the back, where they could park their cars. We all envied them this no end because residents' parking was at a premium in the town. Eventually I was able to rent a garage at the end of the road; it was very expensive but well worth it.

Canterbury Cathedral

Pauline's brother, Robert had earlier been a universally popular Vicar of Sherborne Abbey, so Pauline already had a good circle of friends, particularly among the regular church goers. Robert went on to be Dean of Hereford Cathedral and later Dean of Canterbury. An engaging man, he faced most things with an air of calm, efficiency and good-nature, helped by a very active sense of humour. I visited him with Pauline at Hereford Cathedral and spent two fascinating Christmases with them at The Deanery in Canterbury as well as attending his Installation as Dean there. This was a magnificent occasion, not unlike a mini Coronation in its grandeur. I had visited Canterbury Cathedral once before, purely as a 'pilgrim', but this was quite different and through Robert I learnt a lot about the workings of this great and beautiful centre of the Anglican Church and met so many of those closely involved in it, including Archbishop George Carey. I was surprised to find that he seemed rather younger in spirit than his photographs showed.

The Christmas Services were quite literally 'divine' as was the music and the singing and I felt truly blessed to be part of the all-pervading deep sense of reverence both spiritual and historical in this great Cathedral.

Robert always gives his sermons as if spontaneously and without notes. The Crib Service culminating at the main Cathedral entrance around the crib was very special. The children gathered round and hung onto every word as Robert told a story about a possessive and selfish little spider who lived in the manger where the baby Jesus lay, and who didn't want to share him with any other spiders. It had a moral of course and was a totally enchanting story even for we adults.

After attending Matins on Christmas Day, I accompanied Robert and Pauline to the ancient Town Hall where the Mayor was hosting his traditional Christmas Reception. Slightly at a loss as we entered the party, knowing no-one, not even the Mayor himself, my anxieties were quickly assuaged when Robert said: "Hang on to my coat-tail" and as I did so he introduced me as we went round the assembled throng. And of course everyone was friendly and welcoming and I enjoyed every minute. Once back at The Deanery, Robert proceeded to prepare the traditional Christmas Dinner for us all and very good it was too and included a gluten-free Christmas pudding for me and a chocolate pudding for another of his guests who couldn't eat a normal Christmas pudding.

Soon after I arrived he showed me round the Deanery Library, the walls of which were hung with portraits of former Deans. As we came to The Reverend Hewlett-Johnson, also known as the Red Dean, I muttered: "Silly old fool!". "Why so?" queried Robert. "Because he was said to be a communist," I replied. Later in my visit I felt that the Red Dean may well have had a tiny revenge for the simple reason that when I went to pack an immaculate skirt I had worn at a drinks party given by one of the Canons and his wife the previous evening, the whole hem was hanging down, although I was sure it had been intact when I put it away the night before. In these days of 'political correctness' I would probably have held my tongue rather than giving my views on the Red Dean and saved myself the job of re-doing the hem!

Friends in Sherborne

By the greatest of good fortune, a couple whom I had known slightly when living at Hooke, Owen and Virginia Scholte and their younger son Matthew, moved to Sherborne on exactly the same day as I did. They moved from Pilsdon near Bridport amid some of the most beautiful Dorset scenery with a view over the hills to the sea. We soon became very good friends, helped by Peter Bevan, a mutual friend. Owen and Peter were at prep school together a lifetime ago. Peter's sister Polly was the wife of Sir Antony Duff, a former Ambassador and later Intelligence Coordinator at the Cabinet Office and Director-General of MI5 during Mrs Thatcher's Premiership. He was held in great awe and affection throughout Whitehall, but a more unassuming man it would be difficult to find. He and Polly eventually retired to Dorset, not far from Sherborne and I was able to get to know them both a little better. Tony Duff died, very sadly, in August 2000 but I still enjoy keeping in touch with Polly and seeing her on my visits to Sherborne. They had both been involved in charitable works for many years and Peter, cast in the same mould, had done a long stint helping at the Joseph Weld Hospice at Dorchester and as well as being of enormous help to his friends and is always on hand to assist at Conservative events and suchlike in and around Beaminster .

I saw a great deal of Owen and Virginia during my years in Sherborne and it was always great fun being with them. What made it such an easy friendship was that I was and still am very fond of them both and believe the feeling is mutual. So often the husbands of friends, particularly those I had known before they married, found it difficult to accept me as a friend of them both. They knew me as an old friend of their wives and in some cases seemed to resent our long-standing friendship. Sometimes when I went to stay with one such couple for weekends I seemed by my very presence to change the whole chemistry of their relationship; they would begin to snipe at each other and an uneasy atmosphere would build up and in the end I preferred not to stay with them at all. Funnily enough it seemed to work better when they came to stay with me.

On the 24th of August 2001 I celebrated my 70th Birthday with a buffet lunch party on the lawn outside The Orangery in the grounds of Sherborne Castle.

The setting was wonderful, surrounded by ancient trees and flower gardens and with a clear view over the lake. It was a glorious day and we milled about in the shade of the huge gingko biloba tree. Some old friends such as Mary née Rutherford, my old flatmate of 50 years ago, came from as far away as St Andrews in Fife and Anne née Glendinning, whom I'd known since 1967 when we served in Caracas together, from Beverley in Yorkshire and Rosemary née Norden who I first met serving in Berlin in 1964 from Nottingham. John and Tita Shakeshaft provided the champagne and wine as a birthday present and a very generous one too. They came the night before as did Rosemary and as we unloaded the wine at the Castle together that evening with the help of the Castle Administrator, I realised that we were all ex-members of the FCO – even the Administrator, so it was a bit like old times abroad. We were some 40 in all and I felt it was something of a highlight in my life to be in a position to host such a party and in such an historical and lovely spot.

The castle, or the New Castle as it is called had been built by Sir Walter Raleigh in 1594 on the site of an old hunting lodge, not far from the Old Castle of which only ruins now remain. I think Sir Walter just might have been able to see us all from his favourite seat in the park overlooking the town. John Shakeshaft proposed a toast and gave a splendid little speech, to which I was able to reply with no nervousness, thanks to the champagne and it really was one of the happiest days I can remember, surrounded by so many friends from so many phases of my life.

XXXI

More Holidays Abroad

Sweden

I paid fairly regular visits to Haverdal, either to join in Irma and Christer Borlind's family Christmas or a summer break when the children and grandchildren were there. It was always a lot of fun and I enjoyed meeting up with their friends who I had come to know well after so many years. We swam, played golf, wined and dined well at home and with their friends and family.

Very sadly Irma died of cancer in 1993 and her untimely death was a devastating blow to us all. She was warm and spontaneous and in some ways unworldly and in others amazingly shrewd. She was universally liked and was like a sister to me over some 40 years. Her marriage to Christer had been a supremely happy one and with their son, Christian and daughter, Birgitta, now both married with children of their own, they were a very close-knit and happy family.

On a happier note, Hans-August, a Herlenius cousin and a doctor who, among other things, did a stint with the UN Forces in the Gaza Strip, together with his wife Birgit, a Consultant Gynaecologist, began what was to become a regular event: a Herlenius Cousins' Party. It was held during the summer and I very often combined going to this with a visit to Haverdal to see Christer and the family and then he and I would motor up to their home in Falun in

Dalarna. It was, and still is a beautiful home, elegant in the light Swedish style but homely and welcoming, with a vast swimming pool in the rather grand basement area. Birgit in particular tends a most beautiful garden and also keeps bees. We were royally looked after and although we were often as many as ten staying over the weekend, our two hosts coped in the most astonishingly relaxed way. Since Hans-August's death in April 2003. Birgit has continued in the same relaxed way with this very jolly annual event.

Their house is a short drive from 'Sundborn', the home of the celebrated Swedish artist Carl Larsson and his wife Karen, whose handwork, weaving and embroidery was on a par with her husband's wonderfully evocative paintings. The house is now an attractive museum, in a magical setting which still reflects the thriving and industrious life they must have enjoyed with their many children, who feature so largely in Carl Larsson's paintings.

Mexico

All in all I went to Mexico to stay with Malcolm and Kerstin on three occasions during my years in Dorset. Each time I stayed with Allan the night before leaving and also on my return. He would drive me to the airport and on the return trip I would catch the airport bus to Reading where he would be there to meet me. I never failed to thank God (and Allan, of course) for this and so many other blessings. I had finally come within a hair's breadth of what I had always longed and prayed for, after meeting up with him again in 1993.

After one nightmare journey from Mexico to New York in 2000 when heavy falls of snow caused all the flights throughout the States to be grounded, I was stranded at Dallas Airport for over 8 hours, along with thousands of other passengers. When eventually I boarded a plane we were kept hanging about on the tarmac whilst luggage was being off-loaded as were a number of passengers, because, the Captain told us, we were overloaded. The Captain sounded almost hysterical, so I, along with one or two other uneasy passengers decided to disembark and seek a less chaotic flight. This was not easy and involved a further wait. The fact that my luggage was on another plane was a problem to be put behind me for the time being.

We arrived in New York at some unearthly hour of the morning and to my utter amazement my luggage was sitting on the edge of a huge pile in the Arrivals Hall. A kindly and astute West Indian porter took hold of it, steered me to the front of the endless taxi queue and whispered a quick word to the lady in charge. Instead of being lynched by the poor people behind I was bundled into a taxi before you could say 'knife' and on my way to my old friend Nickie Benjamin in Park Avenue.

Although I had kept Nickie informed during the various stages of my journey as to when I might arrive to stay with her for a couple of days on my way home to the UK, she was in a state of near hysteria when I did arrive. It had been on such a night that bad weather had paralysed the air traffic and the plane bearing her husband had crashed and she, poor girl, was re-living that terrible night. Needless to say I was mortified to have been the cause of this, but rather than being gentle with her I chose to react rather brusquely to counteract her hysteria. She rallied and as always staying with her in one of my favourite cities was a delight, but tinged this time with sadness.

What I didn't know then was that she had just been diagnosed with the cancer from which she eventually died. It was no wonder that she was in such a nervous state and I regret to this day not being gentler with her. I kept in touch by letter and telephone during her illness, but was never to see her again. It had been a remarkable friendship in that over the space of nearly fifty years we saw each other, either in New York or in England and once in Copenhagen when I was en poste there, no more than about 7 or 8 times in all yet always took up where we left off as if there had been no gap. We corresponded of course in fits and starts over the years and each Christmas I still get an up-to-date photograph from Bob, her son, and his wife Ellenore of their two girls, Susannah and Sarah who are developing into splendidly good-looking young ladies.

The overnight flight back to London from New York after that awful delay in Dallas was trouble-free until I tried to reach Allan on the phone on arrival. I had left a message the day before on his answerphone to confirm the time of my arrival at Heathrow. But now his number was permanently engaged and in desperation for fear of missing the bus to Reading, I rang his wonderful neighbours, Helen and Tim Batty, explained the problem, which they promised to sort out and then just succeeded in catching the next bus to Reading.

Allan was there to meet me, looking slightly bothered, along with the Batty's son, Dan, in their car. Allan's car was being repaired and I never did quite find out what had happened and decided it was better not to press the point. Allan had booked a table at one of his favourite restaurants not far from Henley and after sleeping off the jet lag I was looking forward to a happy and relaxed lunch.

But Allan was out of sorts; he had had a series of difficult commitments, including attending the funeral of his brother-in-law in Cornwall and was pretty exhausted. I realised, too late, that meeting and putting me up was 'a bridge too far'. However robust he had always been, he was now over 80 years and was beginning to slow down. Had I tried ringing him again from New York instead of just leaving a message, things would probably have been different. Although he would have been the last person to admit that there was a problem, meeting arrangements could have been confirmed or altered.

The Break-up

The reason I recount this all in such detail is because it heralded the break-up of our relationship. Such things are never clear cut and no one person can be said to have been at fault, if fault there was. I had accepted when we met up again after so many years that there would be no real commitment on his part and truly believed that I could just go on loving him on those terms. Eventually, of course, it proved to be beyond me. I had vowed that if things got really difficult again, I would give up and I did. It was a big wrench, but nothing like the anguish I had battled with in earlier years, when it almost felt as if I had lost a limb each time we parted. For the umpteenth time I consoled myself with the old adage: 'Better to have loved and lost than never to have loved at all', although I tend to believe that no love is ever really lost and I accepted long ago that, if 'you don't like the heat, get out of the kitchen'. But I chose not to over so many years, so have only myself to blame. I have no regrets, except that I longed to be married and have a family, but it just wasn't to be.

France

While spending a Christmas with Christer Borlind and family in Sweden, it emerged that he was interested in going to France to see the Normandy Beaches and the War Cemetaries, about which he had read so much. So too was I and in all my travels I had only once been to Paris and then only to collect a new Peugeot car when en poste in Geneva in 1974.

A plan was hatched and in October 2000 Christer drove over to Sherborne from his home in Haverdal. After showing him the sights in and around Sherborne for a few days we set off for France. It was such fun to have a travelling companion and one who was happy to do the driving. Christer and I had always got on well and I liked and respected him and enjoyed his sense of fun. In his younger days he could be fairly daunting when he wanted to be as befitted his calling as a judge. He once invited me to sit in on a court case over which he was presiding in Halmstad. As he disappeared into the courtroom I sat with some lawyers all waiting for the court to open. Next to us was the accused with a fair number of his family, a bit too close for comfort I felt and without a policeman in sight. But nothing unforeseen happened and at the end of the hearing the accused was led away and suddenly the presiding judge, Christer, beckoned me forward. As I made my way towards him I almost felt as though I had committed some felony or other. But he grinned and whispered: "See you outside in about ten minutes!" Behind the stern exterior lurked a splendid sense of humour.

We took the ferry to Cherborg where we spent the night and in the morning after visiting the rather stark Liberation Museum there drove down to the Utah and Omaha Beaches, visited the War Museums and one or two of the War Cemetaries. Allan had once described the war cemetaries to me and when walking round one vast cemetary, Batteria des Longues, with row upon row of the graves of young men, struck down in their prime, his words came back to me and I was glad but sad to have been there.

We spent the night at the Marine Hotel at Arromanches and marvelled at the Mulberry Harbour, the remains of which could be seen from the hotel and the beach. That such a harbour and bridge could have been constructed in England, transported and erected so precisely off the French coast all within a fortnight and without the knowledge of the Germans was no less than a miracle. To be used to bring ashore hundreds of men and heavy equipment even when the weather deteriorated into a storm at the eleventh hour was an altogether magnificent effort of planning and sheer indomitability. At the Pegasus Bridge we visited the area where the first Parachute Regiment soldiers had landed, not altogether comfortably and then we read the harrowing accounts in the comfort of the museum there. The whole experience was one of incredulity and admiration.

Greatly moved we then made our way to the more peaceful atmosphere of Claude Monet's home and his famous garden. Maddeningly it poured with rain, but was well worth even a wet visit. I loved the tiled kitchen and the Chinese and Japanese prints gracing so many of the walls of the house and the lake and the bridge one knew so well from his paintings.

We then headed for Paris, calling at Versailles for, sadly, only a quick look at the gardens, but enough to appreciate the history and the grandeur there. We had another whistle stop to look at the Bayeux Tapestry, which narrated events leading up to the invasion of England by William of Normandy and the Battle of Hastings in 1066. Again, it was time-honoured and stirring stuff all beautifully worked and displayed, but the museum was very crowded and one wasn't able to study the Tapestry too closely in the time we had available.

I have to say that finding our way into Paris and our hotel was not the smooth run it had looked when planning our route on the map; it never is, but my map-reading had nothing to commend it. Our hotel was very close to the Arc de Triomphe, which should have simplified things; however, once there we had a head start for seeing the main sights, which we did together each morning and then went our separate ways after, usually, a very good lunch. The very best of these and at a very reasonable price was at the Moulin de la Galette restaurant in Montmartre. It sported a lot of red plush and there were mirrors everywhere, as one might expect from such a venue. Oddly enough we seemed to be the only foreigners, which added to the wholly French atmosphere of the place.

On our way out to dine one evening we found ourselves in close proximity to rows of armed gendarmerie. We followed them with interest. Police sirens battered our eardrums as we made our way down the Champs Elysees. Christer, being more versed in the ways of the criminal classes than I was and a bit more cautious, was all for keeping our distance, but nevertheless we pressed on. The excitement intensified as we neared our chosen restaurant, which was open but empty of customers. I asked the maitre d'hotel who was standing at the door, what all the commotion was about and he simply shrugged in the way that M. Clouzot might have done, faced with an unexpected corpse. It turned out to be a fairly peaceful demonstration of Arabs and Israelis, the reason for which I cannot now recall, who were all milling around the Israeli Embassy nearby. We had a magnificent meal watched with some envy, I think, by some of the demonstrators who peered at us through the windows, but thankfully gradually dispersed Our slight feelings of unease were greatly assuaged by the maitre d'hotel's initial shrug.

One way or another we had time and energy to see most of the things we had planned to see. Christer, who had been to Paris before was happy to come with me to the Louvre where we made straight for the Venus de Milo and of course I was not disappointed. Nor was I disappointed in Paris as a whole which I viewed from the top of the Big Wheel at the Colonade.

At the end of our stay Christer left for his long drive back to Sweden and I caught the Eurostar train back to England. This again was something I had longed to do, but it was a disappointment. The empty seats all seemed to be full of crumbs and the carpets covering the floor were badly stained and shabby. The service and the buffet car were mediocre. Whilst travelling through France we sped along at a good speed, but as soon as we crossed the border into England the train crawled along or stopped for long periods of time, when no explanation was offered. Ashford Station, the gateway to the UK so-to-speak was a disgrace. A lot of construction work was going on so it is possible that this has now resulted in a more impressive and welcoming milieu. To add insult to injury the Eurostar arrived very late at Waterloo and there was an ugly rush to get out through the doors and away. Despite a concerted dash through Waterloo Station I missed the train to Sherborne and had to wait another hour for the next one. It was chilly and I caught the cold to end all colds and spent the worst of it penning a disgruntled letter to the Eurostar management. Surprisingly, it evoked a polite and positive reply and a single free ticket to Paris, which went a long way to quelling my grievances. I haven't been back, so can only hope that the improvements promised in the letter have now been made.

Mexico again

Early in 2000 I went again to stay with Malcolm and Kerstin in Mexico. The highlight of this visit was to drive many miles and to a height of 10,000ft to see the famous Monarch butterflies. These beautiful creatures fly all the way down from North America and Canada to an area in Mexico where they breed. Malcolm drove us as far as he could and then, with a guide, we had to climb for about a mile up a stony track until we reached what our guide explained was one of the best spots from which to witness this amazing sight. The air was filled with millions of these butterflies, huge clusters of which rested on the branches of the surrounding trees. The only sound to be heard was a rather uncanny and very faint rustling of butterfly wings. The best way I can describe it is that it closely resembled the sound of millions of poppies falling down at the end of the Armistice Day Remembrance Service each 10th November at the Royal Albert Hall. We watched in wonder and awed silence for a goodish time before retracing our steps back to the car. It had been a magical experience.

We stayed at a ranch-like hotel, Hotel Rancho, San Cayetano, run by a very sophisticated French lady and her Mexican husband. Some of our fellow guests, several of whom were members of local government, were engaged in hot discussions about this phenomenon and there appeared to be unpopular plans for the area which would have a deleterious effect on this miracle of nature. We didn't hear the outcome of these discussions and suspect that they may still be going on, but we enjoyed a deliciously cooked Mexican meal before turning in for the night and continuing on our way the next morning.

We visited the famous town of Taxco which is surrounded by silver mines so that the shops are predominantly full of silver articles of all standards. For example one could buy jewellry, such as simple stud earrings and bracelets, for next to nothing. But in the very expensive shops exquisite works of art were to be found, many of them a mixture of silver and delicately decorated enamel. A present to the Pope from the President of Mexico had been made in one of the workshops we visited and the owner showed us, with due reverence, a letter of appreciation he had received from the President. I vowed to return when 'my ship comes home'. But so far it hasn't.

On my last evening I treated Malcolm and Kerstin to dinner at the magnificent restaurant 'Los Morales' in Mexico City. Originally it had been a huge privately-owned ranch, but the owner lost so much money gambling that he had to pay off his debt with his ranch, or so the story goes. Suffice it to say that it is one of the best restaurants I have ever had the good fortune in which to dine.

The town of Cuernavaca also boasts a splendid hotel, Los Mañanitas, the gardens of which are home to some beautiful but noisy peacocks and round a vast lawn there are a number of first class Mexican sculptures.

On two occasions I was fortunate to stay in Cuernavaca with Dicky and Marina Skipsey whom I had first met at Malcolm and Kerstin's wedding in New York. Dickie is half Scots and half Mexican and Marina is Swedish and a more charming and engaging couple it would be difficult to find. Their home is full of exquisite works of art and their garden a work of art in itself, with terracotta pots and amphoras amid a swathe of ancient trees and tropical plants. We lunched beside their long, cool and enticing swimming pool and it was like being cocooned in a sort of paradise.

I left Mexico City at some unearthly hour the morning after our splendid dinner at Los Morales. Malcolm and Kerstin stoically drove me to the airport and then the nightmarish trip on to New York described above unfolded. But worse was to befall Malcolm. He had had a niggling pain in his chest for some time, which he had mentioned to no-one. But it had worsened after our recent heavy programme so he decided to have it checked out. It turned out to be extremely serious and within hours he was on a plane to Houston, accompanied of course by Kerstin, and underwent heart surgery there on the recommendation of his son Gustav, who is a transplant surgeon in Sweden.

On my arrival home, I rang Göran, Malcolm's brother, to pass on greetings only to be told of the awful events which had taken place after my departure. Luckily the operation went well and in no time Malcolm rang me from the hospital in Houston to say that he was fine and flying back to Mexico in a couple of days. He mentioned that, when he told his Mexican doctor about our trip to see the Monarch butterflies, the man was astounded that Malcolm hadn't suffered a heart attack then. I must say that it was indeed a miracle as that last slog up the hill at an altitude of 10,000 feet, in relentless heat, was taxing by any standards. I privately put his good luck down to the fact that we did so much laughing that whoever ordains these things just hadn't the heart to spoil the fun.

In 2003 my final visit to Malcolm and Kerstin started off badly. On the way out I had to change planes, this time in Chicago. As I made my way down the endless corridors towards the baggage hall, I suddenly realised that my handbag was missing. I had left it on my seat in the plane. Rather than trudge back, I used one of the emergency phones to alert the airport staff to my dilemma. "Just you wait right there lady and we'll get someone to come to you," the voice at the other end said. I just want my handbag back, rather than someone coming to me, I thought testily. There was a long silence around me, everyone else had gone, and I suddenly realised that my heavy suitcase would be going round and round the conveyor belt unclaimed and would be removed to goodness knows where. I picked up the phone again and the nice lady repeated her first message: to stay where I was and someone would come to me. There was nothing for it but to do as she said. After what seemed like a lifetime a figure appeared in the distance. To my huge relief, as she got nearer, I saw that she was smiling and patting my handbag. She was a plain-clothes policewoman by the name of Heather and after introducing herself she said, "I'm so sorry to have been so long, but I banged my head and had to sit down for a bit." Poor girl. In retrospect this was cause for a giggle, but not at the time. To complicate matters the stewardess on the plane had given me a final plate of fresh fruit, about the third or fourth, in lieu of the set meals containing gluten and it lay in a carrier bag, which I felt bound to declare. Heather took it all in her stride and said, "You'll need to go to 'Agriculture' with that," and pointed the way. At 'Agriculture' I said to the man: "I have a small problem." "Through this door here please," and there I was in the Baggage Hall;

plate-of-fresh-fruit-problem eliminated. My suitcase was being removed from the conveyor belt at that very moment. It had to be checked before my onward flight to Mexico City and as I opened it for the Customs official, I saw to my horror that the little packets of gluten-free bread mix looked just as I would imagine bags of cocaine would have looked. But they were of no interest to either the official or the metal detector which nosed its way through the suitcase and was only interested in bombs. At this point I bade a fond farewell to Heather who had been such a support throughout, despite her banged head, and made my anxious way to catch my onward flight.

Anyone who has been through Chicago Airport will know that it is one of the largest there is and the terminal I was heading for was at least a mile away. I hadn't any US money to get a trolley and in the end, worn down by lugging my bags so far and close to tears, I appealed to a policeman. He metaphorically dropped everything he was doing and carried all the bags the remaining half mile to my terminal. He was kind, courteous and quite chatty, allowing himself only to say in the nicest way: "Might be a good idea to have the odd dollar for a trolley with you next time, Mam". In fact on the way home I changed planes in Washington where the trolleys were free.

On arrival in Mexico City I was gathered up by Malcolm and Kerstin and all the trauma faded. Late though it was when we arrived at their home, we tucked into smoked salmon and champagne and they outlined their plans for the visit. They had arranged for us to drive down to Acapulco and stay for several nights at the 'Las Brisas' Hotel. It's a fairly long drive and although we stopped on the way for a breather, the sun was too hot for us to walk around. The hotel was perched on a hillside overlooking Acapulco Bay. The entrance was at ground level and once we had registered we were driven up the hill in a tiny little 4-wheel drive through a maze of chalets to our own two chalets between which lay our own private swimming pool. The hotel is a well known honeymoon spot and each morning the cleaning ladies placed red hibiscus flowers to form a heart on the table in my room and one on the pillow, together with either a chocolate or a tiny gift, on each bed. More hibiscus flowers were scattered on the surface of the pool and carefully replaced with fresh ones each day.

The first night we dined on the balcony of the hotel dining room, overlooking the twinkling lights around Acapulco Bay and it was all the travel brochures say it is and then some. The whole trip was a treat Kerstin had wanted to lay on for me and I could hardly believe it was really happening.

They took me to watch the famous pearl divers leap from enormous heights into a small area of churning water below. It was fairly dramatic as darkness had descended and spotlights picked out the figures of these intrepid young men who each said a prayer and crossed themselves at little altars behind the ledges from which they then dived, with enormous precision, into the swirling waters below. We later watched as they clambered back up the hillside. They were cheerful and fit and water drops, or perhaps sweat glistened on their well-oiled and firm brown bodies. They were greeted with well-deserved cheers as they reached terra firma again.

Once back in Mexico City each day was spent in a leisurely way but with plenty of gentle sightseeing during the day and delicious meals either expertly cooked by Kerstin or by kind and stimulating friends living nearby in the evenings. Relaxing music of all kinds was always playing quietly in the background. I spent many daylight hours wandering round the magnificent Archaelogical Museum and learning about the history of the Mexican peoples and their lifestyles, visiting various art collections, pausing now and then for light lunches or to rest my feet at an icecream parlour and to watch the world go by. The sun was always shining, the jacaranda trees had just started to bloom and their colour and delicacy added a wonderful lightness to the streets below, which teemed with nose-to-tail-traffic, the inevitable honking horns and police or ambulance sirens; the air thick with the smell of petrol. Every so often at road junctions there were mouth-watering displays of rich colour where florists were plying their trade at the roadside.

The three of us did a lot of serious talking about our respective futures. I had more or less made up my mind to go and live in the sunshine somewhere in the Mediterranean, but where I didn't quite know. Malcolm and Kerstin were still trying to make up their minds whether or not to move back to Sweden. After some 40-odd years of living in Mexico, this was a serious decision to have to make. Both had children and grandchildren in Sweden and this was one of the great draws. Although they were used to spending part of their summers there, Swedish winters are quite another thing and they were in the process of debating this and all the other issues such a draconian move would entail.

Cyprus

With my move to the sun in mind, Eve Walsh-Waring, an old Foreign Office friend, invited me to stay in the villa she rented each winter in Paphos in southern Cyprus. I went a couple of times and loved it. There were so many ancient sites and ruins to be seen, which we did in a leisurely fashion in a little hired Landrover. The beaches weren't quite as unspoilt and golden as those I'd been to in Malaysia, but the sunshine and warmth on a January day was a far cry from home in the UK.

I stayed there with Eve a couple of times and on the last occasion spent part of the time with Eve and then moved on to a smaller house which I had rented myself and was joined there by Jane Gross. We toured the many popular sights which Eve had shown me on earlier occasions. As we were wandering round the ruins of Old Paphos, I suddenly stopped at the sight of what looked like a shrivelled and brown dead snake. Jane thought it was a snakeskin which had been shed by its owner. "Let's just wait a minute and see if it moves," I said. And it did, gliding suddenly and silently into the undergrowth. We reported it to the officials at the entrance to the site, who, after asking us to describe it, exclaimed that it was a very poisonous snake. As I had just been about to step on it in my sandaled feet, I was grateful for the sixth sense that had stopped me in mid-step.

Although Cyprus had much to offer I decided that, although it was lovely for a holiday, I couldn't see myself living there permanently. The atmosphere was just not quite right and I had a feeling there might be problems with regard to Turkey and its wish to join the European Union, vis-a-vis the division of the island into Turkish and Greek areas. Also its proximity to the Middle East, in its usual state of flux, led me to look for somewhere else in the sunshine of the Mediterranean. It was then that the 'still small voice' suddenly whispered: "What about Spain?"

XXXII

Considering a Move to Spain

Now Spain was a country I had visited on my way back from Caracas in 1969, where with an office colleague as guide we had done a quick tour of Madrid and then in pouring rain she had driven me with great stoicism to Toledo. I remembered very little about it, except that I bought a copy of Don Quixote's sword which I had mounted into a stone, like Excalibur, and gave it to Allan for his birthday, intended as a door-stop, accompanied by an encouraging message, but with hindsight a rather pompous one, which said: "When you succeed in drawing the sword out of the stone, the secret of life will be revealed to you!" Romantic stuff, which bore no fruit at all of course.

Now, on a typically cold and dreary February day in 2003, back in Sherborne, I realised with more and more conviction that I needed to give up my life there. Everything seemed grey, particularly the skies above and life seemed to be standing still. Having read a bit about Spain and talked to friends who knew the country, it seemed to have a good deal to recommend it both as a country and as a prospective home.

My researches were encouraging enough to take me to an Overseas Property Exhibition at Grosvenor House Hotel in London in March 2003. Jane Gross came too and we wandered round the endless stands full of posters of tempting villas and apartments in the sunshine. Exhausted, I asked one of the stall-holders if I might just sit down for a minute. "Yes, of course," she said, then added "And I know you only want to sit here because you are tired." "Well its up to you to prove otherwise," I answered with a smile. And she did. Her sales patter was sensible and sympathetic, so much so that within a day or two I was on the phone to her to ask if she could fix me up with a little apartment in the seaside town of Moraira, just north of Alicante where her agency was based. Again, she did so. Not only that, but she and her ex-policeman husband met me off the plane at Alicante late at night and delivered me safely to the apartment which was to be my base for the next three weeks. I had no idea whether this part of Spain would be what I wanted, but had to start somewhere.

Needless to say, these forays into the unknown needed financing, and I had taken along to the local auction rooms in Sherborne my one diamond ring, an heirloom from my Godmother, Auntie Gee, a pair of pearl and diamond drop earrings, a Christmas present from Elsa and Jonas Herlenius and some gold jewellry I had bought myself over the years. They were all pieces I cherished and had enjoyed wearing on high days and holidays, but now they had to be translated into ready cash. I parted with them with great sadness, but needs must.

Visiting Spain

The apartment I rented in Moraira was an annex to a villa owned by an English couple who had left the UK some 8 years previously, mainly for health reasons. They were kindness itself throughout my stay. One evening there was a very heavy rainstorm and the lights went out. There were candles to hand and Linda, the owner, arrived with more. Soon after she left, I noticed that the rug by the door was changing colour. The rain was so heavy that it had come flooding in under the doors quite silently. Within minutes there was about a foot of water everywhere. Linda and her husband Derek came in and we spent the next couple of hours mopping it up. The wardrobe was the worst and my shoes and slippers were sodden. Otherwise the three weeks passed without mishap.

I did a lot of exploring in and around Moraira and went as far as Alicante to the south and Valencia to the north. But I knew that this area, attractive as it was, was not for me. Many foreigners had settled there and in Moraira these were predominantly British. They had lost no time taking over and running little general shops and had set up charity shops and clubs to cater for every possible hobby or interest and of course there were endless sandy beaches and promenades with restaurants galore. The ex-pats all looked 'as happy as sandboys' in their new and sunny environment. But I had to look further.

The FCO gave me the names of several ex-Office staff who were living in Spain, of whom I knew just three. Again, the Office came up trumps and wrote to tell them when I would be in Spain, giving them my telephone number at home and inviting them to get in touch before I left if they felt so inclined. Two of them did and as they both lived much farther south and no great distance from each other I planned the long trip down by car to see them and explore other areas of this vast and beautiful country.

The first couple invited me to lunch at their home in Frigiliana a few miles inland from the coastal town of Nerja and it was lovely to see them again and conversation flowed easily until it was time to drive on up to the little town of Periana where Heulyn Rayner lived.

The last time I had seen Heulyn was when she and her husband John Rayner gave me a farewell lunch at The Travellers Club in Pall Mall as I was about to retire from the FCO. When John died some years later, I wrote to Heulyn to offer my condolences and in her reply she wrote: 'Let's keep in touch'. I kept her letter for years, but when doing some weeding of accumulated letters just after deciding to move on from Sherborne, I thought: I doubt if I'll see Heulyn again and destroyed her letter. Little did I know what a superlative friend she would become.

She and John Rayner had been coming to Spain for a number of years and had a little house at Moya near Periana. After John died, Heulyn built a charming and elegant house overlooking Lake Viñuela, with the most magnificent views from every window of the lake and the surrounding mountains. I spent the night there and Heulyn was able to give me an idea of what it was like to live there in particular and in Spain in general. It all sounded too good to be true and I went on my way the following morning fired with enthusiasm.

I had a look at the coastal town of Nerja, which is a bit like Moraira, but a lot bigger and slightly more cosmopolitan and then to La Herredura, ten minutes up the coast where Don McNeil, a friend from Sherborne, had an apartment. He had been very helpful in briefing me before I left home on so many things I needed to know about living in Spain, as only an ex-Army officer could do, but after this long trip I still had no firm idea where to settle.

I made for Malaga, thinking to spend a night there and then return to Moraira, taking the Seville motorway rather than the coast road on which I had come down. It had been an interesting but rather deadening route, with so many of the coastal strips, like Benidorm, just a mass of high rise apartment blocks, seething with holiday makers. It was also slow with a lot of traffic near the towns.

I reached Malaga late in the afternoon, tired and with little idea quite how big the city would be. Looking for a likely hotel for the night while negotiating the traffic was not easy and when I saw a sign to The Parador I followed it. The Paradors are State-run hotels dotted all over the country, some of them in old and beautiful castles or stately homes, others modern but all attractive, comfortable and well-run. The one at Malaga was high above the city with a wonderful view over the vast harbour, but it was completely full. I was rather thankful because it was considerably more expensive than my budget really allowed. Without my even suggesting it, one of the Receptionists offered to ring round other hotels for me. A typical example of the kindness and helpfulness of the Spanish people. But he drew a blank. There was a film festival taking place in the town and there wasn't a room to be had. I must have looked fairly tired and forlorn by this time because he said "We have a Parador in a little town 45 kilometers north of Malaga; would you like me to see if they have a room?" I nodded. After telephoning he told me that they had one room and would know "in 5 minutes" whether I could have it. It was a very long 5 minutes but eventually to my joy and relief he signalled that the room was mine.

Finding my way out of the city just as offices were closing proved to be no easy task, but once on the right motorway I went zinging along to the little town of Antequera. The Parador was well-signposted and in no time I was safely and comfortably ensconced and running a soothing bath. As I looked across the plain, which was fast becoming a sea of bobbing lights as darkness fell, I knew instinctively that I had come home.

The following morning, despite being faced with the long drive back to Moraira, I made time to visit an estate agency in the main street, an elegant thoroughfare which bore out my instincts that this was a town of great aesthetic style and substance. I explained to the house agent that I would be returning within a month or two and would like to rent a property for 3-6 months in Antequera with a view to buying a house there; would he please look for something suitable. He promised to do this and I left my address and phone number and went on my way back to Moraira rejoicing.

I thought it would be unkind to tell my estate agent friend there of my plans at that point although actually she hadn't shown me any properties as my Sherborne house wasn't even on the market, but she did spend one afternoon showing me round the immediate area. She was also enthusiastic about living in Spain herself and took me to see the house that she and her husband were having built. We parted good friends and when eventually I did ring to tell her of my plan to buy something in Antequera, I found that, sadly, she and her husband had split up and she was back living in England. The house they had been building together and which she had shown me with such pride and excitement had had to be sold.

House-hunting in Antequera

Once back home, it was all systems go and the house in Sherborne I had put so much into went onto the market. I heard no word from the estate agent in Antequera but the intrepid Jane suddenly announced that I needed to return to Spain to look seriously for something to rent and that she would be happy to come with me. She found on the Internet a charming hotel in the middle of a national park about an hour's drive from Antequera. This may have been considered impractical, but in fact it was lovely to come back each evening after house-hunting to this peaceful hotel in the forest, where a family of wild boars came down from the hills each evening to have supper. The hotel staff put out delicious orange peel and other delicacies to tempt them and the animals provided us all with regular entertainment. It was June and the heat was less potent there than it was in Antequera, which is renowned for being very hot in summer and very cold in winter.

The all-pervading feeling of peace which seems to envelope Antequera struck me again immediately, not only in a couple of the churches we visited but also in the middle of the town amid the bustle of traffic and people going about their busy ways, pausing to chat with friends and acquaintances as they did so.

We looked at only three houses and as we looked at the third, Jane, who had been tasked by my friends to stop me rushing headlong into buying rather than renting something first, whispered "Buy it"! My initial offer was not accepted so I agreed to pay the asking price and put down an initial deposit of € 3000 there and then to secure it. The owner's wife sidled up to me during the second viewing to say that they had another buyer and the first one to put the money up front would get the house. I didn't actually believe her, but couldn't afford to disregard this comment.

It transpired some years later that I was wrong; there had been another buyer. An English family suddenly appeared outside my house one day in 2006 and seemed to be taking an interest in it. We got into conversation and they told me that I had gazumped them over the house, which they had wanted to buy. I think this must have happened through an estate agent other than mine; mine knew of no other buyer when I asked him. Luckily, they said, they had found a lovely house just outside Antequera where they had put in a swimming pool, which they certainly couldn't have done had they bought my house. They were happy to see round the house and we parted friends.

Leaving the UK

Although the sale of my house in Sherborne seemed to have been going through smoothly when I left for Spain, there was a completely unexpected last-minute hitch involving the second link in the chain. This meant having to borrow the money for the formal 10% deposit from my bank. A worrying thought, but one that Jane dismissed lightly and in the event sensibly. As luck would have it all turned out well sooner rather than later, but the knife-edge timing was such that my solicitor wrote after completion that she didn't think many of her clients could have coped as calmly as I had done with the delays. Little did she know that this client was inwardly in a state of semi-collapse over it all.

After leaving my house in Sherborne, I was lucky enough to be lent a dear little one-up-one-down cottage by Sheila and Edwin Rideout, friends from Beaminster, who had moved to Sherborne on the same day as I had in 1999. The cottage was across a little passageway from their home and unoccupied. There were three houses down this passageway which came as a surprise as one opened a little green wooden door off the main road. It was called Tuffins Passage. Each house had a tiny garden and it was all very quiet and secluded and a real haven after the trauma of giving up my house and preparing for the move to Antequera. The Rideouts were kindness itself, as were Sheila and Allen Hill with whom I stayed in Hooke on my last night in Dorset, after a farewell dinner at a seaside restaurant at West Bay near Bridport with Winfy and Jim Spicer. Other friends gave me a good send-off too and all commented on how brave I was to make this draconian move so late in life.

If I were to examine my own feelings at leaving, I can only say that, sad as I was to be leaving friends who had been so much a part of my life in Dorset over some 14 years, I was spurred on by some inner compulsion which left little place for serious fear or regrets. After attending Sung Eucharist at Sherborne Abbey just before leaving I bade farewell to the Vicar, Canon Woods. When telling him that I was moving to Spain, he asked: "Have you got family there?" To which I replied: "No there's just me and The Almighty," and although it elicited no reaction from him, it was for my part the truth. I couldn't have done it all by myself.

XXXIII

A New Life in Antequera

The plane which was to bear me off towards a new life was very late in leaving and we touched down at Malaga just before midnight. The girls at the car hire company at the airport were anxious to get home and gave only cursory instructions on how to operate the car's electronic starting system with a card, something I had never come across before. Just after turning off the motorway to Antequera the car stalled and stopped. It was almost 2 am and I was tired. The girl had told me to put my foot on the brake briefly as I inserted the card. Nothing happened. Cars passed me by but I wasn't anxious to stop one, which might have landed me in an even deeper mess. Had I known then how kind and enormously helpful the local inhabitants usually are, I would have had no hesitation in doing so. Suddenly after about twenty minutes my efforts bore fruit and the engine engaged, the secret being to keep one's foot firmly on the brake whilst putting in the electronic card. The porter on duty at The Parador was expecting my late arrival and as he showed me to my room, I told him: "I've bought a house here." He sensed my excitement and responded with an encouraging smile.

The following morning, the very nice Dutch estate agent who was holding the keys handed them over with due ceremony. It was an enormous bunch of keys and none of them were marked, so it took me some time to actually get into the house. I mentally berated the former owners for not labelling them. But once inside I realised that the house was something special; a good start I thought, with some relief.

It was a tall house in a row of different sized houses in a road which led only to the magificent Santa Maria Collegiate Church, one of the finest of the 32 churches in the town. When looking at the photograph of the house in the estate agent's window, I had noticed the tip of a stone wall on the other side of the road, which probably meant that there was an uninterrupted view. I was right. The view was of mountains, a little farm in the valley and a hilly field where two horses were grazing. To the left lay part of the town, the centre of which was only a seven minute walk, downhill all the way. One of the most singular features of the view was a massive rock in the middle of the plain below called La Piña de los Enamorados. The legend surrounding this rock is that a Muslim boy and a Christian girl who were very much in love, were forbidden to marry, so they climbed up to the top of this rock and hurled themselves down to their deaths.

The other feature, besides this sad story, was that the rock resembled a man's face looking peacefully up into the heavens and the extraordinary thing was that the profile was that of my beloved Allan; yet another reason to enjoy living there.

The house itself was charming and had a grand marble staircase with a beautifully carved mahogany bannister and plenty of living space. There was a generous patio in the centre, which divided the house into two, a further two terraces and a garage. It stood just outside the newly restored walls of the Alcazaba (Moorish castle) and it was now mine.

It wasn't long before my next door neighbour-to-be came up to greet me with a kiss on both cheeks. I wasn't yet used to this traditional Spanish greeting, but soon became so. Other neighbours followed suit. They were simple and friendly Spanish womenfolk, with names like Dolores, Encarnación and Socorro (meaning, respectively, Suffering, Succour and Incarnation) and I immediately felt welcome and somehow safe.

Although my goods and chattels were due to arrive within two days of my arrival, they were delayed and I decided to stay on in the comfort of The Parador and hang the expense until the van arrived. Returning from an evening swim in the hotel pool some four days later the phone rang. It was the furniture removal man saying that they were stranded on the Cordoba motorway and had all but done their driving limit for the day. Although I had provided a map of the town showing where they should park, they had ignored this and tried to drive their 18 metre van along the narrow streets into the centre of the town and very properly had been turned back. I drove to where they were waiting and took them along a peripheral road to within a short distance of my house where they spent the night in their van, which was equipped with bunk beds. In the morning I took them to the garage from which I had hired a smaller van, to cope with the narrow roads to the house. Once the furniture and a daunting number of boxes containing my precious possessions were safely installed, Heulyn insisted on coming over to help me unpack and what a noble and much appreciated act of kindness that was.

A Brief Visit to the UK

A couple of weeks later I set off to the airport en route for the UK again to sell my car and tie up one or two loose ends. Unsure quite where to leave my hired car, I stopped at a BP garage at Malaga Airport to ask. Just as I was leaving, a man came up and gestured towards the back wheels of the car. He then pointed to something under the mudguard so that I had to get out of the car. In the twinkling of an eye his accomplice had pinched my handbag from the passenger seat and they both dived into their waiting car and drove off with lightning speed. How easily one can be taken in by such rogues and what a predicament I was now in. As luck would have it my ticket and passport were in another bag, so I could at least take the flight. Another stroke of luck was that John Morley, my brother-in law, was to meet me at Gatwick Airport. It was years since I had been met off an aircraft.

But that was where the luck ended. Fairly distraught, I drove into the public carpark by mistake and of course had no money to get out again. An official let me out and urged me to stop my credit cards immediately. There was a long queue at the car hire firm and although the people in it were happy for me to go straight to the desk in the circumstances, the young woman in charge insisted I had the car checked first. The checking lady was nowhere to be seen and there simply wasn't time to go in search of her. Much against her will the girl at the desk allowed me to hand back the keys, but not before getting me to put my signature to the rental form. More of this later. Dragging my luggage behind me I then sped to the airport police station, but the police advised me to report the theft on my return to Spain as time didn't permit making a report then. I managed to cancel my credit cards thanks to the kindness of a travel agent in the airport who let me use her office telephone to do so.

After checking-in, I sank down on a bench and realised just how hot and bothered I was, but had no money to buy even a drink of water. A man who was standing at the bar, who could have been mistaken for a 'lager lout' with his shaven head and multiple tattoos, swiftly ordered a bottle of water and handed it to me. "Have this on me, madam," he said with a smile. It was hard to hold back the tears at this kind and quite unexpected gesture.

The rest of the trip back went smoothly and John was there to meet me, but in the morning, plans to see more of the family had to be sacrificed for maddening and time-consuming telephoning in the wake of the stolen handbag, one of the worst being the loss of all my telephone numbers. Once back in Sherborne, the sale of my car went well and there were more emotive farewell parties to enjoy with friends. I left for Antequera full of excitement and optimism.

Waking up on my first morning back, I stretched to switch on the light and fell out of bed, catching my chin on the bedside table. This resulted in a small cut and a big bruise, which put paid to calling on the police to put in a report on the theft of my handbag. Their curiosity and suspicions, albeit unwarranted, might well have been aroused, so it simply wasn't worth it.

However there was something that did need prompt action. A bill for some €200 was waiting from the car hire firm for damage done to both rear wings of the car I'd hired. The damage was certainly not done by me, but it took all of six months and continuous letters from both me and my bank to convince them of this and the money which had been debited to my credit card finally returned to me. It had been a fight worth persevering with.

Casting my mind back to the settling in period, with all the delights, the dramas and the pitfalls, I can do no better than quote from a Christmas letter I wrote to family and friends after my first three months in Antequera in December 2003 instead of a Christmas card that year:

'...The town lies on a plain surrounded by hills and mountains. It is 45 kms north of Malaga and has been a town of considerable significance from time immemorial. Outside the town are burial chambers (dolmens) dating back to 2500 BC. It has therefore the remains of a succession of changes from the Moors and before, the Romans and one of its most flourishing periods was during the Renaissance, so it has much that is beautiful. It has always been a prosperous town and some of the Spanish nobility still live in palaces and large houses in the centre. There are some 30-odd churches here and behind all the present-day bustle there is a great sense of peace and tranquillity. One of the most outstanding churches is some 200 yards from my house.

The house is one of a row of white houses just below the Castle (Alcazaba) at the top of the town. I can walk down to the main square and thoroughfare in about 7 minutes, coming back is rather slower as it is up lots of steep steps. The road in front of the houses leads only to the Collegiate Church of Santa Maria, which is now deconsecrated, but used for concerts, exhibitions and civic meetings. Traffic is confined to that of those living here plus the odd ambulance which comes to take the elderly or infirm to the local hospital; and also little white vans shoot up here daily hooting ferociously to deliver fresh comestibles. The unrestricted view from my bedroom balcony, where I am now sitting in hot sunshine - after a fiendishly cold night - is of mountains, little white houses well below, a farm where the goats live, but they tinkle up and down the hillsides during the day, and a field where three horses graze. Part of the town of some 44,000 souls can be seen to the left. On the other side of the boundary wall in front of these houses grow small conifers and tiny orange trees, now laden with fruit.

My neighbours are all unpretentious Spanish families who generate plenty of life. They are kindness itself and immensly helpful, although my present lack of coherent Spanish inhibits proper communication. Dogs of every shape and size proliferate - and bark, setting each other off, so that at times the hills resound to their lamentations - that and the buzz of mopeds zooming up and down the hilly roads. In the summer there is a sort of happy hour when everyone sits outside in the cooler air talking nineteen-to-the-dozen at the tops of their voices. It's all great fun.

Settling in has seen a series of dramas. I wish I could relate some of the hilarious and also hairy situations in which I have found myself, but these will have to wait until another time. The main sticking points have been to do with all the admin necessary for me and my car - a miniscule white SEAT - to live here legally. To become registered with an English-speaking doctor, to get a flu jab and cost-free medicines were all fairly fraught occasions, as was having gas cylinders delivered, the gas boiler repaired and hot water restored at the weekend; to having a lampshade replaced when the newly installed glass one in the bathroom fell and shattered minutes after I had left the room. But it has to be said that The Almighty has done me proud, because just as I've thought 'I'm not going to manage this' someone has appeared as if by magic, or else someone has come good after being intransigent and the immediate problem has been solved. At such times I am filled with a great surge of elation. But there have been times when tears have welled up out of sheer frustration at my inability to make myself understood in Spanish. But this is improving with two lessons a week and some homework, tapes, CDs and with plenty of necessary practice. I have a Sky Digital TV so am able to get English news broadcasts, which is a boon.

There hasn't been time for sightseeing so far, but I have done a little with various friends who have passed through. Heulyn, my ex-FCO friend who lives about an hour away, has been immensely supportive and has also provided some lovely social occasions; and I have already given four small lunches here. My house is super, but perishing at this time of the year; however it is possible to survive (so far) as of yore with various puny heaters. It is some 7 degrees centigrade warmer on the coast. Yesterday after attending the Advent Sunday Service at St George's Church in Malaga, I sat on the beach in hot sunshine and then had lunch outside at one of the restaurants overlooking the sea. Yippee!

The Spanish are kind, courteous and eager to please. I am happy and well (touch wood!) and find it all very civilised. Needless to say, I miss all you kindred spirits, but so many of you have kept in touch by phone or letter and this has helped to fill what otherwise might have proved a gaping hole. Thank you!'

Returning home after my first Christmas away from Antequera, which was spent in Sweden, all was not well. The telephone didn't work, the gas-heater had been switched off and couldn't be coaxed into action again. The house was very cold. This, I thought, is what people meant when they said how brave I was to move alone to a foreign country and without knowing the language.

The problems were in part caused by my neighbour, Loli, who had agreed to clean and look after the house for me. Her husband had been bedridden at home for over 20 years after an accident and her lot was not an easy one. I sympathised with her, but when she continued to break things in the house fairly regularly something had to be done. She also had three dogs living in the patio and although a high wall divides the two houses their yelps, cries and barks nearly drove me to distraction. Both problems were eventually solved, but not easily. My Spanish wasn't up to having a heart-to-heart with Loli, but with the help of my Dutch friend, Susan, who with fluent Spanish interpreted my words in the most sympathetic way things changed immediately for the better and a better cleaner, all round help and friend it would be hard to find. But it took all of three years to reach this happy outcome.

The breakage problem had been a serious one because I too began to break things and eventually I came to the conclusion that there must be some rogue elemental in the house. I consulted Robert Haslam, the newly retired vicar from St George's in Malaga who had come to live in Antequera. He had had experience of such things whilst in England, he said, and would be happy to come and say a few prayers and bless the house. The malign influence seemed to be just near the kitchen sink, in the passage leading onto the patio and on the patio itself. This was where most of the breakages occurred. After Robert had said a prayer at each of these spots things were certainly markedly more peaceful. The odd thing was that two days later a page from an old diary was pushed under my front door with two words scribbled on it. The words were 'un energi'. I had had no previous experience of any malign manifestations; the ghosts I had seen or felt at Bisham Abbey were alarming, but never malign, but as I understand it, they are all some form of energy.

Goodbye to Romance

When sending off my Christmas 2003 letter I had a sudden rush of blood to the head and included Allan on my list of recipients. There seemed to be nothing to lose by doing so and I thought he might be interested. I expected no response, so it was a lovely surprise when he rang me shortly after Christmas and was clearly not only interested but also impressed by my move to Spain. He said he knew Malaga and asked with unusual tenderness if I was happy. I assured him that I was. It was a short conversation but one which made me very happy and I sent him some photographs of the house and surroundings for his birthday in March, including his look-alike, the mountain of 'La Peña de los Enamorados'. They arrived right on the day and he telephoned immediately and was obviously tickled to bits to have them. I suggested that he might come out to stay but he said, "No, I'm finished," and he died three months later on the 13th of June. He had fallen and broken a hip and then developed pneumonia from which he died.

A Memorial Service was held for him at Sandhurst on 17th September 2004 and I went over to the UK to attend it. Two couples from the Regiment from Dorset were on the look-out for me so that we could sit together. However, when driving to Camberley the car, which had been lent to me by a kind friend, suddenly slid to a halt. The oil warning light was on so I assumed I'd run out of oil and went into the nearest shop, the Christmas Bakery at Worplesdon, to see if anyone knew of a garage nearby. None of the men I asked could help and finally the manageress let me use her telephone. No luck with any of the garages I contacted. In the end I was so distraught I found myself saying that I was outside the Christmas Brewery instead of the Christmas Bakery. Chris, my brother commmented later: "No wonder no-one would help you!" Finally the manageress sent one of her bakers off to buy some oil and I went out to the car and opened the bonnet. As if by magic two cars stopped in quick succession and the occupants leapt out eager to help. Amazingly one was a mechanic, who quickly ascertained that there was plenty of oil. The culprit turned out to be a small piece of carpet in front of the driver's seat which had become jammed under the accelerator. By this time it was after the 2 pm start of the Service.

My late arrival coincided with the Address being given by General Sir Anthony Walker. The Memorial Chapel was packed so I took a seat just inside the door. It was difficult to hear what General Walker was saying, but there was a lot of appreciative laughter as he recounted some of the stories for which Allan was famous, both in the Army and in the golfing world.

I began to look through the Service sheet and right at the end were the names of two tunes to which the congregation would exit the chapel. One of them was 'Moon River', which had been 'our song'. All the emotion which had been bottled up inside me was released and tears flowed freely. As the Service ended and the music filled the Chapel I was scooped up by my Dorset friends and we made our way into the Indian Army Room in Old College for refreshments, hosted by Allan's two daughters, Jackie and Lucile.

Apart from family and friends there was a profusion of senior officers, including the Chief of the Defence staff, many other military colleagues and a lot of his golfing friends. Early on I bumped into an old FCO colleague who often played golf with Allan and this was somehow cheering. Allan's two girls did a magnificent job hosting the occasion and I chatted to old friends and briefly to the Honorary Chaplain of the Tank Regiment, The Venerable Graham Roblin and his wife and also to General Walker. But I confess that the hold-up on the way there had taken its toll and I probably made no sense at all. It would have amused Allan though.

And so the final farewell was taken of a remarkable man, to whom I lost my heart some 40 years ago. He gave me great joy and a lot of sadness, but it was all worthwhile, and somehow 'meant'. Lucile, Allan's younger daughter, David and their son Harry I see from time to time and it is always good to see and hear from them.

The drive back to Dorset was slow. There was a lot of traffic as it was a weekend and raining heavily. Thankfully, Sheila and Edwin Rideout in whose little cottage in Tuffins Passage I was staying, had prepared a delicious supper and it was a relief not to have to go back to an empty house at that point. But I woke up that night with a serious attack of tachycardia. It was particularly worrying as I was due to fly back to Malaga the following day and was expecting a friend to stay for a week the day after. The National Health Service came up trumps and luckily a doctor from my old practice was on duty. She arranged an immediate ECG at the local hospital which was three minutes away and the machine succeeded in recording the attack. With all the previous attacks the heart had righted itself before each ECG, so this was a lucky break, as a result of which my heart specialist in Antequera was able to treat the condition, so far successfully.

The Pattern of Life in Antequera

What of the next three years? Well I fell in love. Not with some suave Don Juan or with any testerone-rich toy boy, although there were one or two I might have fancied, but not at my great age with the difficulties of close relationships still gnawing away not too far beneath the surface. No, with the Spanish people in general. As a Swedish friend once said: 'There is a King in every Spaniard'. I know what she meant and to some extent this is true. There is an innate civility, almost amounting to nobility in so many of them. It is a joy to walk in the town and see the plethora of young attractive men and women all moving with ease and self assurance; old men chatting in pairs or in groups immaculately turned out in crisp, neatly pressed, clean shirts and trousers and their female counterparts also neatly and smartly turned out for a visit into town. A lot of greeting and chat goes on and there is an atmosphere of natural bonhomie. Of course the sunny climate helps, as does the background of beautiful buildings all the way down the main street. A toothless old man sits playing the accordion day in and day out and when a coin is thrown into his basket he half rises to acknowledge it and to smile. I'm told by my hairdresser that he lives in rather a nice house, so perhaps he just enjoys his music and people-watching.

The tourists stand out as they wander uncertainly along consulting their maps. And the many newly-arrived immigrants tend to have a slightly anxious mien. I expect I had too in the beginning. On Sundays the churches are well-attended and when the congregation spills out onto the pavement after Mass they all seem loath to disperse and again they are smartly dressed. The children, who are openly loved and cherished are adorable: good-looking, well dressed and well behaved, Needless to say, there is an element of wildness in some of the older boys and girls around the town which sometimes gets out of hand. But so far one has had no cause to fear attack, robbery or derision when passing such a group.

However, this wilder element did manifest itself quite recently when a group of about 15-20 youngsters began gathering outside three derelict houses at the far end of the road on which I live. They came come rain and come shine every evening and systematically ransacked the three houses. They also picked all the oranges off the trees which line the road, throwing the fruit all over the area and when I remonstrated with them by banging on my window, throwing one at my window. I wasn't tempted to go out and confront them, but waited in vain for one of my Spanish neighbours to alert the police, but as none of them appeared to have done so, I eventually sent a letter to the Chief of Police, translated into immaculate Spanish by Heulyn. Within days a police patrol arrived and dispersed these trouble-makers. Peace has finally been restored, as have two of the houses. Long may this peace last.

Friendship

Despite having missed out on marriage and the joy and security of being the most loved and important person in someone's life, I have been blessed with a wide circle of friends throughout. Some of them go back 40, 50 and even 62 years and others are quite new. I couldn't survive without them. I believe the secret is that it has to be an equal relationship. Each has to have something to give to the other in human terms. There must be an innate trust and affection usually without the instability of a sexual element. That is probably why women often enjoy warm friendships with homosexual or asexual men. That being said I have had a number of close friendships, which weren't affaires, with heterosexual men, but rarely have they been Englishmen. I have found that some Englishmen of my generation often feel slightly uneasy in the company of women, particularly single women and often find it difficult to be naturally friendly.

It has been great fun having friends to stay. In all some 35 friends have visited me here, mostly during my first two years. My first guests, two couples, came in quick succession just about a month after I moved in. Neither couple stayed with me but both insisted on taking me out for a meal. They loved the house and its situation and came back again the following year when I was better able to provide hospitality.

Malcolm and Kerstin Herlenius were to have been two of my early guests, but sadly this wasn't to be. They had eventually moved back to Sweden from Mexico, but had hardly finished unpacking, when both became seriously ill. Malcolm had been suffering from cancer, but it was thought to be under control, so the sudden worsening of his condition was a shock to us all. Kerstin had been suffering from attacks of dizziness and debility and a nightmare situation befell them. Strangely, they were both treated simultaneously at the same hospital in Stockholm, where, very sadly, Malcolm died on 17 January 2005. His death caused a great light to go out in my life and in the lives of all who knew him. I had loved him dearly as a brother for some 50 years. Kerstin came to stay the following year, still battling valiantly with her own ill health and her shattering grief.

Touring in Spain

Other friends came in quick succession soon after and it was fun putting them up and showing them round the wonderful sights and buildings that Antequera has to offer. Sometimes we went further afield to the famously old and beautiful towns of Granada, Cordoba, Ronda, Seville and Cadiz, to name only a few. To date I think Cordoba is my favourite and I don't think I will ever tire of wandering, entranced, round the magnificent Mezquita and then dining at the old-established restaurant 'El Caballo Rojo'.

My first visit there was with friend Jane Gross. It was in the summer and the heat was crippling. I sank down opposite a beautiful Dutch painting above one of the many altars in the Mezquita and fervently wished that I had a fan. To my utter amazement a fan lay on the bench opposite. I waited a good quarter of an hour for its owner to come and claim it, but no-one did and I accepted it as a welcome gift from The Almighty.

Three other highlights of touring in Spain stand out in my memory. The first was a visit to Jerez de la Frontera, where apart from going on a guided tour of Gonzalez Byass, one of the most famous of the bodegas, to see how they produce their sherry and to drink generous samples of it, we went to a performance at the Real Escuela Andaluza de Arte Ecuestre. (the Royal School of Equestrian Arts). The dressage, to music, was spectacular and so elegant and beautiful that tears began to trickle down my cheeks.

The other two were both bullfights. Robert Haslam, the retired vicar from St George's Anglican Church in Malaga took me to the first. He is an expert on Spanish history and bullfighting and was able to explain the rituals and sequences of the fight so that, uneasy though I was as to the effect it might have on me, I was so busy following the movements and the elegance and excitement of it all, that the gradual and undoubtedly cruel fate of the bull became part of the essence of it all, rather than the central feature. The second bullfight was even more spectacular. The matadors were mounted (rejoneadors) and their task was to weave round the maddened bull, allowing it to come as close as possible without injuring either the horse or the rider. The ensuing footwork by the horses was like nothing I had ever seen. They appeared to be completely unafraid and although the bull was swift, they were even swifter and their legwork so adroit and beautiful. The last of the six fights was the most exciting of all and the rejoneador rode bare-back, guiding his mount into the most intricate movements with only his body, ending with a triumphant gallop across the arena as the bull gave in and sank to the ground. The cheering of the thousands of spectators around the bullring as they waved their white handkerchieves to signify the force of their approval was totally deafening and I had to sit with my fingers in my ears to protect the eardrums. This rejoneador's performance won him two ears and the bull's tail, which was no mean feat.

The Present

Although there is plenty to occupy my mind, the dearth of friends in Antequera itself has become a bit sobering, especially in the winter when the climate can be dull and grey and pretty cold. This paucity of friends nearby is a new experience. On postings abroad when it proved difficult to make friends among the local community, there were always colleagues within the Embassy who in themselves provided a busy social life. Those few friends I have made in Antequera itself are, refreshingly, younger than I am and are interested and very supportive. There's always plenty to talk about, particularly as one or two of them have lived in far flung places abroad as I have.

Heulyn Rayner, with her Periana-based friends: Tony Daniels, an artist of some distinction and a marvellous host, who invariably radiates a rather contagious joie de vivre; Sir Peter Wakefield, a retired Ambassador and his wife Felicity and Martin Young, also a former member of the FCO, have proved to be a real lifeline. Weekends spent with Heulyn, being thoroughly spoilt in every way, often provide opportunities for seeing them all. Without exception they give the stimulation and laughter that I miss in my daily life in Antequera.

Peter and Felicity Wakefield have recently built a most beautiful house on the outskirts of Periana with magnificent views. They have battled with great stoicism through the inevitable problems of such a project and still work like Trojans designing and making the garden a delight and a real work of art, seemingly undeterred by the fact that Peter himself is now well into his eighties. Immediately after his retirement from the FCO he became the first Director of The Art Fund in the UK and set about broadening its base and moving it into a very much more active sphere. The Fund and its members, of which I'm happy to be one, do a wonderful job buying and keeping British works of art in the United Kingdom. He was also the prime mover in setting up Asia House, a charitable society which aims to stimulate closer and broader contacts between Britain and Asian countries in the cultural, political and business spheres.

Martin Young, also in his eighties, is just in the throes of finishing his own new and lovely house, also with stunning views. He too is making a garden to be proud of. I felt very honoured to be his first house-guest on one occasion recently when Heulyn had a full house; and despite builders' dust and packing cases abounding in most of the rooms, my bedroom and bathroom were immaculate and he had gone to great pains to ensure my comfort. I count myself very lucky to have them all barely an hour's drive away.

After nigh on five years living here there is still so much to delight in. I love the way people's faces light up in response to a smile and a "Buenos Dias" or "Hola" when passing them in the street; I love the patience, courtesy and sheer common sense of most of the Spanish drivers in the town, with its narrow and often hilly streets. The motorways are becoming less comfortable though and speed has now become the order of the day, as in the rest of Europe. I love waking up to the predominantly blue skies, the sunshine and the birdsong, always at its height in the mornings and evenings. There are so many birds here and I sometimes wonder if some of them are emigrants from the UK, where the numbers of sparrows, particularly, appear to have diminished recently. Anyway if they are English sparrows they have adapted well and seem as happy as - well - larks. Throughout the day and well into the evenings great numbers of them fly around, then sit around my patio and the two terraces among the miniature tropical trees (in which I think they do their courting, judging by the noise they make).

I love the way the washing dries in the twinkling of an eye and looks and smells so fresh and wholesome. I love the way the staff at the Supermarket checkouts greet each customer with a smile and a hello and pack the shopping into carrier bags and the few who have a smattering of English enjoy practising it on me.

The workmen who have come over the years to install central heating, an electronic garage door and countless other jobs, have worked hard and conscientiously and been a pleasure to have around, with only a few exceptions, despite the language barrier. They usually work from around 9 am to 2 pm without a break and then from 3.30 - 6 or 7 pm. Offers of coffee are greeted with a smile and a shake of the head and they bring their own water to drink.

Grappling with the Spanish Health Service was something of a nightmare to begin with, mostly because of the language barrier and I used to dread going to the Health Centre to see my GP. The Centre is a mass of open-plan waiting areas with rows of metal chairs outside each consulting room; a bit like I would imagine the old workhouses to have been. Throngs of people queue endlessly to make appointments and to see their doctors. Stern notices outside each consulting room request silence. It is well-nigh impossible for any Spaniard to be silent and conversations spring up amongst those waiting, reaching a series of crescendos as more and more people turn up. There used to be a system of numerical appointments, so on arrival one asked tentatively of the person standing nearest the door to the surgery what number they had. After that there was always great discussion as to who was next and there was no chance of missing your turn because a chorus of voices would let you know that you were next. For some reason or other everything has suddenly changed for the better, including my doctor.

My first doctor was a huge figure of a man with an expression which alternated between smiles and grimness and during the grim times he could be positively rude. He spoke a little English which helped and I always felt like laughing at the times when he suspected I was suffering from an attack of cystitis and asked: "Does it hurt when you go peepee?"

Hospital appointments are somewhat calmer although very few nurses or specialist doctors have much English. The heart specialist is an exception but as it is important to be absolutely certain of what each of us is saying, Susan, my Dutch friend, very kindly comes along to interpret, although she sometimes ends up speaking Spanish to me and English to the doctor and we all dissolve into merry laughter. A nicer doctor one couldn't hope to find and one whose diagnoses and treatments have made a wonderful difference to my state of health.

In fact I cannot speak too highly of the Spanish National Health Service as a whole. When something does go wrong it is usually to do with the paperwork and a muddle over names. It doesn't happen often, but it is wildly frustrating when it does. A case in point happened quite recently when I waited for an appointment, instituted by my GP, to check that I wasn't a diabetic. The letter with the appointment came back for 'face surgery'. Perhaps my GP was trying to tell me something!

I am blessed with a wonderful pharmacist, the divine Carlos as I think of him and his pretty wife, Patricia. Their pharmacy is a haven of help and bonhomie to all who use it and Carlos in particular knows most of his customers by name and always asks with great sincerity after their aches and pains. Nothing is too much trouble and he seems to take as great an interest in the results as I do when taking my blood pressure. He insists on practising his steadily improving English on me and as he reaches for the blood pressure gauge he invariably says: "Come on Angela, don't worry, be happy," all with a divine smile which usually causes my blood pressure to rise.

Missing my old friends in England means that I reckon to make two or three visits a year to catch up with them and the family, go to the odd theatre, some museums and art exhibitions in London. Likewise with Sweden, although not quite so frequently, but when I do so everyone is very welcoming and there are open invitations to stay a few nights here and a few nights there with members of the Herlenius family.

One of the musts when visiting the UK is to have a car, as it is becoming more and more difficult to hire one after the age of seventy and with an insurance excess of as much as £600 unless one pays a fairly expensive extra premium. This problem was solved for me quite by chance earlier this year when Don McNeil from Sherborne decided to give up living part of the year in Spain and happened to mention that he had put an advert in the local English language newspaper to find a buyer for his old Rover. On hearing its condition and the price he was asking, I said without hesitation and without thought of where I'd keep it in the UK: "I'll buy it!" In fact all those details proved to be easily manageable, but first I had to get it there. It meant driving up to Bilbao before the summer heat began as it had no airconditioning and then catching the ferry to Portsmouth. Although I planned to take several days to do the trip, Winfy Spicer, practical as ever, emailed to say "Are you sure you are fit enough to drive the length of Spain alone and in an old car?" I realised she was right and set about finding a co-driver.

Motoring to Bilbao

Jane Gross once again came to the rescue and declared herself willing, able and happy to share the driving. Heulyn, who knows the route well, helped us plan and booked our hotels whilst we spent a happy time at her home in Periana the preceding day ending with a merry dinner party there together with Tony Daniels and Martin Young,

We set off the next morning through glorious countryside to join the main road to Granada. The sun followed us throughout and we stopped for lunch at The Parador and some sightseeing in the beautiful town of Ubeda and then spent the night at Almagro. The Parador in Almagro was once an old convent and so it had a special tranquillity. After a brief, but rewarding look round the centre of this ancient town, we moved on to Toledo, Segovia and Avila, all of which lived up to the enthusiastic descriptions in our guide books. Having read Vita Sackville West's biography of St Teresa of Avila, I was anxious to see this little town. I was not disappointed and bought a little ceramic plaque with the figure of the saint bearing the words: 'Sadness and melancholy have no place in my house'. Fingers well-crossed on that one.

The third night we were to spend in a village quite near to Bilbao so that we could make time to have a look at the massive Guggenheim Museum in the centre of the town. Our hotel turned out to be deep in the countryside and took a lot of finding. I mistook the entrance and found myself driving along a path which soon became a garden path and so sure was I that it was the right way to the entrance of the hotel, I was undeterred by the fact that Jane was becoming seriously worried as we swept past overhanging bushes of ceanothis and the like until we really did arrive at the front door of the hotel. I turned to her with a smile of satisfaction, but no sooner had we come to a halt than a series of gently irate figures popped their heads in through the car window and said in no uncertain terms, in undecipherable Basque, that this wouldn't do at all. Full of apologies I had the almost impossible task of turning the car round without seriously encroaching on the garden plants. To my great relief a very positive lady with very dark eyes and maroon hair directed me and eventually we were able to make for the proper entrance, which was badly signposted but certainly more user-friendly than the one before.

There seemed to be no ill-feelings over my gaffe and we were well looked after. The hotel, we discovered, was a commune run by fourteen families. It was clean and simple and surrounded by a beautiful garden at the far end of which, in a dip, stood a large meditation centre with a domed roof. Through the glass we noted an array of small cushions on the floor and a notice which read: 'Please wear white socks to meditate in. These can be purchased at the Reception desk'! We were the only guests, but were assured by the couple who served us dinner and breakfast that the hotel was usually full at weekends. After breakfast the next morning we were directed onto a quick route to the ferry, but sadly there wasn't time to get into Bilbao itself for a glimpse of The Guggenheim Museum.

The ferry journey was extremely comfortable despite a force 10 gale, causing the waves to severely pound the ship's buttocks and we sailed through drizzle and mist into Portsmouth in the early evening. Luckily we were heading for Hambledon, a short drive away, where Tita Shakeshaft was expecting us for the night and this banished the dismal weather blues. We agreed that it had all been great fun and Jane's parting shot was "Next time Siberia!"

XXXIV

An end to my
Captain Cook Researches

Having always vowed to get to the bottom of my family's connection to
Captain James Cook, I put together the results of all my researches to date in
2005 and took them to The Cook Memorial Museum at Whitby to show to
Dr Elizabeth Forgan, Chairman of the Trustees of the museum. While showing
interest in the case, she told me that the vital piece of proof - the birth details
of my forebear Thomas Cook - was necessary for my assumptions to hold water.
As I have been unable to find this information after extensive searching, I asked
Dr Forgan if she would be prepared to support a case for a DNA test if a bona
fide descendant could be found. She explained that she wasn't the person to
help with this and suggested I get in touch with the Chairman of The Cook
Society. In the meantime I found two descendants of Captain Cook's sister, the
only member of the family to have issue, down to the present day and although
one of them, Rod Fleck in Australia, agreed to cooperate in doing a DNA test,
this has proved a non-starter. It appears that DNA testing can only follow male
or female lines and cannot (as yet) cross the genders. And so my avowed quest
to prove my family connection cannot be verified and the great man can now
rest in peace.

XXXV

Finding Contentment

So that is where I must leave any further reminiscences, for better or for worse. While going through an old suitcase full of memorabilia the other day I came across a poem I wrote in 1968. It read:

'There may be time
And maybe not,
But while there is I will not stop
Looking for something I'll never find
Which some call contentment
And others peace of mind.

It may be here,
And maybe there,
But deepest in its all a blur
Of having all and having not
And trying not to give a jot.

This may sound sad,
It isn't really,
This world is ours to live in freely,
But what we do and what we think,
Must somehow make the Devil shrink.'

Forty years on I am still fighting the Devil to the best of my ability, hoping that my judgement of what constitutes the Devil isn't becoming impaired!

The good thing is that I believe I may actually have found contentment here in the sun in Antequera, so something has been achieved. For this I must thank my friends, lovers, colleagues, acquaintances and my family, who have helped throughout my life to provide the excitements, the struggles, the inevitable sadnesses and most of all the fun to make contentment now a real possibility, God willing.